America Sold Out

By Ray Hope

The Coming Persecution and Complacency of the Church

Prologue, Epilogue, and technical editing

By "Al" Cuppett, US Army - The Joint Staff (JCS) Retired

Dedicated to my wonderful family and friends as well as family who have gone on to their eternal reward. Special thanks to Pam and Alex "*Al*" Cuppett who risk their lives daily to be a faithful witness to any and all; and even more so to our Jewish and Israeli "fellow pilgrims" as "the day" approaches.

All Scripture quotations are from the Authorized King James Version of the Holy Bible.

First Edition

Printed in the United States of America

ISBN 1-594671-57-5

Table of Contents

You are hereby advised to pray about how you should use and or interpret the materials contained herein.

Neither, the author, agents , heirs or publisher accept any liability hereof.

Media Interviews are available for Mr. Cuppett or Mr. Hope by emailing
RAYHOPE@AMERICASOLDOUT.COM
Make sure you put the word **interview** IN THE SUBJECT LINE.

Please tell us the name of your news organization, contact person and day, date and time you would like their availability. Requests will be granted in the order received. Requests for interviews are not guaranteed. Limited speaking engagements and arrangements can be made by also emailing the above address and inserting the word Speaking Engagement in the subject line.

A final note from Ray Hope:

I urge you to order a copy of David Wilkerson's latest book "The Vision and Beyond" Prophesies Fulfilled and Still to Come. When you do, include a gift for widows and orphans his organization is helping. They are in NY City, Times Square and they are doing great things. God is moving by his spirit. Email us for his address: RAYHOPE@AMERICASOLDOUT.COM put in the subject line WILKERSON ADDRESS TO ORDER BOOKS.

Also, be sure to visit www.thegoldenreport.com and let Jerry Golden know what an awesome job he is doing to promote the Gospel as well.

Pray for me as we continue to tell the people the truth.

God Bless You for ordering and reading this book.

Ray Hope

PROLOGUE

28 September 2003
Madison, Virginia

The late April 1994, morning calm was violently shaken by four black, unmarked choppers, as they thundered low, 50 feet over my house near Madison, VA! What was this? I am a licensed pilot and this little "trick" was altitude-illegal, and a completely abnormal flight procedure. To wit, choppers do not usually fly "*knap of the Earth*" flights in such rugged terrain! I would soon discover just what it was they were trying to do.

To wit, I was being introduced to my first "black operations-intimidation" over flight. Be advised to get that low over my house, flying east to west, they had to swoop down, after just clearing towering, granite-faced German Ridge, rattle the house, then flare out over the Rapidan River "valley", as they departed the area.

I pondered the incident all day. The next morning the Holy Spirit awakened me at about 4 AM to pray, as per usual. I prayed about the choppers too! After prayer, my Authorized King James Version opened to Obadiah 1, and off the page "jumped", as ONLY KJV text can "jump", "*We have heard a rumour from the LORD, and an ambassador is sent among the heathen, <u>Arise ye, and let rise up against her in battle</u>*". At that moment, I got my answer as to who had sent the choppers. I also, at that point, had received my "orders" for the rest of my life. You will note the "*her*" in the text. This links the "*woman*" in Luke 13:20-21, and refers to the "*whore*" in Revelation. Folks, Rome runs the entire New World Order, until antichrist appears.

Ray Hope is a friend of mine, and although I have not known him long, the Holy Ghost has shown me he has a "*kinship spirit*" in the Lord, and is "*of like precious faith*". Therefore, I have agreed to edit and add to the manuscript, as well as write a Prologue and Epilogue for the book.

Since the New World Order executes most operations by gross deception, be sure you will never get a signed affidavit certifying what they are doing at any given venue/time. For example, there is "Brother Joe", a known, pre-tribulation rapturist evangelical personality from Charlotte, NC, who always demands I give him "documentation" to prove my military and professionally deduced allegations. He fails to realize that the KJV bible states in at least 10 places the following principle, with just about the same wording each place:

> "*In the mouth of two or three witnesses shall every word be established*".

This principle also pertains to any fact or event, and is the bedrock of our English Common Law-birthed system of jurisprudence. Signed affidavits are not necessary! Just two witnesses!

I once told Brother Joe, if he did not believe there were new detention facilities in the US, to look near Butner, NC, near his ministry headquarters, and he would find a massive new "Federal Prison Camp", behind the trees of "Camp Butner". I also asked him, "*If a black chopper landed in your back yard, and little black uniformed and black masked soldiers dragged you and your wife out of the house and flew them to that prison camp, would that not be tribulation?*" He admitted that it would be tribulation. Unfortunately, he still would not accept my evidence. Dear reader, if you make the same mistakes this man continues to make, you shall fare no better than Brother Joe in the days ahead!

Therefore, be advised, Ray Hope has the book firmly based on the "*two or three witness*" principle, when referring to the OVERALL scenario which is about to ensnare most all BORN AGAIN Christians in the US; to include all Jews and supporters of Israel. Moreover, this includes you, dear friend!

Be further advised that when I take a picture of a "*Regional Police*" car in York, PA, and later on receive verbal reports from 10 people across the USA who state they saw strange "*Regional Police*" cars in their hometowns, this serves as *prima facie* evidence there are "*Regional Police*" operating in the US! Furthermore, when two citizens from the same town, after seeing the photo tell me, "*Man, those cops are nasty. They push people around. We do not like 'em! In addition, they all speak "funny English"*", it becomes patently apparent "somebody" is hiring "*Regional Policemen*", and just maybe they are not US citizens! Please note I am conversant in five languages, and spent fourteen years overseas in over thirty countries!

Chapter Six begins with "*Why the Strange Troops, Police, and Events All Across the USA?* Folks, these troops, cops, equipment, etc, have been seen by hundreds of military, police, and intelligence officers, to include numerous retired people who once worked in positions that required familiarity with Chinese, Soviet, and Warsaw Pact operations. Their testimony offsets any doubt or denials that might arise from the civilian sector regarding these ominous signs. Unfortunately, civilians cannot identify a Soviet MI-24 "Hind" attack helicopter! I can! We military folks can! One was over my house at 100 feet! More than once I've confronted foreign pilots surveying my property from an unmarked chopper, on a "pre-operational recon sortie", prior to them executing an over flight in a fixed wing aircraft; then, either spraying some substance, or running a magnetometer-radar or IR sweep!

As a career military enlisted member, and later serving as an *Action Officer* with the Joint Chiefs of Staff, I can declare to you what you are about to read in this book is circumstantially-established fact! I served 31-plus years in the defense of this nation, and 19 of those years were "joint service". There is no other person I know of who served 19 years with Army-Navy-Air Force-Marines! I know whereof I speak and more surely, what I write!

Ray Hope has surely placed his life on the line to write this book. Therefore, dear reader, I too can do no less than, in the short time I had, contribute all I can to help warn YOU!

I never had time to write a book. I merely wrote hundreds of "*Intel Reports*" and individual letters. "One pagers" are read much more easily than a book. However, it is time, for the record, that a book was written and this is it!

Be advised, I could supply enough information for four or five books. It now takes me three days to cover the subject of the Satanic New World Order, now in the USA; especially if you include [which I do] the reason we are now in this situation! Read on and you shall find out why! The info rolls in at alarming rates from scores of savvy people every month. It cannot be kept up with, as events are happening at "warp speed"!

Hosea writes, "*My people are destroyed for lack of knowledge*". When you have finished reading this book, you will not lack "knowledge". However, what you do with this newly gained insight could determine how your life will end; and surely will determine where your soul shall spend eternity – Be you goy (gentile) or Jew!

In the Name of the Lord Jesus Christ, the Messiah of Israel -- Am Israel Chai!

Alexander "Al" B. Cuppett

P.S. Be advised there is "dedicated" command and control data circuits from Brussels, Belgium, to EVERY head of state in the world, including the White House! If you understand the principle of "back channel" communications, the way the government functions, know there are UN troops here, and several other factors, you can readily deduce that the "*actual*" Waco scenario [not what you saw on TV] was a product of orders from Brussels! With all this info, the fact there is a command and control connection to Europe, classified higher than any Dept of Defense medium, and becomes professionally elementary. Folks, the "Beast" is already running the globe! Watch for the last name "*Apostikane*"! It comes to 666 when the proper key and algorithm are applied correctly!

Introduction

God will not be mocked—we will reap what we sow. Are you doing good, then most likely good will come your way. Are you living like the devil? If so, most likely, bad will eventually come your way! America has slaughtered the unborn for over 30 years and the abortion statistics are well into the 40 million plus range. America is the largest producer of pornography, largest cigarette manufacturer, consumer of alcohol and in many cities in America; the police do not patrol at night for fear of being killed themselves.

America has fed many nations, repatriated the oppressed and rebuilt nations it destroyed in war but there is a score to be settled.

God will not sit by; and turn a blind eye and a deaf ear to killing innocent unborn babies. He will deal with America. Does he love America and all nations? Yes, he does. However, since he is no respecter of persons, sin must be corrected. When you read this book, understand that while everything looks bleak and you might feel the urge to give up, God says that those he wounds, he also binds up. Repent for the Kingdom is at hand. Fear not for the Lord is with thee.

It is time we stood up and told organizations like Planned Parenthood, the ACLU and other radical groups that their party is over. It will be over someday anyway but if everyone were as steadfast in the faith as Randall Terry or Flip Benham, the world would have a few more people in it. Terry founded Operation Rescue and Benham worked along side him to protect the rights of the unborn.

I am not suggesting that everyone get arrested by blocking clinic entrances or harming abortion workers. Anyone who takes the life of another is guilty of sin but there are things that can be done to alleviate some of these situations. This book will change the way you look at life. Friend, it is no longer party time or business as usual. One thing I want to make clear is God loves the sinner but hates the sin. God calls homosexuality "an abomination" but everyday, people come out of that lifestyle, get saved and go on to do great works for the Kingdom of God. Abortionists kill babies but some repent and do great things for God and people. He is quick to forgive!

As you read this book, pray and ask God to reveal things to you. This book will change the way you look at life and others. Finally, this information is not here to scare but help you prepare. If you do not call Jesus Lord and Savior, you should read the book regardless because you may find many points in the book that confirm some of the things you thought were wrong with the church. The church isn't perfect and neither is anyone else but through Jesus we have forgiveness for sin and the gift that cost God his only Son, is freely available to you anytime, anywhere but the window of opportunity is fast closing. If you think this is a churchy, touchy feely book, you are in for a big shock! Hollywood loves to demonize Christians and people of faith, but rumor has it that terrorists have a big target painted on Hollywood's party. God has his sights set on the USA. We are arrogant if we think persecution will not come to us because we live in America.

Chapter 1

Perilous Times

Please understand the events described in this book are highly possible and many are currently transpiring in the USA and abroad. Nevertheless, what appears does not have to be. We still have prayer and people who want to do good and not evil.

Terrorism is here to stay. You have no doubt seen and heard what the President said regarding terrorism being "a long-term fight" both in the United States, and on foreign soil. What he did not tell you was that we are very vulnerable to terrorists both foreign and domestic; especially foreign agents now deployed in country. You are virtually on your own. America is also in debt and the dollar is in trouble. What I am about to tell you will not please you, is not popular and will make me very few friends. We are about to see the destruction of America as a financial superpower. Foreclosures are at an all-time record high and getting higher. Yes, I believe that the current President will be re-elected and that for a while, we will win the war on terrorism but there is coming a day when the Democrats may get back into office and that is when the information in this book will be most valuable.

The war on terrorism did not start with 9-11. The war started when global factions decided they wanted to take God out of the equation and now they want to take you out too. This is not a recent event but happened many years ago back during Old Testament times and was decided when an angel of light decided to attempt to become God.

Muslim extremists want to kill Americans and others who do not believe in Islam. This work will not only describe exactly what is prophesied in the book of Revelation but also teach you how to protect yourself and family from the "shadow government" terrorists too. Israel could have remedied this had they followed the instructions from God way back when. Nevertheless, they are now suffering terribly with daily high alert status waiting for the next bomb to blow up. While Israel faces bombs, America is looking down the barrel of Financial Armageddon.

I give my 100% support to the current President of the United States, George W. Bush. Secondly, I pay my taxes, am not a member of any hate groups, militias or any group considered subversive to the USA. I will tell you that inside our country, there are factions, specifically "shadow government operatives", who cannot wait to take away your bibles, guns, freedom of speech, right to worship freely and your children. Furthermore, many of them would rather take away your life; and are making such plans. Indeed, they walk among us!

Does the President know about the organizations who are working night and day to undermine and overthrow the USA? Indeed he does. Fortunately, President Bush listened to Col. Lunev, former high-ranking intelligence official in Russia, who defected but also sat down with the President and briefed him on the dire situation the United States faces. President Bush is well versed on what is happening but he needs support from praying people who are not afraid to do battle on their knees as well as their feet.

Lunev: Source: Newsmax.com

I am a Christian who believes in Jesus Christ, nevertheless, even if you are not, you need to read and heed the message conveyed herein. What you read in this book will affect Christians and non-Christians alike. Some of the information contained herein may save your life and might scare you. You need to understand that America was not plunged into this situation by President George W. Bush; Bill Clinton and friends exacerbated it.

This plot was conceived long before Clinton took office. However, George W. Bush was not supposed to take office when he defeated Al Gore. The election was fraught with voter fraud and the democrats had several people in key areas of the country literally stuffing the ballot boxes with deceased people, felons, and fictitious votes for Al Gore. The way the election turned out angered people in high places but the only person the election did not faze was God himself.

When the Democratic handlers made their estimate of how many phony votes they needed to carry each of the precincts in order to win the election without the need for a run-off, they failed to calculate that they really are not in control. God is! Now if you don't believe in God, that is something you will have to live with but I can tell you with all authority that while Republicans were sweating and Democrats were plotting, the Lord knew exactly what would happen. Mr. Gore did not have to face down the Chinese over the plane incident in China, nor surrender our country over to the UN during the 9-11 crises.

How did I learn the information that you will be reading about? (No "classified" *military* secrets are published in this book) As a youngster, I became very interested in Military Affairs and investigations. I assisted a certain three-letter government organization with an investigation nearly 2 decades ago and they wondered how I managed to grab a certain report that was sealed. Some would say, he stole it, others might deduce I obtained it surreptitiously. These were good guesses but what actually happened was I knew someone who knew someone and they made a mistake by giving them the report "*out of school*", without knowing, it was sealed. Was I lucky or was it divine providence?
In life, you have heard it said it is not what you know but whom you know. In order for me to stay alive, it has been both who and what I know. I had no idea it was even a sealed report. It was not my skills but my faith that has allowed me to accomplish great things.

No doubt, you have kept up with the news and the reports of alerts and terrorism. It is what the government is not telling you that could shorten your life, or the lives of your loved ones. I make no apology for the next statement but ignorance thereof may cause you to end up in a concentration camp near you. I am not kidding! They still exist and shall be utilized in this conflict. Later, I will discuss at length where the camps are, who runs them, and why you might end up there. Calm your nerves as we go into the dark world that the "Shadow Government" has no plans to tell you about.

There are Nazi-style (circa 1934) lists of names. The "*Red and Blue*" lists have been confirmed. The "*Green List*", if it exists, should surface eventually. Most Christians, gun owners, patriots and folks who believe in God, the bible or the Constitution are on one of the lists. If you do not own guns, do not believe in God or the Bible, and hate America, you may also be on a list [expected to be the" *Green List*"]. This list is for those who have hope under the Shadow Government of being "reeducated". For now, I want to address those like me who hold the basic traditional values, and who shall appear, or are now on, the *Red and Blue* Lists.

Inside various old military bases, many closed under the direction of former President Bill Clinton in order to save money, you will find a house of horrors. Clinton's role in the virtual demise of America is clearly becoming apparent as we see many [and shall soon see all] of our forces shipped off to foreign shores to allow foreign forces to help train and keep watch over America and Americans. I spoke at length to a recently retired Green Beret who spent time in Africa on "missions of minimal importance at best" who was aware we were being shipped off to foreign lands while the real battles will be right here in the USA.

Our borders are wide open! Although, the Border Patrol and US Customs are doing their best, some of our other neighbors could not care less whom they let in or out. Many areas are virtually free access with no checkpoints. Just cross at will and welcome to America. However, soon, getting out will be OUR personal problem!

Even government knows something big is up. Vice President Dick Cheney said "it's not a matter of if we are attacked, only a matter of when". He is telling the truth. He and the President, George W. Bush, know what is happening with terrorism but they are also aware that they are fighting a two front war, Terrorism and the agenda of the United Nations. The UN wants all firearms off the streets, particularly the streets of the USA. [Ed. Note: After 9-11, it was reported that Dick Cheney and "the shadow government" was hunkered down in a secret location, probably Mt Weather, in Virginia. However, a shadow government is patently ILLEGAL! We are supposed to have an elected government! Senator Daschle even stated he had "never heard of any shadow government". You never heard him mention it again either! Why? His New World Order (NWO) "handlers" told him to shut up about issue – or else!]

In fact, at Fort Polk, Louisiana, Special Ops soldiers and even foreign troops train for urban assault/pacification operations, and house-to-house combat.
What they are really practicing for is gun confiscation here in America. Clinton sold secrets to China who wants to dominate the USA and eventually take it over. First, through stealing jobs and finally taking over the USA with Chinese troops. The fastest growing Country in the world is China. [Ed note: The Chinese troop issue was one of several, which caused the murder, not suicide, of Admiral Mike Boorda!]

Do you think gun confiscation will make America a safer place? Just ask the Australians who like sheep led to slaughter turned in their weapons in exchange for a safer place to live. Crime rates sharply increased but it was too late, they had bought the lie. In America, we will not go down quite that easy. Secret plans are being continually revised to bring about events to facilitate a total gun confiscation and usher in *Martial Law*.

What does martial law mean to you? In the event of a large-scale terrorist attack, the stock market crash, or urban rioting out of control, the Shadow/Federal Government would institute MARTIAL LAW. Part of this would mean curfews, total government control of the food supply, water, utilities, and other necessary services. Some would say, that does not sound that bad. There are authors who will tell you what the problem is, nevertheless, few who offer solutions. If I can show only one person what to do in order to position them for what is coming, I have discharged my duty to God. {Ed note: It is the UN troops and cops who will eventually enforce and oversee martial law declaration!]

Red List: Source: Al Cuppett, US Army/The Joint Staff, (JCS) Retired.

Let us examine why you would not want to live under Martial Law. First, if you put away any extra food for a rainy day, the government would have the right to come in with force to seize it. There are a tremendous number of Executive Orders allowing any President to control, Utilities, Communications, Food, Transportation and a myriad of other critical components of the infrastructure of the United States. We are facing dark times and why aren't more of our Pastors speaking out and telling us what is going on?

My Grandfather was telling me bits and pieces of these things when I was a young man but I just laughed at him. I said, "Grandpa, this is America, Guillotines and taking the bible out of the church, that isn't going happen!" Well it is happening!

Look at how they tried to murder the comatose woman in Florida, Terry Shiavo. It was the righteous of the nation, through prayer, fasting, and administration of Legislators and Governor, Jeb Bush who made the way for the feeding tube to be re-inserted. There is an element in Society who wants to murder the unborn, the useless and throwaway people of all nations. Do you think for one moment we could not wipe out hunger in America or even worldwide? Of course, we could but not everyone likes the idea. The U.N. and others really want population control and starvation is simply nature's way (so to speak) of eliminating the problem.

The Posse Comitatus Act would prevent this from happening – right?
Wrong! Under Martial Law, PCA would be invalid. Imagine your extra soup or garden veggies falling into the hands of troops. I am not talking American troops, I am talking about foreign-trained troops who are instructed to confiscate, with or without force, food supplies, weapons, ammunition, and firearms.

You would also be told to relocate to a Federal Government internment camp or a FEMA "detention" center. FEMA is the Federal Emergency Management Agency.
You would have little or no time gather any belongings; and bibles would not be allowed in the facility because it might offend someone else in the camp and cause a disturbance. Once loaded onto a Chinook helicopter in your Cul de Sac, or at your rural retreat, you are loaded onto a black unmarked chopper or white van or bus. This vehicle might have the words UN on the front or side. You are now off to camp for "routine" processing; or so you may be told.

At this point, you hope this book is a work of fiction but take another sip of whatever you are drinking because it is not. Upon arrival, you are processed into the facility and you feel safe because the soldiers there are armed with machine guns and the fence is high to not allow anyone in. However, you fail to notice that the barbed wire is turned top-inside, not out. This fence is to keep you in, but unless the detainees have had military experience, they would not recognize the fact that they are in serious trouble. I have many accounts from reliable former Military people including Colonels and even Generals. These camps were used during the Japanese internment and for the Cuban's during the Carter Administration.

Upon check-in, you are searched and separated from your family and issued a number. This most likely will be the chip implanted into your forehead or right hand. All of your vital information including military history, medical records and financial information are on the chip. This chip is already in use by the US Military and in other branches of service worldwide. (Ed note: Two mothers of both Marine and Army recruits, stated their sons have recently taken "chips" in their right hands!]

It is *THE MARK OF THE BEAST. This is in form of an ID card at present but with the escalation of war and security a high priority, the chip implant technology will not go to waste. It is ready for immediate deployment.*

What will facilitate this camp situation? Most likely, it will be [choreographed] terrorism in the form of Nuclear, Chemical, or Biological Weapons of Mass Destruction. (WMD). The likely scenario will play out with a suit case nuke ["back-pack nuke"] being detonated in Washington D.C. or New York, which sends the people who survive in those cities, into a dreadful panic. National Guard troops, if any remain in the US, and the 100,000 extra "reserve" [actually imported foreign] police officers called up under Clinton's plan to regionalize police forces will go into effect. Foreign cops will take no thought to shooting down armed or unarmed American civilians. They did not at Waco!

Next time you see an officer dressed in "generic" black, go ask him a question and see how good his English is? You may be shocked to discover that his English is broken at best. I learned much of this information fromAl Cuppett, a former Department of Defense (DOD) employee who spent 21 years in the Army, won the Bronze Star and Purple Heart, and served 8 years with the DOD, which included 6 years with the Joint Chiefs of Staff. He also received the Secretary of Defense Civilian Service Medal upon retirement in 1990. He converses in five languages, and has personally talked to these foreign cops and troops.

They are coming after you in other ways! Have you noticed that your retirement is slowly or in some cases rapidly disappearing? Wall Street greed mongers have misappropriated your money. They do not care if the market is up or down because they make money on both sides of the trade buy or sell.

Recently, several large mutual fund firms have settled with the SEC (Securities and Exchange Commission) regarding after hours trading where they took your money and traded these mutual funds on the float, after hours. This has literally cost investors probably a billion dollars or more in lost profits. Will they go to jail? No way! Nevertheless, they are ushering in the crash of the market as fast as any terrorist is. The brokers are in fact not to be trusted. You have heard the old adage; it seems like when I use my broker, I become broker.

This work is not about bad news, in fact, it is more about the good news that all of these events do indeed fit directly into God's plan and are not beyond his comprehension. I could use the book to quote you many scriptures but what you need to know about scripture is in the bible, what you need to know is right here and I will provide you scripture verses later to support the statements presented.

Did you notice recently that a particular Wall Street Executive received a bonus of $140 million dollars? This happened while your retirement fund, 401K, stocks, and savings accounts went down in value. In the economy, if someone is winning big (Obviously, this NYSE executive was), someone else is losing big.

As this was being written, Richard Grasso lost his job as the Head of The NYSE (New York Stock Exchange in September 2003. I will not go so far as to say anyone's compensation should be limited, this is still America, however, as a regulator, and his compensation should be less than $50,000 per day.

Wall Street is nothing more than Las Vegas in New York. You have many people placing bets (buying or selling stock) some think a particular stock will go up, others think they are headed down. They even have options you purchase or sell. Perhaps you want to play it safe with your money that you once earned 7% interest on when you had it in the bank. Now, it earns maybe 1%.

I cannot keep pace with the financial headlines as the SEC and NASDAQ are investigating Prudential at this time. As you, become more aware of what to look for in the news, you will rejoice for your "*redemption draweth neigh*".

What is transpiring is they are wiping out the money supply and taking your ability to earn money from your investments. How about that generous 1% interest your CD now pays. They have sucked the wealth out of this country, and the NWO, a.k.a. the United Nations (UN), is planning to collapse the USA, and is in fact mandating such an event.

When the money is gone, a one-world currency can then be issued and America will lose its sovereignty and its place as a superpower. Then the UN, with their troops and cops, steps in and the USA loses its sovereignty.

Do you think the CEO's of America's corporations care if you lose? Bill Gates recently sold a huge block of his stock, as have many others who knew it was time to cash out on the backs of the little people who have been told by their broker to buy and hold. As you are taking the brokers advice, you are becoming "broker" and they are selling stock at inflated prices and laughing all the way to the bank. In addition, most SEC actions are minor insignificant punishments and they could care less about the individual investors.

By now, you have been introduced to a number of things you never knew existed. You may still watch Network news on the Big Three Networks, NBC, CBS, and ABC. If this is the case, you are as a sheep led to the slaughter. In case you have failed to notice, the network anchors have agenda and that agenda falls right in line with global governance and a one-world system. If you are a Christian, you are the biggest threat to One World Government and the liberals carrying out their plans for utopia. Their goal is to eliminate the Religious Right! (Ed note: Eliminate Jews and "born-again" Christians –period!]

Did you know you are already considered a "*domestic terrorist*"? If you read the bible, fly a flag, and believe in the Constitution, own a gun, home school your children, you qualify.

Reading certain magazines also places you on the blue, red, or green lists. Every piece of information you provide to your doctor, the social security administration, the IRS, and even the police, is stored in a central database in Brussels, Belgium where the SUPER COMPUTER keeps track of everyone and everything, worldwide. This information is disseminated and carefully chronicled and produces a real time dossier on the subject. (YOU!)

By now, some of you are living in fear, others are mad, and some just do not care because they think this book is pure fiction. Let me address the fearful reader at this time. There are certain things you can do to safeguard information and prepare for the possibility that America, as we know it, may change due to terrorism or NWO "black operations". Black operations are what happen when a government must keep its subjects in the dark on what is really taking place. [Ed Note: Such operations are being executed, now, against scores of US citizens!]

It is time to stand up and be quiet! That is right, be quiet. Let people like me take the risk, but you need to make your plans, follow the instructions in this book and the bible -- if you believe in the bible. Even if you do not believe in the bible, you will be following the bible anyway because what we do lines up with the word of God; it always has!

Since many of you have never thought that anything out of the ordinary was going on in the federal government, now you know otherwise. You will need to pay close attention from here on out. If you miss one sentence, you may cost yourself, or a loved one, their life.

We now understand that there is an agenda and that Christians and patriots are considered terrorists. Since we have identified the problems (us), we must seek a solution. You can hide, move overseas, get pro-active, harm yourself, and/or head for the insane asylum. Alternatively, you can recognize what the agenda is about and get to work. How can we do this? In prayer. Prayer [specifically at 3 or 4 AM] wins battles, changes circumstances, and will see you through. Of course, faith without works is dead, so we must put the feet to the faith and show our faith by our works. Be prepared to lose friends. Jesus lost friends, even the disciples abandoned him as did his own family. However, if God be for us, who can be against us.

Foreign troops are here in America training at various clandestine bases and along side our own troops in the USA. Why? *Project Harmony*. A Clinton brainchild to allow these cops access to America. These cops [many are Muslims] will have no qualms firing on you, raping your wife or daughter, or shooting down innocent civilians when they are called upon to confiscate guns, ammunition, and or food stocks. [Ed note: The foreign troops are here under the auspices of "Partnership for Peace" (PfP) Program. They even carry blue and white HMO cards labeled, *"Partners for Peace - Medical"*.]

A few years ago, a marine commander asked his troops this question. "If your country called you up to confiscate guns would you [and would you] shoot American civilians in the process?" Over 25% of the marines said yes they would. Since the US could not handle a large-scale mop up operation with a small percentage of its combat troops in country, the need for foreign troops becomes clearly apparent. The UN troops will do what US troops will not.

My grandfather was a preacher who ran across a truck driver one day who was hauling a load of guillotines (see Rev 20:4) to a large southern state bound for the capital of that state. You might be wondering what those are for? When the time comes, you will be asked to deny Jesus Christ, and live; or proclaim Him and die by the guillotine. Revelation 13:16 <u>And he causeth all, both small and great, rich and poor, free and bond, to receive a mark in their right hand, or in their foreheads: 17 And that no man might buy or sell, save he that had the mark, or the name of the beast, or the number of his name. King James Version. - Cambridge AKJV Bible "83"</u>.

FEMA may attempt to rescue those in peril, but they will not help the Christians in the great and awful day of terrorism. In fact, it is likely they will help you only long enough to make it to one of their camps. I have information that many new prisons have been built and are "house kept" by some local sheriffs; we are asking them why they are standing watch over empty, new prisons?

One facility is a 4000 bed facility in L.A. waiting the time of unrest; or is it set for something, or someone else?

You hear a lot about the UN but little truth is told about this organization. President George W. Bush is one of the only Presidents to openly defy and stand up to the UN but he is hated by most of the countries except for a few of our closest allies, Israel, Great Britain, and Taiwan.[Ed Note: George Bush jawboned with the UN but his "handlers" staffed everything he said. Seek wisdom on all this.]

The UN wants guns off the streets of America and Christians silenced sooner rather than later. If you think the Secretary General of the UN is your friend, guess again!

Fort Bragg North Carolina is home of the Special Ops and Special Forces Green Berets. A friend of mine was an Army Colonel and former Green Beret for 26 years with a top-secret military clearance and he confirms we have a problem. With the background briefing you are privy to, you may find yourself doing more research. A word of caution to you…Do not! Much of the information on the internet is polluted and has been sanitized as well as a great deal of disinformation propagated as well. [Ed note: Try much prayer and reading your KJV bible at 3 and 4 AM! The Holy Ghost is a better Teacher than the "WWW".]

This did not happen over night and it will not go away overnight. Nevertheless, there is a way to foul up the plans of the New World Order.

2 Corinthians 10:4 "For the weapons of our warfare are not carnal, but mighty through God to the pulling down of strong holds;) 5 Casting down imaginations, and every high thing that exalteth itself against the knowledge of God, and bringing into captivity, every thought to the obedience of Christ; 6 And having in a readiness to revenge all disobedience, when your obedience is fulfilled.

Take heart dear friends, your redemption draweth nigh.

In Malachi Chapter 3 verse 1: Behold, I will send my messenger, and he shall prepare the way before me: and the Lord, whom ye seek, shall suddenly come to his temple, even the messenger of the covenant, whom ye delight in: behold, he shall come saith the Lord of Hosts.

2. But who may abide the day of his coming? And who shall stand when he appeareth? for he is like a refiners fire, and like fullers' sope:

Verse 14: Ye have said, it is vain to serve God: and what profit is it that we have kept his ordinance, and that we have walked mournfully before the Lord of hosts?

Verse 15: And now we call the proud happy; yea they that work wickedness are set up; yea, they that tempt God are even delivered.

Verse 16: Then they that feared the Lord spake often to one another: and the Lord hearkened, and heard it, and a book of remembrance was written before him for them that feared the Lord, and that thought upon his name.

Verse 17: And they shall be mine, saith the Lord of hosts, in that day when I make up my jewels; and I will spare them as man spareth his own son that serveth him.

Verse 18: Then shall ye return, and discern between the righteous and the wicked, between him that serveth God and him that serveth him not. AKJV Bible.

If you thought I was joking about the guillotines, here is scriptural proof. Revelation 20: verse 4 And *I saw thrones, and they sat upon them, and judgment was given unto them: and I saw the souls of them that were beheaded for the witness of Jesus, and for the word of God, and which had not worshipped the beast, neither his image, neither had received his mark upon their foreheads, or in their hands; and they lived and reigned with Christ a thousand years.*

"Control the food and control the population" as one famous diplomat once put it while addressing a gathering at the United Nations in New York. Therefore, we have established that they will behead us at some point, but Christ will reward us. A few readers are now ready to possibly reconsider their Christianity at this point. Many will say, "My preacher never told me that part" or like Peter, deny they ever knew Jesus. However, you must stand firm, for only those who do shall be saved.

Now is the time for action! You have seen and read enough by now to be ready to do battle with the left wing liberals, New World Order nutcases, and the radically extreme environmentalists. Just you and your mighty weapons of war, God's word and prayer. The word tells us to put on the helmet of salvation; and that helmet and the breastplate of righteousness will withstand the attacks of the enemy. Reading this book makes you a terrorist. When you have God on your side, you are a feared and hated individual. If you want to win the battle and the war, get serious about prayer.

In a few chapters, we will be getting into the Hit List. Call it Clinton's top 100.
For those who dealt with Clinton, few lived to tell about it, and several have crossed the line like Larry Patterson, Larry Nichols and a host of others who have managed to survive only by the grace of God; and by knowing so much were demonized by the mainstream press and came off looking like paranoid nut cases. I spoke a few times to Nichols and the last time I spoke to him, a red truck was watching him. As of this writing, he is still alive but I know he does not live in fear.

You recall former Commerce Secretary Ron Brown who died in a plane crash but my sources indicate he died not from the crash impact but a dry ice bullet fired into his skull. It was a dangerous thing to go against the Clinton's and several of his chopper pilots found out the hard way with premature deaths, all accidental of course. [Ed Note: Near-real-time intelligence reveals Airman Shelly Kelly, a flight attendant on the doomed flight, was walking around on the ground! The Pentagon fully expected her home. She died of a slit femoral artery three hours after the actual crash! This is only one fact about this "take out" flight.]

The deaths of people in the Value Jet Crash, TWA 800, and even the more recent downing (AA Flt 587) over Far Rockaway, New York, have some people convinced that these were all "accidents" because the National Transportation Safety Board (NTSB) says that is the way it happened. The fact is, these and many others not mentioned herein, were brought down by "black operations", and executed by foreign operatives within the USA! The NTSB, the UN, and the shadow government wants you flying, for now, so do not expect them to tell you what really happened. You know, the ones they said were already here. [Ed note: The presence of foreign operatives within the US MUST be kept secret at all costs!] However, do not fly unless you absolutely have to or you know the LORD has ordained it.

Recently I spoke to a friend of mine who has a Top Secret clearance. He made the mistake of flying and was greeted by two Marines armed with machine guns; he was identified by name and told to have a nice flight. He is former military, but is this how we must now treat US citizens; even ex-military men? This was prior to the plane's departure. He was with Air Force Intelligence.

The Vice President has a secret and highly fortified radiation proof shelter in his backyard. The Greenbriar Hotel in West Virginia is also a heavily fortified compound with underground tunnel systems. Speaking of underground, between the mountains near Culpepper, Virginia, and Pennsylvania, there are a series of complex underground bunkers, which were ostensively built to house all the infrastructure of the Government. I believe in America and I know we have some good politicians on both sides of the Congress; however, the Socialists in the camp want to bring down the USA.

How about the New Air Marshal Program. I hope when I fly I do not have to sit next to an Air Marshal. Why? Because he might haul me away because I have my bible out, reading it on the flight while he lets the two Arabic speaking passengers carry on their conversation about how they hate America and Americans in the next row.

Do not be naïve - it happens. [Ed note: The Justice Dept's 1998-99 "*Emergency Response to Terrorism Program*", principally identified "right wing Christians", not Muslims, as "the terrorists".] See Al Cuppett's, Prophecy Club video, "*Black Operations and Prophecy*" for the proof!

CEO's are leaving their companies, building fortified retreats, and investing in gold. The government has purchased over 100,000 gas masks and protective gear for Pentagon, first responders and DOD employees.

We will, not may, be looking at a massive reign of terrorism that will be unleashed against the USA by Islamic Extremists who are actually Sleeper Agents that will answer the call when it goes out to attack the USA. I assure you firsthand that the FBI, CIA, NSA, and a host of other "straight" Government agencies are working around the clock to prevent the next 9-11. However, off the record, some I have spoken with say, it is not a matter of if we are hit, its when. [Ed Note: There are enough UN/Soviet agents deployed in country to perform any NEW terrorist acts, the blame being put upon whomever the New World Order finds "in their way"]

So why is the shadow government behind the camps and round ups? It really isn't the legitimate ["straight"] people in government, but it is the numerous left wing ideologues, many who are devout atheists, communists and wacko environmentalists, as well as power hungry, blood thirsty politicians who must have it there way; who don't believe in God or Country. Yes, Satanists are real and very dangerous. Ever wonder why we have so many disappearances? I warn you that leaving your children unattended is dangerous.
The [choreographed] terror attacks are coming sooner rather than later, and the shadow government knows; it and now so do you.

We will be covering what to do in case of a dirty bomb, suitcase nuke and if you still believe that Oklahoma City was the work of Mc Veigh and Nichols, the mainstream media have duped you again! They had help and it was Islamic extremists, or in-country agents who made it possible. I could write an entire book on this subject but we cannot occupy the time by focusing on the past, we must live in the present. An ANFO fertilizer bomb cannot cut reinforced concrete past 23 feet. The brisance wave is too slow! The truck was 35 feet from the building! Enough said.

If you live in any of the major cities, get out if you can. If you cannot, or do not have relatives or friends, then do what comes natural, Trust God! I spoke to a former Green Beret, a demolitions expert, and he told me that the media has blown certain aspects about the dirty bomb out of proportion. We may have upwards of 70-100 suitcase nukes (back-pack nukes) here on US soil. You still have to have the know how to arm and use them. While none of these statements is comforting, we know two things: God is in control and terrorists are misguided. Why else would they strap themselves with explosives and blow themselves up? Sometimes, they blow up when there is no one around. Not a real smart move, is it? [Ed Note: Back-pack nukes, deployed or not, UN-choreographed "terror paranoia" is what they foster in the public's mind set]

Some would call this book a down and dirty version. Just the facts, no hype, no fluff! Therefore, I am going to teach you to think like a Green Beret, have the confidence of a well-armed unit, and to turn off the regular media outlets and listen to those in the know.
Turn off CBS, NBC, and ABC now! Get it on Fox and lose the CNN, although sometimes you get some great photos and live coverage. Remember Ted Turner wants to be around to show the end times and he may get his wish unless he repents of his sins and calls upon the name of the Lord. {Ed Note: Even Fox News is "programmed", and is not giving you the entire "bottom line"; they only make you think you have the truth!]

David Wilkerson, the NY Times Square Preacher, who has never been wrong, and who publishes a newsletter every three weeks wrote in a prophetic vision he had a few years ago. "I saw a thousand fires burning at one time in NY City" I believe what he had the vision of was people (or foreign agents) setting fire to buildings when they find out their retirement went up in smoke, their jobs were lost, and that DC was hit by a nuke. A blast of cold hard desperation. I must tell you it grieves me to write this book but if I do not, God will hold me accountable for lives lost because I refused to obey him. I actually have a family and have a great job. Writing this book at this time was a labor of love but mandatory.

Wilkerson's vision may also have been after the crash of the stock market. In addition, currency becoming worthless along with stocks and retirement programs. Whatever the case, he is never wrong, because he is God's Watchman and Servant.

The mere letters, WEAPONS OF MASS DESTRUCTION (WMD) have been emblazoned on our hearts, minds and souls but Jesus said "be of good cheer, I have overcome the world" We will get through these tough times and either make a great nation, or be with the Lord if we accept his gift of salvation. If you do not know Jesus, please turn to the last page of the book now; and pray. Then continue reading.

There have been some serious atrocities committed against people like Randy Weaver who was shot and his wife and child killed in Idaho. We might not have agreed with their sheltered lifestyle but to gun them down in cold blood and then have the government pay them off to the tune of 3 million dollars seems perverse.

My Joint Staff friend says if the New World Order crowd can take a way the physical power, GUNS, FOOD and FUEL; then all that stands in their way of the takeover is [any remaining] spiritual power. Getting rid of the Christians, who can speak the pure Word, is all that stands in the way at that point. [Ed Note: The whores of Revelation, a.k.a. the Jesuits, have, for all practical purposes, taken away our spiritual power with perverted bibles. Also, see Luke 13:20-21, noting the "her". They have "leavened" the whole kingdom of God!]

"No weapon that is formed against thee shall prosper; and every tongue that shall rise against thee in judgment thou shalt condemn. This is the heritage of the servants of the Lord, and their righteousness is of me saith the Lord." Isaiah 54:17 King James Version

God is going to give you power and you will not be condemned when you are brought before kings and rulers for the sake of the Gospel of Jesus Christ. He is the King of Kings and the Lord of Lords. Need more evidence of how much you are loved? *Jeremiah 29:11 "For I know the thoughts I that I think toward you, saith the Lord, thoughts of peace, and not of evil, to give you an unexpected end". King James Version.*

BANKS AND YOUR MONEY:

Banks have made bad financial bets called "Derivatives" These are hedged 10 to 1 and even 100 to 1 with depositor's money. Suckers like you and I believe our money is safe in the stock market and or the bank as long as we do not exceed $100,000.00 in order to be insured by the FDIC. The bank has a way around that in a crisis. They will only allow you to draw down $100.00 -$400.00 a day and do not have to let you have any of it. Just ask anyone who was around in 1929. The current market we have makes 1929 look like a picnic.

So what to do:

1. I would immediately divest myself of Dow stocks
2. Convert to government treasury bonds
3. Hold some gold----that gold I spoke of has gone up about 100.00 an ounce when I told everyone to buy it.
4. Keep some cash at home and a limited amount in the bank
5. Retire while your money and stocks are worth something. You will be so far ahead of the money game and the curve that you will thank me later.
[Ed note: Many storeowners can only positively identify US silver dollars/coins; as gold coins were before their time. Moreover, specie [gold or silver] will buy something only if there is something on the shelves to buy. Stock up on tangible goods.]

Real Estate is headed for the cellar. If you own it, sell what you do not need. Keep your home and Do Not wait, the economy is out of control. Ignore what the talking heads on the financial TV shows tell you. Ask the Lord to show you where to be!

The game is over; Alan Greenspan cannot re-start the economy with all the rate cuts. The analysts and talking heads are all lying to save their filthy jobs, and the banks make loans to stay afloat; but America has shipped all the jobs to overseas and we are now a debtor/consumer nation. I love this country but I also recognize the problem and it is not the President, but what has been done prior to his election; and if you factor in the massive numbers of refinancing, credit card debt, zero percentage car loans, and the tapped out consumer, America is in trouble! We have borrowed our way to prosperity and now there is nothing left to borrow. {Ed. Note: G.W.Bush is not guiltless; however, his "handlers" are making sure he goes along with most of their program. If he does not he could be in danger by high order of the same people who had the Kennedy boys killed!]

I have been aware of the things written above for a long time but they can no longer be ignored. Remember back when you were making money, or staying about even when everyone else was losing their butts because they trusted their broker? If you are going to trust someone else with your money, send it all now a Christian relief agency, at least you will not have to see it go up in smoke from bad financial advice or company misappropriation. Even decent Dow component stocks will be decimated with news of financial mismanagement and cooking the books [Ed. Note: Donate only to ministries which use the KJV bible – ONLY; and who do not "correct" it with Greek and Hebrew!]

Factor the stock market that rolls with the banks and vice-versa, one can affect the other but the party is over and insider selling of major Dow component stocks has hit a feverish pace. Every little so-called rally is a means for these cretins to dump their stock while your broker participates in this massive fraud. Why? Because he makes money as long as someone is buying or selling! Pump and dump is illegal unless you are a broker or have a public company.

TV talking heads say "buy and hold" that is how they trap the unsuspecting sheeple into riding it out ...these are the dummies who wake up on Monday morning and flip on CNBC and see they lost 50-90% of their investments. How did it happen? They trusted someone who did not have their best interests at heart.

Watch mortgage rates go through the roof, which will trigger foreclosures and bankruptcies at record rates. Interest rates will rise but that will not happen until after the banks collapse...they will not be totally wiped out, just bad enough that the stock market will be around Dow 5000 and NASDAQ 800 and most folks will not have the knowledge or guts to get back into the market. By now you are saying forget it all. In the end times, God is going to show his mighty power through you and all you must do is trust him to get you out of debt; however, you will need to repent.

And they overcame him by the blood of the Lamb, by the word of their testimony and because they were faithful unto death! "Revelation 11:12 (Ed Note: They did not overcome by "praise and worship".)

Chapter 2
The role of the UN (United Nations)

The following document is from the Department of State and it is not classified.

Freedom from War

The United States Program
for General and Complete
Disarmament in a Peaceful
World

U.S. DEPARTMENT OF STATE

DEPARTMENT OF STATE PUBLICATION 7277
Disarmament Series 5
Released September 1961

Office of Public Services
BUREAU OF PUBLIC AFFAIRS

For sale by the Superintendent of Documents, U.S. Government
Printing Office, Washington 25, D.C. - Price 15 cents

INTRODUCTION

The revolutionary development of modern weapons within a world divided by serious ideological differences has produced a crisis in human history. In order to overcome the danger of nuclear war now confronting humanity, the United States has introduced at the Sixteenth General Assembly of the United Nations a *Program for General and Complete Disarmament in a Peaceful World.*
This new program provides for the progressive reduction of the war-making capabilities of nations and the simultaneous strengthening of international institutions to settle disputes and maintain the peace. It sets forth a series of comprehensive measures, which can be taken in order to bring about a world in which there will be freedom from war and security for all states. It is based on three principles deemed essential to the achievement of practical progress in the disarmament field:

First, there must be immediate disarmament action:
A strenuous and uninterrupted effort must be made toward the goal of general and complete disarmament; at the same time, it is important that specific measures be put into effect as soon as possible.

Second, all disarmament obligations must be subject to effective international controls:
The control organization must have the labor, facilities, and effectiveness to assure that limitations or reductions take place as agreed. It must also be able to certify to all states that

retained forces and armaments do not exceed those permitted at any stage of the disarmament process.

Third, adequate peacekeeping machinery must be established:
There is an inseparable relationship between the scaling down of national armaments on the one hand and the building up of international peacekeeping machinery and institutions on the other. Nations are unlikely to shed their means of self-protection in the absence of alternative ways to safeguard their legitimate interests. This can only be achieved through the progressive strengthening of international institutions under the United Nations and by creating a United Nations Peace Force to enforce the peace as the disarmament process proceeds. (Ed Note: "*Peace keeping machinery*" means foreign cops on US soil [i.e., secret police and black operations here], and subsequent confiscation of all private firearms!)

There follows a summary of the principal provisions of the United States *Program for General and Complete Disarmament in a Peaceful World*. The full text of the program is contained in an appendix to this pamphlet.

FREEDOM FROM WAR

THE UNITED STATES PROGRAM
FOR GENERAL AND COMPLETE DISARMAMENT
IN A PEACEFUL WORLD

SUMMARY

DISARMAMENT GOAL AND OBJECTIVES

The over-all goal of the United States is a free, secure, and peaceful world of independent states [nations!] adhering to common standards of justice and international conduct and subjecting the use of force to the rule of law; a world which has achieved general and complete disarmament under effective international control; and a world in which adjustment to change takes place in accordance with the principles of the United Nations.

In order to make possible the achievement of that goal, the program sets forth the following specific objectives toward which nations should direct their efforts:

- The disbanding of all national armed forces and the prohibition of their reestablishment in any form whatsoever other than those required to preserve internal order and for contributions to a United Nations Peace Force;

- The elimination from national arsenals of all armaments, including all weapons of mass destruction and the means for their delivery, other than those required for a United Nations Peace Force and for maintaining internal order;
- The institution of effective means for the enforcement of international agreements, for the settlement of disputes, and for the maintenance of peace in accordance with the principles of the United Nations;

- The establishment and effective operation of an International Disarmament Organization within the framework of the United Nations to insure compliance at all times with all disarmament obligations.

TASK OF NEGOTIATING STATES

The negotiating states are called upon to develop the program into a detailed plan for general and complete disarmament and to continue their efforts without interruption until the whole program has been achieved. To this end, they are to seek the widest possible area of agreement at the earliest possible date. At the same time, and without prejudice to progress on the disarmament program, they are to seek agreement on those immediate measures that would contribute to the common security of nations and that could facilitate and form part of the total program.

GOVERNING PRINCIPLES

The program sets forth a series of general principles to guide the negotiating states in their work. These make clear that:

- As states [nations] relinquish their arms, the United Nations must be progressively strengthened in order to improve its capacity to assure international security and the peaceful settlement of disputes;
- Disarmament must proceed as rapidly as possible, until it is completed, in stages containing balanced, phased, and safeguarded measures;
- Each measure and stage should be carried out in an agreed period of time, with transition from one stage to the next to take place as soon as all measures in the preceding stage have been carried out and verified and as soon as necessary arrangements for verification of the next stage have been made;
- Inspection and verification must establish both that nations carry out scheduled limitations or reductions and that they do not retain armed forces and armaments in excess of those permitted at any stage of the disarmament process; and
- Disarmament must take place in a manner that will not affect adversely the security of any state.

DISARMAMENT STAGES

The program provides for progressive disarmament steps to take place in three stages and for the simultaneous strengthening of international institutions.

FIRST STAGE

The first stage contains measures, which would significantly reduce the capabilities of nations to wage aggressive war. Implementation of this stage would mean that:

- The nuclear threat would be reduced:
  All states would have adhered to a treaty effectively prohibiting the testing of nuclear

weapons.

The production of fissionable materials for use in weapons would be stopped and quantities of such materials from past production would be converted to non-weapons uses.

States owning nuclear weapons would not relinquish control of such weapons to any nation not owning them and would not transmit to any such nation information or material necessary for their manufacture.

States not owning nuclear weapons would not manufacture them or attempt to obtain control of such weapons belonging to other states.

A Commission of Experts would be established to report on the feasibility and means for the verified reduction and eventual elimination of nuclear weapons stockpiles.

- Strategic delivery vehicles would be reduced:

  Strategic nuclear weapons delivery vehicles of specified categories and weapons designed to counter such vehicles would be reduced to agreed levels by equitable and balanced steps; their production would be discontinued or limited; their testing would be limited or halted.

- Arms and armed forces would be reduced:

  The armed forces of the United States and the Soviet Union would be limited to 2.1 million men each (with appropriate levels not exceeding that amount for other militarily significant states); levels of armaments would be correspondingly reduced and their production would be limited.

  An Experts Commission would be established to examine and report on the feasibility and means of accomplishing verifiable reduction and eventual elimination of all chemical, biological, and radiological weapons.

Peaceful use of outer space would be promoted: The placing in orbit or stationing in outer space of weapons capable of producing mass   destruction would be prohibited.

States would give advance notification of space vehicle and missile launchings.

- U.N. peace-keeping powers would be strengthened:

  Measures would be taken to develop and strengthen United Nations arrangements for arbitration, for the development of international law, and for the establishment in Stage II of a permanent U.N. Peace Force.

- An International Disarmament Organization would be established for effective verification of the disarmament program:

  Its functions would be expanded progressively as disarmament proceeds.

- It would certify to all states that agreed reductions have taken place and that retained forces and armaments do not exceed permitted levels.It would determine the transition from one stage to the next. (c) The manufacture of armaments would be prohibited except for those of agreed types and quantities to be used by the U.N. Peace Force and those required to maintain internal order. All other armaments would be destroyed or converted to peaceful purposes.(d) The peace-keeping capabilities of the United Nations would be sufficiently strong and the obligations of all states under such arrangements sufficiently far-reaching as to assure peace and the just settlement of differences in a disarmed world.

- [Ed Note: Warning, "..*by peace shall* [he] *destroy many*.." (Dan 8:25) All of the above means UN troops will be policing the USA, and all private firearms confiscated! Thus through "peace" [keeping] many shall be killed.

Chapter 3

Who is on your side?

American Sovereignty Restoration Act of 2003 (Introduced in House)

HR 1146 IH

108th CONGRESS
1st Session
H. R. 1146

To end membership of the United States in the United Nations.

IN THE HOUSE OF REPRESENTATIVES

March 6, 2003

Mr. PAUL introduced the following bill; which was referred to the Committee on International Relations

A BILL

To end membership of the United States in the United Nations.

> *Be it enacted by the Senate and House of Representatives of the United States of America in Congress assembled,*

SECTION 1. SHORT TITLE.

This Act may be cited as the `American Sovereignty Restoration Act of 2003'.

SEC. 2. REPEAL OF UNITED NATIONS PARTICIPATION ACT.

(a) REPEAL- The United Nations Participation Act of 1945 (Public Law 79-264, 22 U.S.C. 287-287e) is repealed.

(b) TERMINATION OF PARTICIPATION IN UNITED NATIONS- The President shall terminate all participation by the United States in the United Nations, and any organ, specialized agency, commission, or other formally affiliated body of the United Nations.

(c) CLOSURE OF UNITED STATES MISSION TO UNITED NATIONS- The United States Mission to the United Nations is closed. Any remaining functions of such office shall not be carried out.

SEC. 3. REPEAL OF UNITED NATIONS HEADQUARTERS AGREEMENT ACT.

(a) REPEAL- The United Nations Headquarters Agreement Act (Public Law 80-357) is repealed.

(b) WITHDRAWAL- The United States withdraws from the agreement between the United States and the United Nations regarding the headquarters of the United Nations (signed at Lake Success, New York, on June 26, 1947, which was brought into effect by the United Nations Headquarters Agreement Act).

SEC. 4. UNITED STATES ASSESSED AND VOLUNTARY CONTRIBUTIONS TO THE UNITED NATIONS.

(a) TERMINATION- No funds are authorized to be appropriated or otherwise made available for assessed or voluntary contributions of the United States to the United Nations or any organ, specialized agency, commission or other formally affiliated body thereof, except that funds may be appropriated to facilitate withdrawal of United States personnel and equipment. Upon termination of United States membership, no payments shall be made to the United Nations or any organ, specialized agency, commission or other formally affiliated body thereof, out of any funds appropriated prior to such termination or out of any other funds available for such purposes.

(b) APPLICATION- The provisions of this section shall apply to all agencies of the United Nations, including independent or voluntary agencies.

SEC. 5. UNITED NATIONS PEACEKEEPING OPERATIONS.

(a) TERMINATION- No funds are authorized to be appropriated or otherwise made available for any United States contribution to any United Nations military operation.

(b) TERMINATIONS OF UNITED STATES PARTICIPATION IN UNITED NATIONS PEACEKEEPING OPERATIONS- No funds may be obligated or expended to support the participation of any member of the Armed Forces

of the United States as part of any United Nations military or peacekeeping operation or force. No member of the Armed Forces of the United States may serve under the command of the United Nations.

SEC. 6. WITHDRAWAL OF UNITED NATIONS PRESENCE IN FACILITIES OF THE GOVERNMENT OF THE UNITED STATES AND REPEAL OF DIPLOMATIC IMMUNITY.

(a) WITHDRAWAL FROM UNITED STATES GOVERNMENT PROPERTY- The United Nations (including any affiliated agency of the United Nations) shall not occupy or use any property or facility of the United States Government.

(b) DIPLOMATIC IMMUNITY- No officer or employee of the United Nations or any representative, officer, or employee of any mission to the United Nations of any foreign government shall be entitled to enjoy the privileges and immunities of the Vienna Convention on Diplomatic Relations of April 18, 1961, nor may any such privileges and immunities be extended to any such individual. The privileges, exemptions and immunities provided for in the International Organizations Immunities Act of December 29, 1945 (59 Stat. 669; 22 U.S.C. 288, 288a-f), or in any agreement or treaty to which the United States is a party, including the agreement entitled `Agreement Between the United Nations and the United States of America Regarding the Headquarters of the United Nations', signed June 26, 1947 (22 U.S.C. 287), and the Convention on Privileges and Immunities of the United Nations, entered into force with respect to the United States on April 29, 1970, (21 UST 1418; TIAS 6900; UNTS 16), shall not apply to the United Nations or any organ, specialized agency, commission or other formally affiliated body thereof, to the officers and employees of the United Nations, or any organ, specialized agency, commission or other formally affiliated body thereof, or to the families, suites or servants of such officers or employees.

SEC. 7. REPEAL OF UNITED NATIONS EDUCATIONAL, SCIENTIFIC, AND CULTURAL ORGANIZATION ACT.

The joint resolution entitled `A joint resolution providing for membership and participation by the United States in the United Nations Educational, Scientific, and Cultural Organization, and authorizing an appropriation therefore' approved July 30, 1946 (Public Law 79-565, 22 U.S.C. 287m-287t), is repealed.

SEC. 8. REPEAL OF UNITED NATIONS ENVIRONMENT PROGRAM PARTICIPATION ACT OF 1973.

The United Nations Environment Program Participation Act of 1973 (22 U.S.C. 287 note) is repealed.

SEC. 9. REPEAL OF UNITED STATES PARTICIPATION IN THE WORLD HEALTH ORGANIZATION.

The joint resolution entitled `Joint Resolution providing for membership and participation by the United States in the World Health Organization and authorizing an appropriation therefore,' approved July 14, 1948 (22 U.S.C. 290, 290a-e-1) is repealed.

SEC. 10. REPEAL OF INVOLVEMENT IN UNITED NATIONS CONVENTIONS AND AGREEMENTS.

As of the date of the enactment of this Act, the United States will end any and all participation in any and all conventions and/or agreements with the United Nations and any organ, specialized agency, commission, or other formally affiliated body of the United Nations. Any remaining functions of such conventions and/or agreements shall not be carried out.

SEC. 11. REEMPLOYMENT WITH UNITED STATES GOVERNMENT AFTER SERVICE WITH AN INTERNATIONAL ORGANIZATION.

Nothing in this Act shall be construed to affect the rights of employees under subchapter IV of chapter 35 of title 5, United States Code, relating to reemployment after service with an international organization.

SEC. 12. NOTIFICATION.

Effective on the date of the enactment of this Act, the Secretary of State shall notify the United Nations and any organ, specialized agency, commission, or other formally affiliated body of the United Nations of the provisions of this Act.

SEC. 13. EFFECTIVE DATE.

Except as otherwise provided, this Act and the amendments made by this Act shall take effect 2 years after the date of the enactment of this Act.

There are many good people in Congress, however, only a handful, actually know what the diabolical dark forces have planned. You have heard about population control and do not be naïve to think that there is not an agenda to separate those who are sick, retarded, of little value to a contributing community to be sent away and silenced. Prison populations are expanding at an alarming rate. People who commit crimes should be dealt with; however, the current system is a massive for- profit operation, which is currently being executed against the people of the United States.

Chapter 4

The Brave

Alexander B. "Al" Cuppett committed Christian, former *Action Officer* and Command and Control and Intelligence Communications Inspector for the Joint Chiefs of Staff, and the Department of Defense, with 31 years of federal service in the military, nine with the Department of Defense, including two years with the Air Staff. He holds the Bronze Star, the Purple Heart, the Defense Meritorious Service Medal, three awards of the Joint Service Medal, all of the Vietnamese awards, as well as the Joint Meritorious Unit/ Defense Meritorious Service Medals.

Al revealed disturbing information about New World Order efforts to destroy and enslave America. When he retired a few years ago, he was awarded the Secretary of Defense Civilian Service Medal. He has been around the world to 31 countries on four continents, and speaks five languages. He tells of the coming American Holocaust and the Shadow Government's plans for dealing with the so-called enemy combatants. (Christians and Jews)

He spoke of the infrastructure currently in place, which facilitates incarceration and eventual execution of "listed" Americans. He disclosed the locations of the facilities to be utilized for these purposes, including photographs.

"The infrastructure is set up". There are at least 142 major [funded] concentration camps, including quietly modified facilities which have sprung up, and continue to spring up, across the country, seemingly devoid of activity, yet requiring abnormal accoutrements such as barbed wire-topped fencing (with the tops turned inward) and helicopter wind socks. Most have good logistical supportability, with major highways and railroad transport facilities adjacent to the sites.

"These facilities, many in remote areas across the USA, are set up to become concentration/detention camps, complete with gas chambers, for resisters and dissidents. They are set up for dissenters who will not go along with the New World Order. The resisters are gun owners who refuse to give up their weapons; the dissidents are Christians, Patriots and Constitutionalists [and surely Theocratic Jews]. These camps are real and I personally have seen several, one is a crematorium.

"On August 6, 1994, I toured the Amtrak Railcar Repair Facility at Beech Grove, Indianapolis, Indiana. There are at least ten maintenance barns at this facility, covering 129 acres, with two separate fences with the tops leaning inward. The windows of several buildings have been bricked up. Hence, you have three levels of security for Amtrak repair barns. There are three helicopter 25-knot aviation windsocks (which are not the correct ones to use for chemical spills, which require 10-knot windsocks).

I have the address for Al's two video tapes after you finish the book and you may purchase and view them. Note: Al gets no monetary income from these videos.

There are high security NSA-style people turnstiles, and high intensity/security lighting for 24-hour operation. The boxcar (gas chamber) building fence is marked with special RED/BLUE Zone signs! [There are the "Red-Blue" criteria again!]

This corresponds to the mission of the RED/BLUE Lists, which surfaced in June and July of 1996. Under martial law, this will become a death camp. They are only going to handle Category 1 and Two (RED and BLUE) people there. This boxcar facility will be used for execution.

"One of the barns is large enough to put four box cars into. There are powered vents on the top of the barn to vent the gas out of the building after the boxcars have been fumigated. All of the buildings have newly installed six-inch gas pipes and furnaces installed in all railroad barns. Since August 1994, FEMA has allocated $5.9 million to modify the walls and roofs of the buildings. Under martial law, this facility could be utilized as an SS-style termination gas chamber. [You need to get, from Al, "*Anita's Dream*", a shocking dream given to a handmaiden of the Lord featuring "*four car*" trains! She had never seen his "*Straight from the Joint Chiefs*" video!]

"On January 27, 1995, The Indianapolis News ran an article titled", Amtrak Lays off 212 at Beech Grove: 170 Lose Jobs at Maintenance Center Today." Why perform $6 million worth of renovations, and then lay off 212 people? Because the people doing the final executions will not be Americans. Thus, the slots of the 212 will [eventually] be filled with non-Americans. They will hire foreigners for this "capo" task. Cappo ("chief" in Italian) was the title of the trustee prisoners who actually killed many Jews for the SS butchers at Dachau, and at other Nazi crematoria across Europe. The news article also said, "...hopes the yard may be able to solicit work repairing private train cars, and perhaps subway cars from Washington, DC, or other urban areas."

The repairing of private trains is a dead giveaway to death cars! The article went on to say, "Late last year, Congress ordered Amtrak to spend at least $5.9 million patching holes in the roof and fixing masonry on the walls of the giant machine sheds at Beech Grove." These buildings have been "sealed." They are [suitable or] airtight. The facility is constructed to allow gas to be blown into all the buildings via the newly installed, two-story, and hot air [blower] heating furnaces."

"The RED List is for pick-up and execution before unobtrusive preparations for martial law is initiated. The BLUE List is also for execution, but later (within six weeks of martial law declaration.) There are no 're-education' plans for either category, just execution. When you get picked up on a RED pick-up, they'll take you from your home at night (probably around 4 a.m.) and put you in a black van, then drive you to a helicopter waiting to fly you to an intermediate point.

There, you will be loaded onto a big 64-passenger CH-47 Chinook helicopter all black, unmarked and illegally operating under the "*Treaty on Open Skies*". Then they'll fly you to one of 38 cities where you'll board a 747, 737, or 727 aircraft."

"You may be taken straight to a temporary detention facility. When you are RED listed, you will be taken to a red camp. Then you'll be executed." "At some point, martial law will be declared. (Martial law is the writ of Habeas Corpus 'to have a trial by jury' is suspended. Instead, of going to the judge, you go straight to jail for a limited time.)

I suspect there will be a major outage, or some other crisis, which will be the reason to declare martial law. {Ed Note: Both videos were made in 1998. Note what congruent "events" have happened since then!]

At this point, the BLUE listed people will be picked up. At that time, the country will be regionalized into ten regions, which are already designated by FEMA. Be advised that it has been proven (in Wyoming and at least one other location) that the black choppers have state-of-the-art radio frequency (RF) wideband jammers, and can jam cell phones and CBs while they're executing black operations missions. This means that your cell phone could be jammed just before and/or during any action against you." You recall during 9-11 virtually every cell phone in America but especially on the entire east coast was rendered inoperable. {Ed Note: a Continuous Rod warhead missile, fired from a chopper employing a "spoofer" transponder to spoof the terminal radar at JFK facilitated the shoot-down of TWA 800. The chopper was flown by a foreign pilot!]

"In June of 1996, an FBI agent got hold of the Region Three BLUE List (from a CIA agent), and found his own name on it, and those of several others he knew in Virginia. The Regional BLUE List stated that the names on the BLUE List would be picked up 'within six weeks of the actual martial law declaration.' This parallels the Nazi RED/BLUE List policy almost to the letter. Heinz Hohne published the parallel Nazi plan in his 1966 book, "*The Story of the Nazi SS: The Order of the Death's Head.*"

"People say, 'It won't work.' Nevertheless, it will work if the several million covert Soviet troops currently here can get the [confiscate] guns. The name of the game is to blackball the people to get the guns...make the militia look bad, make guns look bad, make everybody give up their guns. Once they get your gun, they have you, UNLESS you have the angel of the Lord at your door. If you've got the Angel of the Lord out there protecting you, it's another story."

"The ones doing all of this are operating out of the highest places in the Federal Government. [By that, we/I mean the post-911-identified "shadow government".] They are cooperating with 'spirit guides and mediums' and using astrology and numerology. (Hillary Clinton was openly doing this and a former Secret Service agent revealed to me the debauchery going on in the White House by many.) The spirit guides are telling them what to do, and the entire thing is being orchestrated at the highest spiritual levels of Illuminism, Satanism and the occult Skull and Bones. Every base has been covered. They have thought of everything. (Note-EXCEPT the Eternal GOD factor!-PS) If you notice, they often do things on the 13th of the month. [Alternatively, on full moons or other Satanic holidays]"

"Who will be doing the actual picking up? Foreign cops (United Nations Internal Security Forces). Over 30 foreign military bases under the United Nations flag are already set up in the US. All with the approval of special [shadow government] appointees in high Federal positions.

These bases are already manned with over TWO MILLION troops from Russia, Poland, Germany, Belgium, Turkey, Great Britain, Nicaragua, and Asian countries. Why are they here (and the 2 million includes those in Canada and Mexico as well)? Because unlike our own troops (many of which along with the Guard and Reserve of 24 states are being deployed overseas) they will have no qualms about firing on U.S. citizens when the time comes.

There are more than 2,000 Russian tanks, military transport trucks, and chemical warfare vehicles just outside Gulfport, Mississippi. They began arriving in January of 1994. There are 180 foreign troops at Fort Reilly, which was confirmed to me by a Brigadier General. 300 came into the Birmingham, Alabama airport on a big white Russian cargo plane on December 13, 1995. As of 1995, there were 10,000 and foreign troops at Fort Chafee, Arkansas reportedly making preparations for 20,000 'detainees.' This is going on all over the country. (I know a soldier who was in Special Forces [also known as Delta Force, although he revealed no secrets, he confirmed that these suggestions by Mr. Cuppett are possible].

German troops are known to be at Holloman Air Force Base in New Mexico, Fort Bliss, and Wright-Patterson Air Force Base in Ohio, Dulles Airport, and Fort Hood, Texas. Chinese troops are known to be at the Long Beach Naval Station in California. There is not going to be some future event when the invading troops are going to show up. They are already here! When martial law is implemented, these foreign U.N. troops will be policing our country, carrying out the plans of the New World Order." {Ed Note: There is/was a German Armed Forces (Bundeswehr) HQ Base at Reston, VA.}

Another expert on the subject is Colonel Jim Ammerman. Col. Ammerman is a retired Army Chaplain who remains in charge of the Chaplain program for the Army. All of the information on his radio shows and in his seminars is unclassified.

The CIA/shadow Govt operatives do censor the major news media - and make certain that the news that you digest is carefully controlled. I thought that it was interesting that some of the people (or patriots) that I talked to afterwards said, "I've heard all of this before". So have I - but none had ever "connected" it for me quite as well before.

Our Constitution is gone. There is no more balance of power since the President (and Presidents for many years now) rules by Executive Order (a de facto dictatorship); the Judicial System makes the Laws - since the Courts are based on "case law"; and Congress is caught between the other two branches; including a Congress too gutless to impeach President Clinton. [Ed Note: The Congressmen/Senators do not want to get Sony Bono-ed! They suspect the foreign forces are here!]

Furthermore, the Congress failed to rid themselves of Clinton because Hillary had everyone's FBI Files and knew all the dirty laundry. If you saw the credit and FBI reports of a number of your congressional representatives, you would say, "We're in trouble." The New World Order is in place and has been for several years now.

Have you noticed how much internal fighting there is in the Intelligence Community? Note: There were also fist fights reported in the Pentagon when JCS Action Officers dared to defy downward directed [Clintonian] orders to destroy our military prowess and defense programs. The "Action Officers" are the real "worker bees", and as Admiral Boorda did also, they recognize treason when it comes from the shadow Govt, or the White House!

EXECUTIVE ORDERS: All Executive Orders issued by the President become law in 30 days if not challenged by Congress; and are entered into the Federal Register and become Public Law.

FEDERAL RESERVE: It is NOT a government agency but a private corporation controlled by bankers all over the world (IMF and World Bank) and only three live in the U.S. (all three in NY) with the others in England, Germany, France, Italy, and the Netherlands. They control the world's economy - and our Congress!

OUR MILITARY HAS BEEN TAKEN OVER BY THE NWO: Want Proof?

F.E.M.A. - is the controlling Agency for MJTF (National Police Force of federal officers - FBI, ATF, BLM, and other federal agencies) with HQ at Ft. Monroe, VA. The MJTF holds joint operations with the Military and have been conducting exercises over major cities in this country call M.O.U.T. (Military Operations in Urban Terrain) - i.e. Pittsburgh, Houston, St. Petersburg, Mobile, and New Orleans (aborted in Ft. Lauderdale thanks to a coalition of citizens!!!).

The MJTF has been cross training with foreign troops at Ft Polk, LA. The MJTF had at one time, at least 3,000 Black Helicopters to use in these exercises. The M.O.U.T. operations are coordinated out of 29 Palms Marine Corps base (remember the infamous questionnaire from 29 Palms: "Would you fire upon U.S. citizens who refuse or resist confiscation of firearms banned by the U.S. government?). One of the exercises conducted by the MOUT operations has been to disable a major telephone switching station. Since there are only five major switching stations, the whole country could be immobilized in a very short period!). "Gun Grabs" are already taking place across the country - beginning with police and military personnel under the Domestic Violence Act passed under the cover of the Omnibus Budget Bill - the beginning [these people have to practice!].

Roadblocks are being set up in school zones checking vehicles for firearms. [Ed Note: Foreign troops have been reported setting up "short term" roadblocks, and are arresting US citizens. The road blocks are "short term" because these creeps know the militia guys might show up! These have been reported in Illinois, Michigan, and Alabama, to date. Never give out your social security number to a strange sounding "officer", in a black uniform, with a palm pilot in his hand, and a Makerov 9mm on his hip!]

FEMA has many underground operations, the largest of which is in Mt. Weather, VA, just outside Washington, D.C. FEMA is under the control of the many detention centers built in every area of the United States - 142 in all, with many more being built. These will be operated by the MJTF/ eventually composed of UN troops, who are now "practicing" house-to-house searches and seizures, when martial law is declared. The largest of these facilities is located in Beech Grove near Indianapolis, IN). Primary practice area is Ft. Polk, Louisiana. {Ed Note: All 34 FEMA bases are guarded by foreign troops!]

The RESERVE Forces of the United States have been under F.E.M.A. Command since 1995 when they were placed under 10 Regional Commands. This is patently illegal but it happened under the Clintons. However, as of 24 Sept 03, it appears the Guard and Reserves will be deployed to Iraq, leaving few US combat troops of any Service here. Al Cuppett was warning of this possibility as early as 1994!

These ARCOM Commands have been reduced by many closings (Willow Grove, PA; East Point, GA; Columbus, OH; Forest Park, IL; Ft Meade, MD; St Louis, MO; and Nashville, TN. Many have been reduced in size: San Antonio, TX; Ft. Jackson, SC; and Harrison, IN. Since the National Guards (under our State Governors) have been cross training with the MJTF, it is obvious that they too are under FEMA command.

Please email RAYHOPE@AMERICASOLDOUT.COM if the next page in this book is blank.

For a chart on top to bottom New World Order Command and Control

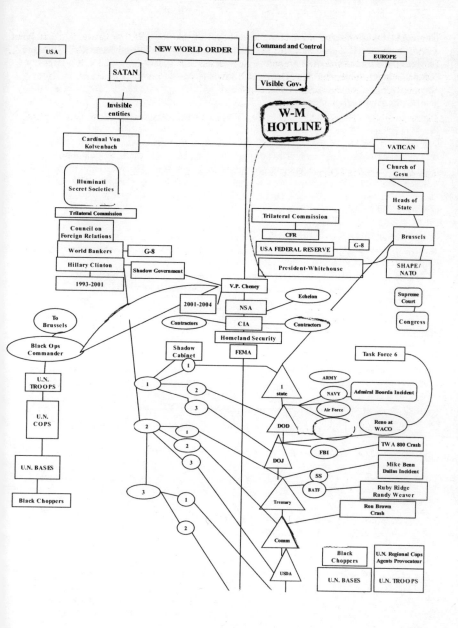

USA

NEW WORLD ORDER

Command and Control

EUROPE

SATAN

Visible Gov.

Invisible entities

W-M HOTLINE

Cardinal Von Kolvenbach

VATICAN

Church of Gesu

Illuminati Secret Societies

Heads of State

Trilateral Commission

Trilateral Commission

Brussels

Council on Foreign Relations

CFR

World Bankers

G-8

USA FEDERAL RESERVE

G-8

SHAPE/ NATO

Hillary Clinton

President-Whitehouse

1993-2001

Shadow Government

V.P. Cheney

Echelon

Supreme Court

Congress

2001-2004

NSA

Contractors

CIA

Contractors

To Brussels

Homeland Security

Black Ops Commander

Shadow Cabinet

FEMA

Task Force 6

U.N. TROOPS

1

1

state

ARMY

NAVY

Admiral Boorda Incident

U.N. COPS

2

3

DOD

Air Force

Reno at WACO

2

1

TWA 800 Crash

U.N. BASES

2

DOJ

FBI

Mike Benn Dallas Incident

Black Choppers

3

SS

3

1

BATF

Ruby Ridge Randy Weaver

Treasury

Ron Brown Crash

2

Comm

Black Choppers

U.N. Regional Cops Agents Provocateur

USDA

U.N. BASES

U.N. TROOPS

37

The BLM (Bureau of Land Management) is now part of the "National Police Force" and has its own police force and swat teams and the authority to seize property from "violators". The Forest Service is being equipped with APC's (Armoured Personnel Carriers) painted White. (UN color) Colonel Ammerman knows the contractor who is painting these vehicles in Texas. [Ed Note: There are (as of April 2002) four APC's hidden in a 4H Camp at Bittinger, MD, of which the Sheriff was completely unaware!]

The MJTF is now in place in our major cities and working with local police and Sheriff's Departments. The units are equipped with the latest high-tech equipment, including black helicopters enabled to see into houses and see guns, etc., can disable cars by scrambling their computers, and can strip search you naked without touching you! {Ed Note: Only those sheriffs who have been duped into abrogating their constitutional authority are working with these unconstitutional and illegal forces. One Iowa sheriff, who figured out what was going on, even deputized 200 men!]

FOREIGN TROOPS: It is estimated that anywhere from 400,000 to one million foreign troops are now in the United States. They are located on our military installations and in our National Parks. Any pilot will tell you that we now have Restricted Airspace over all of our National Parks (now U.N. controlled). That is because there are already foreign troops there or soon will be there. Biospheres are also being created so that these troops will have more places for facilities and will be under the control of the United Nations.

These forces now cross-train with our Active Duty Military Forces - presumably under the guise of "peacekeeping" operations. Germany has an official Air Force Base in New Mexico and a Command HQ in Reston, VA - both flying the German flag. German troops also train at Ft Hood, TX and Shephard AFB - and other bases across the country. The Russians are at Ft. Drum, NY. Many come in and out and have trained at nearly major military facility of the U.S.

THE KURDS - 15,000 Iraqi Kurds are now in Guam and to be moved soon (if not already) to Michigan. Will they join this force already training in America? Probably.

OTHER CONFISCATIONS:

The Long Beach Naval Station (closed in the BRAC of 1991 and 1994) has been sold to Red China in 1996 and is to become a cargo port in late 1997. (See Safan 317).

President Clinton seized 1.7 million acres of private [high-grade coal] land in Utah without prior notification to the Governor, the Legislators, or the People of Utah, and no notification to the Congress of the United States.

The Presidio is now the HQ of the Gorbachev Foundation and is the home of Mikhail Gorbachev (who is NOT in exile) with offices around the world with HQ. in Moscow.

BOSNIA - President Clinton lied to Congress about the number of troops sent to Bosnia - supposedly 20,000. However, at least 52,000 were sent initially.

When 15,000 troops were sent home, over 5,000 troops were sent over from Ft Hood, TX - and now it is estimated that over 42,000 troops remain in Bosnia [in squalid conditions!] It was recently discovered that the remaining troops are not allowed bullets or ammunition for their weapons. This is especially disturbing to many of them since the Muslims in their midst rape and gang rape their own Muslim women and are now raping the women in our military - and the American men have no bullets to stop them. [Ed Note: Al Cuppett talked to two returning US Army Sergeants in 2003 and they confirmed the ammunition problem! You wonder why honest UN peacekeepers fail to assist local people in foreign countries? They have about 200 rounds of ammo! Nevertheless, be sure the UN troops will have ammo HERE!]

The U.N. Organizations are already in control of the World through N.A.T.O. and S.E.A.T.O. and L.O.S.T. (Law of the Sea) Treaties, which controls all waters - oceans and inland waterways. The NWO held a dinner at the Gorbachev Foundation (over $8,000 a plate) with Ted Turner as Moderator.

Present were Sr. Bush, Thatcher, and other "former" world leaders. It was stated at that dinner that over 40% of the world's population must be eliminated!

SCHOOLS:

Anyone who doubts that the U.S. has not been taken over by the NWO does not have a child in school. Goals 2000, a U.N. Mandate, has already rewritten the history books in our Public Libraries and Schools and removed important events in our history, such as Pearl Harbor, and stating that our Revolutionary heroes (writers of our Bill of Rights and the Constitution) were criminals.

THE 10 COMMANDMENTS

Being moved in Alabama and other places in the United States. Look for more home and Commandment seizures in days to come.

AIDS - Created to destroy "people" - evidenced by the fact that AIDS patients should have been quarantined on the onset of the disease in this country if the standards had been followed since Aids is 100 times more dangerous than the diseases now requiring quarantine.

THE JUDICIARY: U.S. Judge Advocate School at Maxwell AFB, AL, and (all military) held a mock trial, found George Washington guilty, and shot him.

THE CHURCHES: Are all-illegal - except for the churches whose religion is nature. Clinton declared implemented in an Executive Order. If you want your church to be free from regulation, perhaps ridding yourself of the 501 C-3 Exempt statuses would help. Otherwise, the government will control you and you already cannot tell people how to vote. It will get worse.

HEALTH INSURANCE BILL (S 1028) and (HR 3103) passed in April 1996 had a rider which originated with the World Health Organization (CODEX) to control food supplements (herbs and vitamins) - and part of the GATT Treaty. This gives the FDA authority to close down health food stores since vitamins and herbs and other food supplements can only be dispensed by a physician's prescription.

TWA-800 CRASH - Pierre Salinger risked his life in his revelation that the French Government knew that there were two men on the plane carrying documents "that would bring down the Clinton administration". The CIA-controlled U.S. press does not carry these particular "stories", so it is common for individuals to fly information to London, Paris, and Luxembourg for publication. {Ed Note: However, for purposes of obfuscation, every and any theory was allowed to be press-advanced in the TWA shoot down. All except the missile-firing, "foreign-piloted-chopper" theory! Why? Because it would reveal that UN forces are operating in the USA!

DRUG trafficking is controlled by the CIA (shadow Govt-appointed officers) and the Mafia. Only intruders are arrested. The CIA introduced crack cocaine to the streets of L.A. and used the money to fund black operations in South America. The money had to come from somewhere; the Congress, at that time, would not appropriate any funds.

TRAITORS in our own government did carry on two wars that we could not win causing the deaths of our soldiers in the Korean and Vietnam Conflicts. Right on!

OKC BOMBING - The Fire Chief of OKC was notified prior to the bombing that it was going to happen and bomb squads were on the scene at the time of the blast. Gen. Ben Partin said that there were definitely TWO blasts - as confirmed by seismographs taken by the Oklahoma Geological Survey.

Col Ammerman personally knows several Sheriffs in Texas who are deputizing Civilians and vow their counties will NOT be federalized. One of the most interesting things Col. Ammerman said was - "Take this scenario: If the President is indicted, he will declare martial law. Nixon was getting ready to declare martial law but was talked into resigning instead by the Generals and Admirals of his time. What stopped Clinton from declaring was the plot for martial law was leaked and publicized and his plans for a third run at the Presidency was negated.

Everyone knows that after 2 terms, you are finished, except Clinton. {Ed Note: The Chief of Naval Operations, Admiral Mike Boorda, wanted Clinton tried for treason before a military tribunal, but one [or more] of the Joint Chiefs squealed to the ["shadow Govt"] on him; thus, he died with three bullets in his body! Thus, this patriotic Jew became a martyr for his country.]

Somalia: I have purposely left out the Somalia debacle where Clinton and his idiots, principally [once Wisconsin Congressman and] military-hating Secretary of Defense, Les Aspin, failed to deploy armored vehicles, artillery, or close air support (CAS) to support the infantry ground contingent, thus, eighteen Army Rangers/Green Berets were killed and dragged through the streets. Carter was no better with his poor planning and the lives lost in his failed operation "Desert One". After all, these guys Clinton and Carter both love the UN and they may have wanted these men killed? Anything is possible. If they were not intentionally doing it, they will go down as the biggest idiots to claim the title "Commander and Chief" {Ed Note: The game is to destroy US forces in any manner, and wherever possible!]

Chapter 5

EYEWITNESS PERSPECTIVE

From Pam Schuffert, reporting from Germany

I received a report from a military veteran "Watchdog") and his watchdog group regarding ultra-sophisticated Russian and German tanks brought into America for the hour of martial law via Canada through Prince Edward Island. Every six months, German troops are being brought into North America through this channel as well. These tanks are painted in camo colors, and have a mini-nuke launching capacity. Special body protection suits for these foreign troops, developed by the Russians for the UN and the operators of these tanks, include special filters and protective measures so that, following launching these mini-nukes into their targeted areas, they can move in after one hour for mop up operations. Operators of these tanks will be German, Russian, and Czech. A recent email informed me that German troops are now prepositioned across North America in over 100 locations. Such tanks are expected to be deployed under martial law. [Ed Note: The foreign troops, equipment, and an entire national support infrastructure have been built, and are ready for employment as of 25 Sept 2003. Fact: Most highway bridges, across the US, have been rebuilt in the past 12 years to support 70 tons. A bakery truck does not weigh 70 tons!

From SATANISM IN AMERICA TODAY by Pam Schuffert)

When I spent ten years traveling and researching for my book exposing SATANISM in America, I was stunned by the large admissions of human abduction and sacrifice that occur annually, as confirmed by former FBI investigator of Satanism, Ted Gunderson, and many former high-level Satanist leaders in America. Satanists coming out of it to expose the truth, such as former high priestess Phoebe Brown of South America, have made the startling admission:" SATAN IS DEMANDING MORE AND MORE ACTS OF HUMAN SACRIFICE TO GIVE HIM POWER TO BRING FORTH HIS NEW WORLD ORDER!" Satanists I interviewed in America agreed completely. Admitted one former high priestess for 17 years of a large region in the USA, "Satan was demanding Christians for sacrifice, and we obliged...we carefully targeted, stalked, and abducted our victims...and they died like all the rest".

HOW did they die, I asked. Eyewitnesses and former participants spared me no details. Once abducted and thrown into the back of Satanist vans, for example, they were quickly injected with a knockout drug, and their hands, feet, and mouth were bound by duct tape. They would wake up chained to Satanist altars or being nailed to crosses, and often tempted to deny Christ and their faith and join the Satanists in order to be spared.

Moreover, when Christians refuse, they are virtually tortured and killed. Often skinned alive, tongues ripped out to keep them from praying or witnessing about Jesus Christ, brutally raped, nailed to crosses, burned, dismembered, electric torture, pregnant women ripped open and both mother and unborn sacrificed. One coven admitted to inventing a cross which, after the victim was nailed to it, the cross could be separated in the middle and the victim torn into pieces. In addition, much more...I will spare you the details.

The Satanists across America admitted that they believed that Satan was demanding more and more sacrifices so he could be given power to help them BRING FORTH THE NEW WORLD

ORDER. {Ed Note: Red List, Category 1 people, as reported by Serge Monast, before they killed him, revealed the Satanists plan to abduct Christian women and girls for satanic sacrifice. This is the Fourth Reich folks! In addition, they plan to go after Jewish people first, since they are a minority and can be demonized easily. Al Cuppett has been trying to warn Jews to Aliyah to Israel for five years! That is because most Chrisyi]

WHY am I sharing this? Because SATANIST INFILTRATION IS INTENSE IN THE MILITARY AND THE INTELLIGENCE COMMUNITY AND THE US GOVERNMENT. I SHOULD know: I lived in the Washington DC area for many years, grew up totally surrounded by the military, and endured the hell of my own father being a high-level military Satanist. These Satanists occupy often high places in the Pentagon, CIA, FBI, etc...all of which will be used heavily to bring America under martial law and to deal with resisters. Such Satanists all share the beliefs I have listed above: that every person sacrificed to Satan counts as one more to give Satan power to bring forth the New World Order.

They explained that THIS IS WHY THE RESISTERS OF THE NWO UNDER MARTIAL LAW WILL BE TREATED ESPECIALLY SEVERELY AND THEN TERMINATED. Each person arrested on government lists under martial law (Christian resister, Patriot, militia, etc.) WILL BE COUNTED AS ONE MORE SACRIFICE TO SATAN TO BRING FORTH THE NWO. This is why, in part, the treatment of resisters will be so horrific in the FEMA-military detention-termination camps under martial law.

Admitted a former Satanist whose father was a high military Satanist on the west coast and involved intensely in NWO military planning and mind control": We Satanists would sit around planning the termination techniques for people arrested under martial law. We decided that we would prolong the torture of Christians and other resisters for as long as possible before they would be terminated. "Such Satanists ought to know this reality: They are already practicing this on abducted victims across America on Satanic altars by night.

It is estimated that Satanist sacrifices across America annually average into the upper hundreds of thousands of victims (as confirmed by Ted Gunderson of the FBI and many insiders.)

US Military Training Rapidly with Foreign Troops Here in Europe for US Martial Law.

I have been researching in Germany for 5 months now, and everything indicates rapid training of our troops to work side by side with cooperating foreign troops for the coming conquest of AMERICA UNDER MARTIAL LAW. As I read the European edition of STARS AND STRIPES almost daily, numerous military publications plus European news journals and newspapers, and interviewing actual military here, I am coming to realize the extent that THE AMERICAN PEOPLE HAVE BEEN DECEIVED AND BETRAYED INTO THE HANDS OF THE NEW WORLD ORDER BY HER VERY OWN GOVERNMENT AND MILITARY!

One military publication shared about a major operation involving three branches of the US military in which they were learning to work intensely together IN A CONTINGENCY EXERCISE. CONTINGENCY means MARTIAL LAW. Here in Europe, Americans are being rapidly trained through the Balkan crisis to work side by side with Russians, Germans, and other foreign troops ALL UNDER THE UN BLUE AND NATO. They are being trained in various exercises as weapons seizures, intimidating resisters to surrender and lay down their weapons, how to operate prisoner detention camps holding resisters of this UN MNTF "peacekeeping" effort complete with guard towers, and more. JANE'S DEFENSE magazine has published pictures of German Bundeswehr (military) looking over large caches of weapons seized from

4

"insurgents, militants, etc.," all in this obvious training exercise in the Balkans designed to prepared American and foreign troops FOR THE HOUR OF MARTIAL LAW IN AMERICA.

I interviewed three German Bundeswehr MP´s fresh from Kosovo, pistols strapped to their sides and white MP armbands on their arms. Here are their revealing comments (This interview took place at the train station in Munich.)

"Oh, yes, we know about our German troops in America. Fort Bliss and Holloman AFB..." I asked, "Do you know WHY they are there...for the hour of martial law, to help arrest Americans and seize their weapons and fire upon them if they resist?" The spokesman for the group said, "Yes, we have heard all this, AND IT IS TRUE." Yet so many of my fellow Americans DO NOT!

Looking at him intently, I asked him this question: "IF martial law is declared in America, could you fire UPON ME?" He would not reply as he looked at me. His cold, steely eyes reflected the position of a professional soldier hardened by German military training and experience in Kosovo. Stiffening, he abruptly excused himself and his two companions and hurried off to their train. We understood each other perfectly.

US military are also being hardened through their experience in the Balkans. They are being conditioned to serving under UN BLUE and NATO, much as they will do in America under martial law. They are being conditioned to deal with "militants, insurgents, resisters," which is exactly how all Patriot resisters under martial law will be labeled as by the US government and military. Fellow Americans, it is time to wake up to the reality of the coming quest for America...and to realize the extent to which we have been betrayed and deceived in this matter. As Chuck Colson once admitted, "It is not inconceivable that, in the future, the US military will be used AGAINST THE AMERICAN PEOPLE." I tell you, <u>I am watching with my own eyes the preparation and conditioning of our American troops for that very hour.</u>

(Was it not great to see the Military in the USA totally reject the Blue UN Berets that we were being asked to convert to a few years ago?) (These berets were blue (UN color) and MADE IN CHINA)

A previous trainer of foreign troops in MOUT exercises at Fort Polk LA admitted to me when he read my book, PREMONITIONS OF AN AMERICAN HOLOCAUST (regarding coming martial law,) <u>"Ma´am, everything in your book IS TRUE, and I am leaving America with my wife and child as soon as I can. Because MARTIAL LAW IS COMING...AND IT WILL BE TERRIBLE WHEN IT COMES.</u>"

What the US news media is desperately trying to hide from the American people, I am watching firsthand here in Europe as so many joint military exercises take place one after the other, and each one points to preparation for COMING MARTIAL LAW (And why not? IF the Russian threat and the cold war are OVER, WHY ALL THESE EXERCISES?) WAKE UP!

<u>Reporting from Germany, Pam Schuffert</u>

Germany glorifies 666 and Satanist Pentagram Goat head.

In the five months I have been investigating and reporting from Germany, I have noted the rise in Satanism, Theosophy and esoteric teachings that once fueled and fired Adolph Hitler and his previous Nazi, new World Order madness. While interviewing one German Bundeswehr in

Munich, he opened his wallet and pulled out HIS GERMAN NATIONAL ID CARD, REQUIRED BY ALL CITIZENS. He showed me the back of his ID card. "What do you see," he asked. I held the card and studied it. All of a sudden, I was stunned. "I see THE CLEAR OUTLINE OF BAPHOMET, THE SATANIST PENTAGRAM GOAT HEAD!" He looked at me and said, "You are right...and IT IS ON THE BACK OF EVERY GERMAN'S ID CARD!" When I started to show my German Christian friends, they were shocked, and sickened. NOW they understood what the strange symbol was on the back of their ID.

Earlier in the winter, in the Bavarian Alps (where Bavarian Thule and Illuminati originated, and with it the Hitler's madness and the New World Order PLAN) I attended an outdoor ski festival. A stage was erected in the village square, and a band with young singers began to sing and play. Suddenly, the song changed, and I heard the German words for "6-6-6-" begin to be sung by the band. Immediately, I turned to look at the crowd. I noted how many had knowing smiles on their faces, and how many began to sway and sing along as if mesmerized as the band belted out "six-six-six". This confirmed what a missionary had reported earlier, how 666 was being glorified now in Germany. Many cities are sponsoring esoteric festivals, such as in Murnau, in which the very teachings that fueled Hitler and the doctrines of "the Master Race" (by Helena Petrovna Blavatsky, who taught that Lucifer is God and that the German Aryan root race is the race from whence all future evolutionary perfection must spring forth, and hence all lesser races must be terminated.)

My German Christian friends are very wary of such developments. I am reaching Germans young and old with free Bibles and Christian literature in German, including German military. Please pray for Germany and the salvation of many...even in the midst of THE BEAST RISING FROM THE ASHES TO FULFILL BIBLE PROPHECY.

Reporting from Germany, Pam Schuffert

Satanists in CIA WANT martial law-Christian torture-death!

(From PREMONITIONS OF AN AMERICAN HOLOCAUST and SATANISM IN AMERICA TODAY; by Pam Schuffert).

"We Satanists in the CIA lusted for the hour of martial law, in which we could finally get our hands on those Christians and terminate them...we hated them and the God that they serve, because THEY ARE THE MAJOR THING THAT STANDS IN THE WAY OF OUR NEW WORLD ORDER. "The very concentration camps you are now investigating, I helped to draw up the blueprints for within the CIA. Under martial law IT WILL BE BRUTAL RAPE, TORTURE AND DEATH for the Christians once they are arrested and taken to the camps because every Christian arrested and terminated under martial law WILL COUNT AS ONE MORE SACRIFICE TO SATAN TO GIVE HIM POWER TO BRING FORTH THE NEW WORLD ORDER!" I have many friends who are not only former Satanists, but were also hired for CIA assassin roles as well. They are now Christians and talking. I spent one month in Florida living with a former Satanist assassin (female) and her family in order to interview her regarding coming martial law.

Now a Christian for many years, she shared things with me that she had never revealed before. However, I found her information confirmed what other former Satanists had revealed to me regarding the truth about coming martial law and the New World Order.

The Satanists in the United States military share the above sentiments equally. Satanism is rampant in the US military. In addition, such Satanists, with a motto of "show no mercy", often sit in the highest levels of the US military, Pentagon, and more. Moreover, they ALL know that the NWO is "their thing". Satan-Lucifer is in fact the spiritual leader of the coming New World Order.

Ask any Satanist...if you dare. Go to the Bible: it plainly declares that the coming world government with its cashless society is fully under Satan's control and those that worship him. (Revelation 13.) In my ten years of researching Satanism throughout America, I heard this consistently...and that PLANNED martial law is their means by which they can initiate America's removal from under the Constitution and begin to come under UN world government and Satan's coming world reign of darkness. Hence, Satanists have been infiltrating their people heavily into the military community, the intelligence community, and our government into the highest levels (and I can name names.)

Repeatedly, they admitted across the nation as I sat and interviewed them that , "yes, the Satanists of America (and worldwide) are fully aware of coming martial law, and how it will be used to initiate persecution and death of millions of resisters of their New World Order.

Christians and Patriot resisters are the major targets". They told me "they KNEW Christians would not accept a world government under Lucifer nor accept his mark for the cashless society. Many of the FEMA and other camps I am investigating are not so much for long term incarceration, as under Hitler, but rather for TERMINATION TO GET RID OF THEM!"

"All of us in the intelligence community know about the concentration camps in America and their purpose. We all know that they will be used to TERMINATE RESISTERS OF THE NEW WORLD ORDER as it is brought down in America UNDER MARTIAL LAW!"-(personal admission made to me from former CIA-Naval Intelligence Michael Maholy, now presumed terminated for going public with this and related information. Go to www.Google.com, type in "Michael Maholy".

For this reason, although I used to be a total pacifist and unarmed (Bible college student and missionary, etc., for 30 years), I now advocate that Americans take full advantage of their 2nd Amendment rights prior to martial law, because they do NOT want to be taken alive under martial law...especially to the camps! I know what awaits them, and I am pleading with the Christians and patriots in America to WAKE UP! Trust in God first, and apply His word for grace and protection, but realize that our Patriot forefathers fought for our freedoms with a Bible in one hand, and a loaded musket in the other. I should know...my ancestors (on my mother's side) arrived on the Mayflower and fought in the Revolution! "Having done ALL, stand...," declares the Bible.

The Satanists of America let me know how they would spare neither man, nor woman nor child under martial law, and what they did in secret BY NIGHT on satanic altars to abducted children and Christians; they would feel free to do openly BY DAY to every Christian-Patriot resisters of their NWO seized under martial law.

(Did you know thousands of children go missing daily?) Source: Ray Hope

WHY would Satanists share these deep secrets? Go to "www.Google.com" Type in "Jake Schuffert". This is my father, now deceased. You will see how famous he is on many websites in the USAF Indeed. However, what the websites dare not reveal is that, while the New World Order tragically recruited working for the Pentagon, my father into the military vision of the conquest for America. He was not only recruited into the agenda (as many others in the military and working for the government are) but he was recruited into the religion of the NWO...hard-core Satanism.

Although millions have read his USAF cartoons, and they are published to this day in the USAF publication, AIMMAN MAGAZINE, few (except USAF Satanist insiders) knew that he was a hard core Satanist for many years I lived with personal horror in my home as I struggled to be a Christian, attend Bible college, hold prayer meetings, etc. He would come home from the Pentagon attacking my mother and I and our faith in Jesus Christ. In addition, HE FULLY KNEW ABOUT THE COMING MARTIAL LAW AND THE CONCENTRATION CAMPS!

He said cruelly to me one night after coming home from the Pentagon, "EVERYONE WHO BELIEVES IN GOD AND MIRACLES SHOULD BE SENT TO CONCENTRATION CAMPS!" Oh, how I would weep over my father and plead with him to be saved. Finally, as he lay dying of bone cancer in 1998, he asked me to come home and take care of him. I did so, and confronted him with his Satanism and the need to repent and accept Jesus Christ.

 Finally, Daddy came home. His former high priest in Virginia Beach, J____., told me everything and has become a Christian. Col. Jim Ammerman, famous military Patriot and exposer of martial law and the NWO, sent one of his top military chaplains, Chaplain Ailsworth, to our Washington DC home to confront my father and to call him to repent. Ammerman was on board a flight a few years ago and was injected with Lyme's disease but has since recovered. (No weapon formed against us shall prosper without the approval of the Almighty God).

My father repented totally, asked Jesus into his heart, and became a totally changed man. I fought the battle against the New World Order and Satanism in my own home for 30 years, AND WON THROUGH JESUS CHRIST!

The Satanists in America opened up to me in part because of my father's tragic connections in that dark world. So many knew my father. Only God can know the personal heartache I have endured for so many years because of him and his dark ties with NWO Satanism.

Nevertheless, I have emerged as a survivor, to the glory of God. Moreover, although by daring to go public with this dark secret, I am opening myself up to severe Satanist wrath and retaliation for daring to go public with such revelations, I consider you...my beloved fellow Americans, Christians, Patriots and all who are the targets under coming martial law... WORTH IT ALL TO TELL AMERICA THE TRUTH!

Being able to WAKE UP AMERICA TO THE COMING HORRORS UNDER MARTIAL LAW IS WORTH EVERYTHING God will call me to suffer for my testimony and openness to fellow Americans. I know I will undoubtedly die quite a martyr's death for my faith and my public stand against Satanism and martial law, BUT JESUS CHRIST IS WORTHY! (Besides, many of you will die for you faith as well...)

Fellow Patriots, DO NOT SURRENDER UNDER MARTIAL LAW! Do not surrender to the WORLD'S SATANISTS! You will only lay down your weapons and surrender yourselves to brutal torture, your daughters to be raped and sodomized and sacrificed by Satanists, and worse. It is time to lay down your lives for your nation, your religious freedoms and heritage and the future freedoms of the coming generations.

Loving you and praying for you all, Pam Schuffert
(Please forward this out ASAP)

I received a report from Pensacola, Florida about one Pastor and his visitation by several FEMA officials. They told him, "Pastor, we've decided that UNDER MARTIAL LAW we are going to SEIZE YOUR CHURCH and use it for our base of operations here."

Does FEMA or the government have the power to do so?

ABSOLUTELY... under martial law, as our Constitutionally guaranteed freedoms are swept away and we are forced to come under pre-existing PRESIDENTIAL EXECUTIVE ORDERS that deny us our previous liberties under the Constitution. UNDER MARTIAL LAW, FEMA can seize your home, family members and separate them, your vehicles, and your land and possessions including food supplies, you are Church, and more.

The Presidential Executive orders will turn America into a police state and military dictatorship, denying Christians and other groups the previous RIGHT TO FREELY ASSEMBLE. Which means that you and your fellow Christians can be SUBJECT TO ARREST for failure to disperse when you meet for Church gatherings on Sundays or any other days, gather for prayer meetings, etc?

There are excellent website that publish and discuss the PRESIDENTIAL EXECUTIVE ORDERS THAT WE ARE GOING TO COME UNDER AS THE SIGNS OF MARTIAL LAW PROGRESS AND THE PRESIDENT CONTINUES TO EVOKE EMERGENCY POWERS that are increasingly taking away from our freedoms and civil liberties.

Churches in America should be prepared for the great persecution that is soon to take place on American soil. When Jesus Christ declared", *Ye shall be hated of ALL nations*..." speaking of the end times specifically, realize that ALL NATIONS must include the United States of America!"...*And then shall they deliver you up to tribulation and to be put to death...BUT HE THAT ENDURETH TO THE END SHALL BE SAVED.*" NOT "he that shall be raptured", but rather "*he that endureth to the end*". (From Matthew 24)

[Ed Note: While in Vietnam [since my childhood pastor had severely chastised me after I "*wrongly*" preached on Matt 24, as a new bon-bible schooled Christian] I prayed for three days about the "pre-trib rapture"; asking the Lord for guidance. The fourth day a booklet arrived with no return address, entitled." *Watchman, What of the Night?*" My prayers were answered! There shall be no pre-trib "rapture". Al Cuppett

Christians who have anxiously been following events in American indicating coming persecution and testing have also been hoping intensely that a Rapture will take them out BEFORE they will be tested and tried for their faith (as other Christians worldwide have been tried severely in recent decades.) I remind them that no "quickly Rapture" came to save the millions of Christians who were imprisoned or slain under communist takeover in Russia, China and many other nations. No Rapture came to rescue Sudanese Christians from Moslem persecution and literal crucifixion in many cases. No Rapture saved the many Cuban Christians who died with Jesus Christ on their lips in front of Fidel's communist death squads.

They were allowed to be tested as by fire for their faith. According to the many words of prophecy, I have collected from Pastors and prayer groups regarding these coming events (which confirm end time Bible prophecy), I personally believe that the TRUE Christians in America are going to face the great trial of their faith. Ultimately, this will result in imprisonment and literal martyrdom for their steadfast faith and confession of Jesus Christ. (I speak of millions of persecuted and martyred Christians in the times to come in America.)

Admitted one youth Pastor in California whom I interviewed while distributing my book, PREMONITIONS OF AN AMERICAN HOLOCAUST,

"Ma'am, none of what you are sharing with me is a surprise. God showed me in a vision TWICE a few nights ago that MARTIAL LAW WAS COMING, and I saw it all happen. I saw myself arrested and dragged before a modern guillotine, and asked, 'Pastor, are you willing to renounce your faith and work with us, or die?' I remember being very sacred, but I would never renounce my faith in Jesus. I was then beheaded. I woke up, wondering what it all meant. I went back to sleep, and the same vision repeated itself, only this time I was put into a prison to 'rethink' my decision. Nevertheless, I still confessed Jesus as Lord, and was beheaded. I always know, when God repeats a vision that it will come to pass."

Friends, the tools of our persecution are all in place. The hundreds of thousands of modern guillotines manufactured in Japan and China are here, waiting for the hour of martial law and the termination of all deemed "resisters of the NWO". Revelation 20:4 is clear on the persecution/martyrdom if those end time believers in Jesus who refuse to cooperate with the New World Order and its cashless society "MARK".

"And I saw the souls of them beheaded for the witness of Jesus and the Word of God."

The concentration camps are all in place to "terminate resisters of the New World Order" as it comes down under martial law. {Ed Note: While speaking in Odessa, TX, the host told me that the sister sitting three people away, was told by her brother in Oakland, CA, the following: *I was operating a crane, when a container dropped. It broke open and inside was four foot high guillotines". They were marked for shipment to a FEMA site!*}

"Oh, all of us in the intelligence community know about the concentration camps in America. We all know that they are to terminate the resisters of the New World Order under martial law...," admitted my friend Michael Maholy, 20 years Naval Intel/CIA and previously a dedicated worked for the NWO under Bush Sr. Michael became a Christian and decided to blow the whistle on the NWO agenda.

"We Satanists in the CIA hated the Christians, because they were the one thing that stood in the way of our implementing the New World Order in America. Therefore, we came up with the concentration camps you are now investigating. I even helped to draw up some of the blueprints for some of them.

Although I greatly regret my role now, nevertheless they stand to this day and will be activated UNDER MARTIAL LAW. We lusted for the hour of martial law when we could finally get our hands on them legally...I tell you, it will be BRUTAL RAPE, TORTURE AND DEATH for them once they are arrested and taken to the concentration camps under martial law..." (Admission of my friend, former CIA assassin and satanist high priestess, now Christian lecturer/author exposing the NWO and Satanism.) The boxcars and shackles are in place across America to haul all resisters away, Nazi style, to the death camps of America under martial law.

"God has been giving me dreams of Christians being arrested in America and taken to railroad boxcars and hauled away like cattle to be slaughtered in concentration camps," admitted one Montanan Christian who I met at a Derek Prince prophecy conference. "I used to wonder what this meant, but with your explanation of what will happen under martial law, I NOW UNDERSTAND WHAT GOD WAS TRYING TO TELL ME!" I advised her that there were several concentration camps and sightings of boxcars and shackles already in Montana, waiting for that hour.

Christians in America, I write these things NOT to instill a spirit of fear, which God never gives us, but rather to illustrate the reality of Bible prophecy regarding end time persecution of all believers and how it will be manifested in our nation.

Most Pastors have NOT prepared you to face this reality. They have constantly swept God's warnings through visions and prophecies and books such as mine aside and instead given you an "exit" mentality revolving around the Rapture. While it is absolutely true that Jesus Christ IS coming soon, nowhere in Scriptures do we find ANY verse guaranteeing that We, the Church in North America, are SO special that WE WILL BE RAPTURED prior to end-time persecution and the trial of our faith! No, the Christians in many other countries can go through end-time persecution and martyrdoms, but NOT US.

I have found this false theological doctrine and subsequent "escapist" presumption rampant across America as I have traveled and lectured, and it has saddened me greatly. Those who believe in this type of teaching will scarcely take the time to prepare their hearts before God to suffer and die for their testimony of Jesus Christ and their refusal to deny Him before men. Moreover, as Scripture soberly declares, there WILL be a GREAT FALLING AWAY before Christ returns.

What frequently causes a falling away BUT PERSECUTION!

You are watching with your own eyes the beginning of the END of America as we have known her, and the beginning of the great persecution of the Church in America is about to commence. I suggest you take the time to fall upon your faces before the Living God and implore Him to give you the grace to endure throughout the coming persecution.

Purpose in your heart to confess Jesus Christ as Lord both in word and deed faithfully, even if this means a fiery trial of faith and the tools of persecution I have documented that are prepared against the Christians in America for this coming hour. We must never be moved to deny our faith under fire! It is a matter of your eternal salvation.

Chapter 6

Why the Strange Troops, Police, and Events All Across the USA?

This "staff letter" was begun in 1998 with weekly incoming data, has been updated 27 times since then!

By: "Al" Cuppett (US Army/The Joint Staff (OJCS), Retired)

I recently completed a sponsored speaking tour, which began in Feb 98 [and now] covering 75 or more venues, in 28 states, and 3 countries. I met/spoke to thousands of people, including untold thousands on radio/TV, or by videocassette. Moreover, with what they have either written or told me, I am now going to encapsulate some of the data into a brief "staff" letter. As I do, I am reminded of the stark reality of the sign behind General Prather's [then-XOK] HQ USAF Air Staff desk in the Pentagon, which read, "*What you don't know won't hurt you... It'll kill you!*" It's with the general's sign in mind, and based on prima facie evidence, both spoken/written, which I now 'know or possess, that I write these paragraphs, in a continuing and desperate effort to awaken you, dear reader, to the 'clear and present danger' that's now upon us! Remember Hosea 4:6 "*My people are destroyed for lack of knowledge*"?

Although rarely reported by any local or national media, all across the US tens of thousands of Chinese/Soviet/UN troops and police, under the guise of United Nations/Clinton's "Partnership for Peace" (PfP) and "Project Harmony" operations are now poised/operating, or in place. Furthermore, in accordance with the Soviet Order of Battle in collusion with the UN/FEMA and other [basement cabinet/now "shadow Govt"] controlled federal agencies, T-72 tanks, MIG-29s, Makerov 9mm pistols, AK-47 rifles, BMP-40 armored cars, SAM-8 missile batteries, 130mm howitzers, Zil trucks, K-9 dogs, bio-chemical units, and myriads of other Soviet gear, are all in place, ready to strike at the right time, i.e., a set time, being planned by a 'Globalist' UN cabal, and their New World Order (NWO); to be directed from Brussels/Moscow/Iraq, depending on which has attained "first strike advantage" when our "Martial Law Declaration/D-Day" arrives! [9-11-01: Somebody got "first strike" on us!]

In the states VA/TN/PA/MA/TX/NM, WV, CA, MI, and OR, to name a few, the foreign "Cops [on the Street" funded] have been identified as "Regional Police". In the states of AZ/GA/MS/CA/OH/OK/LA/KS/IN/MD/WI/CO/OR/VA/ FL, and IL, they've been wearing indicia/badges, driving vehicles, or have tags which read either, "Red Dog Strike Force ,MOXCBA (Moscow) Police, Kansas State Police, Tennessee Military Police, International Crimes Enforcement Police, International Police, Multi-National Force Observer-UN Honorary Pro-Counsel, Polizei, Wausau [WI] Community Police, Federal Police, American Police, U.S. Police, Enforcement Officer, Parole Officer, Secretary of State Police, National Police Force, and Border Patrol". [5-10-01 Note: The fed funded program is the, "Community Oriented Police/Policing"; i.e., the "secret police (SS)"!]

*In most places, they are carrying FEMA/State Dept-issued federal ID cards! To wit, thousands of troops are bivouacked in US parks, and on "closed" bases; and in one instance they gunned down three guys whom ATV-ed into a remote park area. Moreover, they are executing "black operations" in choppers, and vehicles against #"*Red-Blue*" listed Americans everyday! Scores of PfP troops were taped goose-stepping on Camp LeJune, NC. They are here folks, and Clinton has ordered our Guard/Reserves, to turn in all ammo stocks & MGs as "terrorists might get them"!

In the last 10 years they've built (FEMA/State Dept-established) infrastructures of buildings, aviation weather towers, EMP vehicle arrestors, video imaging cameras, C2 commo nets, etc, which are hidden in "front", or clandestine facilities, in nearly every county in the US; including yours! This includes the sinister GWEN system, which does more to us than they have told us. Moreover, the 34-plus US FEMA bases are now guarded by PfP troops! Just try to approach one, either ginseng or squirrel hunting, etc, or in a taxi -- as happened near Cismont, VA, at the Peter's Mt base!

To put on paper the 20 hours/masses of data, pictures, maps, diagrams, and testimony, would be nearly impossible. However, maybe the following will alert you to the reality of the above facts: The son of a friend was stationed at F.E. Warren AFB, WY. He once called his dad and said, **"Dad, we have foreign officers in charge of these [Minuteman] silos, who can hardly speak English - and we have to salute 'them!" [He has since left the AF]. Furthermore, there were PfP troops in NC, wearing 10th Special Forces unit patches, "helping" to search for Eric Rudolph. I have the first person report from an Army SFC involved in the search, which, by the way, is contrary to "Posse Comitatus", if anybody even cares. The local NC folks were/are actually fearful! Rudolph was not captured, he surrendered to the authorities. [Regardless, the "game" is to get all our combat guys overseas peacekeeping/fighting, and the UN troops/cops here; and all the private guns confiscated!] To wit, it's "*Ordo Ab Chao*" - A New Order out of Chaos; i.e., a [Satan] controlled "New Order" out of the soon coming chaos "they" shall create!

Excuse me, but I didn't receive "The Secretary of Defense Civilian Service Medal & Joint Meritorious Unit Award, The Bronze Star & Purple Heart, et al", based on my smile while running' around 'Nam, or in some 31 other odd lands, or even through Pentagon halls for 31 years; rather, I was awarded all for dedication/service to the USA! The unthinkable is about to happen, both physically/spiritually, to the USA. It is all here, coming soon to your county. Godspeed, you will soon need it, because the UN will soon be policing the USA!

Respectfully, with just, and only] the cold, ominous tip of the iceberg,

Signed: "Al' Cuppett

Footnotes: # most folks receiving a copy of this letter should be considered to be on the UN/FEMA's "Red" or "Blue" Lists! *It has all happened right before your TV-watching' eyes. Moreover, our current [UN!] logistics support is so overtaxed/degraded that our people o'seas, [in over 140 countries] in the event of a major US crisis, could starve to death! I am sure the 9-11 "hiatus" caused great concern for Pentagon logisticians. Seven Sep 02: They are shipping thousands overseas everyday as the Iraq war looms ahead including the NG and Reserves! ** NWO "Damage Control", now "caught-in-the-act", surely has removed these officers from the silos (Nov 2000.) --- Shalom,

Al Cuppett

P.S. Whatever you do, do not "wax" [turn] anti-Semitic. God has a COVENANT/deal with that ethnic group. Do not make the mistake of running them down, other than the "biggie" Illuminists, like Greenspan, Waxman, Schumer... Do not get on the Lord's wrong side by cursing the seed of Abraham. Many do it and they shall be the first ones the NWO catches, as they will have no

Divine help. Bless the Jew,' because he has a "Plan" that God made with Abraham! One third of Israel [the people existing in the land at the time of the end] shall be saved!

Ed Note: Check the Appendix and look for a photo of the "*Regional Police*" car. They are operating in at least 10 states! "Two witnesses, one man, and one woman, have told me they are "bad cops"!

Col. Stanislav Lunev –The highest-ranking military officer ever to defect to the United States. He left Russia in 1992, after having attained the rank of a full colonel in the Soviet Military. Col. Lunev advised the rank and file of the suitcase nukes, which will be used to bring down the USA. [The official term is "*back-pack nukes*".]

The plan by the enemy would be to position strategic nuclear devices (suit case nukes) and detonate them simultaneously, while bringing down several major cities, the stock market, and cause utter chaos. After the cities are neutralized, foreign troops would be brought in, Martial law declared and the UN Peacekeepers and others would in essence keep the peace. At that time, gun confiscations, house-to-house searches, and red/blue list pick-ups would begin. [This terrible scenario *was* planned for 1 Jan 2000! See below.]

The camps would be used to house not only those who need shelter but resisters to the plan of Martial law. This scenario came close to being played out during the Clinton administration, as his goal was to stay in office for an unheard of *third term,* he felt better about simply getting Al Gore elected and being the man behind the scenes.

Evidently, Clinton's handlers advised [see below] him to delay the planned scenario due to the sheer number of gun owners and outraged population who somehow were made privy to his plans. Word was someone on the inside leaked his plans and now works for a cable T.V. Network. [Ed Note: The Hebrew Bible Code confirmed this diabolical plot, plus more, and a prophet of God ["Robert"] saw it in a vision. It was set for 010001 Jan 2000. However, the prophetic word got out on short wave radio on 27 Dec 99, and later, on 31 Dec 99, at 1100 hours the Code was run again on the whole scenario. Blessed be the Lord, the whole plot was "*friend delayed*". But only delayed!]

There is little question that America is a hated nation. Hated for the good it does and hated by the Muslims because we are viewed as the great Satan. This view is derived from the fact that we kill babies by abortion, we drink alcohol, we gamble, and we flaunt porno, homosexuality, and sex on T.V. While I disagree totally with the ways in which the terrorists get their points across, I do not disagree that America has become an evil place with evil people.

Source: Col. Lunev: Newsmax.com   Source: Al Cuppett

If I had anything to say to soon-to-be "The Late Bin Laden", *I would tell him that you are fighting a war you cannot win. God is not on your side but telling us about our sins here isn't a bad thing, but killing us for our sins is. Furthermore, this so-called peace loving religion I keep hearing about, even from our own President makes me wonder if you are not just a big turban-wearing hypocrite? Don't you realize that God himself is sparring you as he did Saul on the Damascus Road? Don't you know that unless you repent, you will not only perish as those on 9-11 but your fate will be eternal hell as well? Israel could eliminate the problem in minutes Mr. Bin Lying and so could the USA. Why don't you empty the waste from your shorts, come out of your cave and face the fact that you are fighting a losing battle.—Ray Hope*

We can begin to see why some radical Muslims feel the way they do. It is as bad as Christians who go off the deep end and bomb abortion clinics and shoot doctors. How can you call yourself a Christian and commit these awful acts?

There is a war on for you mind. Are you spending hours a day listening to garbage radio or mind numbing television? Have you become absorbed in court cases on the tube that you have forgotten your real purpose? Have you spent time doing things that just aren't productive? If so, (we all have) then you are a victim of mind control. You see, Satan would like nothing better than to have you in front of the TV or under those headphones 24-7. You become ineffective for God when you are. There are exceptions. I know a man whose sole employment is derived from watching television and that is a service he performs to instruct us in what is harmful to watch on TV.

Duct tape and plastic sheeting will not fix the problem unless you are trying to suffocate it. Do not criticize Homeland Security Chief Tom Ridge for making the statement about duct tape. These items have many uses and it was good for the economy, people went out and spent money but this brings us to our next issue.

The economy was not good even under the Clinton Administration, even with the Dow going past 10,000 points. I saw numerous publications in my mail box that told me I must buy a certain stock and spend every dime I had doing it and that I would make a killing. I watched the stock a couple of days. Invested a hundred dollars and sold when I made a 10% gain in about 2 days. After that, the stock went down the tubes and everyone who took the advice of the stock guru lost their shirts and some even worse than that.

Japan stock market has suffered and the Japanese economy was not stimulated when they cut their interest rate to zero. They have dug out through job creation, bank closures and taking their medicine. This is what the USA must do to keep the economy up. Cutting rates again will not work; Greenspan has refused the last two Fed meetings to cut the rates because he knows if he cuts them, he has no place to go. As a prudent individual, if you cannot afford something and do not have cash, do not buy it. These are simple, biblical economics.

American companies are cutting jobs in order to become profitable. This is dangerous as is moving their production facilities to foreign shores. RJR just cut 40% of its workforce that is 2600 jobs gone. This should prove to you that America is in serious trouble. Believe me, I get no satisfaction in being the purveyor of gloom, and doom, any more than David Wilkerson derives pleasure from being God's Watchman but to whom much has been given, much will be required, according to the word of God.

If you are unemployed, maybe that is not so bad after all. God has given all of talents and us different skills. Why not think of what you love to do and do it! When we like our work, we excel at it. It makes all the difference. The Amish are a strange breed of people, no electricity, no cars, and no phones but they never seem to lack anything. I think that is because they worship and honor God and they are oblivious to the cares of this world. They are self-sufficient and they have their own economy that is not predicated upon how well the stock market or the interest rates. I like that! I wish I lived in Pennsylvania but even if we cannot live there, we can read about the Amish at the library and on the internet. They must make and sell many candles.

What are the basics of life? Air, water, food, shelter and clothing, plus transportation are necessary. Let us look at the Amish and see if we can learn anything. Good clean air, well water, fresh farm grown food and when the Amish need something built, it is built in a day by everyone in the community. It does not take 4 months and 20 permits. They have their horse and buggies to pick up supplies and get to church and their tractors are iron wheels, not rubber.

Do you get the message here? Simplify, because in doing so, you'll not only save money but you can start using the money you were spending on food, expensive shelter and clothing and invest it in the Kingdom of God and for your family, plus have something left over to help others.

Do you recall how your parents or grand parents had a food pantry that was always full? Now, under terrorism laws, they consider these folks hoarders. Someday, you will be in the grocery store and you might buy too much of a certain item and here come grocery cops saying, "We have a hoarder on 3". Growing a garden is prudent and the word of God says, "My people perish for lack of knowledge".

I ran across a fellow in Utah recently who was a Mormon and he told me that a can of seeds that allow for replant season after season would someday get you a brand new Mercedes? Could be? The Mormons are also self reliant and prepared for tough times but most Americans cannot fathom fasting, let alone missing a meal due to some catastrophic event. I am not a Mormon but it is good to be prepared, just ask the BOY SCOUTS.

An issue we have failed to deal with is what to do when marauding gangs come to seize your home, food supplies and Lord knows what else. This scenario would play out before any foreign troops arrive to help you off to camp. If you are a gun owner, you a have a good measure of protection but I think, it is more prudent to have not only a firearm but also the power of God on your side. You can hunt with the firearm if you get hungry, protect your property or lives if need be but even if you do not own one, there is a God who created you and loves you and knows the very number of hairs on your head and he marked out your days from the beginning. Therefore, you see, there is no need to fear, only listen to his voice, and read the word. *"No weapon that is formed against thee shall prosper" Isaiah 54:17 God will provide for you even if you have little or nothing. He did it for the Israelites and he will do likewise for you.*

For years, pressure has been building against "telemarketing", a term most people apply to any phone call from someone you do not know, who is trying to get something out of you. They may offer you a vacation. They may want your vote. They may want you to answer a polling question, donate to support homeless, veterans or those with learning disabilities. They may want you to change your long-distance service or buy insurance from your credit card issuer. Now the government has stepped in, and introduced a *"do not call list"*. If you sign up, telemarketing calls will go away. Right?

The government service only applies to the vacation sort of phone call. All the others are exempt. Non-profits can call. Politicians can call. Long-distance carriers can call. Therefore, can any company you currently do business. Nevertheless, Washington does not define any of these as telemarketing.

The list of approved and unapproved calls is not arbitrary. Government is always prepared to nail the merchant class and make it the victim of regulation. However, it keeps its paws off large businesses you are already doing business with (credit cards), and especially leaves the top two political parties alone to pester you.

As for the merchants it permits, you will notice the bias in the game. If you have done business with the company in the last 18 months, it can call you all it wants. This subsidizes established businesses at the expense of start-ups. One can see, then, why large companies would favor this legislation, if only to reduce the number of competitive solicitors. Note too that the companies to which the list applies must actually shell out money to buy it!

What is in it for the state? Aside from the revenue from list rental, with this service, government can claim that it is doing something to assure that you have a quiet dinner hour even as it permits the kind of phone calls most important to the political class and its connected interest. As usual, government is not serving us; it is serving itself.

It is absolute, due to the devious cooperation of most CEOs of telecommunications companies, that they can 'trap' your on-hook phone, and hear you eat your dinner, or what you do in your bedroom, according to Al Cuppett.

Chapter 7

Concentration camps: Real camps for real people.

There over 600 prison camps, or detention facilities, in the United States, operational and ready to receive prisoners. They are all staffed and even surrounded by full-time guards, but most are all vacant. These camps are to be operated by FEMA (Federal Emergency Management Agency) should Martial Law need to be implemented in the United States.

The Rex 84 Program was established on the reasoning that if a mass exodus of illegal aliens crossed the Mexican/US border, they would be quickly rounded up and detained in detention centers by FEMA. Rex 84 allowed many military bases to be closed down and to be turned into prisons.

Operation Cable Splicer and Garden Plot are the two sub programs, which will be implemented once the Rex 84 program is initiated for its proper purpose. Garden Plot is the program to control the population. Cable Splicer is the program for an orderly takeover of the state and local governments by the federal government. FEMA is the executive arm of the coming police state and thus will head up all operations. The Presidential Executive Orders already listed on the Federal Register also are part of the legal framework for this operation.

Most of the camps have railroad access, as well as roads leading to and from the detention facilities. Many also have an airport/heliport nearby. Many of the camps can house a population of 20,000 prisoners. Currently, the largest of these facilities is just outside of Fairbanks, Alaska. The Alaskan facility is a massive mental health facility and can hold approximately 2 million people. [Ed Note: Did you know FEMA employees hold not only TOP SECRET SECURITY CLEARANCES, but CODE WORD also? Code word clearances for "flood and mud" operations? We are in trouble folks!]

There are many camps located in southern California. One camp is located in Palmdale. It is not operating as a prison now but is masquerading as part of a water facility. The fences that run for miles around this large facility all point inward, and there are large mounds of dirt and dry moat surrounding the central area so the inside area is not visible from the road. There are three large loading docks facing the entrance that can be observed from the road. Observed were white vans patrolling the area.

This facility is across the street from the Palmdale Water Department. The area around the Water Department has fences pointing outward, to keep people out of this dangerous area so as not to drown. Yet, across the street, the fences all point inward, to keep people in, not out.

There are also signs posted every 50 feet stating "State of California Trespassing Loitering Forbidden by Law Section 555 California Penal Code". The sign at the entrance says Pearblossom Operations and Maintenance Subcenter Receiving Department, 34534 116th Street East.

There is also a guard shack located at the entrance. Beyond that lie, miles of fences with the top points all directed inward. A railroad track runs next to the perimeter of this fenced area. The loading docks are large enough to hold railroad cars.

This facility could easily fit 100,000 people. Another site is located in Brand Park in Glendale. There are newly constructed fences (all outfitted with new wiring that point inward). The fences surround a dry reservoir. There are also new buildings situated in the area.

There were four armed military personnel walking the park. Since when does a public park need armed guards? Another site is in the San Fernando Valley, adjacent to the Water District. Again, the area around the actual Water District has fences logically pointing out (to keep people out of the dangerous area). In addition, the rest of the adjacent area that went on for several miles arrayed with fences and barbed wire facing inward (to keep what or who in?)

Also, interesting was the fact that the addition to the tops of the fences were new as to not even contain any sign of rust on them. Within the grounds was a huge building that the guard said was a training range for police officers. There were newly constructed roads, new gray military looking buildings, and a landing strip. Police cars were constantly patrolling the several mile perimeter of the area. Nearby, an area contained about 100 black boxes that looked like railroad cars. We had heard that loads of railroad cars have been manufactured in Oregon outfitted with shackles. These may be of that nature. [Ed Note: Gunderson Steel of Portland made The 102,800 steel boxcars. They have shackles and chains, and such has been confirmed. Al Cuppett]

There are similar sites around the country. (In addition, more literally, popping up overnight... do they work all night?) They are manned, but do not contain prisoners. Why do they need all these non-operating prisons? What are they waiting for? We continuously hear that our current prisons are overcrowded and they are releasing prisoners because of this situation. However, what about all these facilities? What are they really for? Why are there armed guards yet no one to protect themselves against? Moreover, what is going to be the kick-off point to put these facilities into operation? [Ed Note: Camp Butner, NC, now changed to "Butner" on the road map. Has two massive Federal Prison Camps. However, a deputy, in 1994, said they were sending NC prisoners to Rhode Island for lack of space"??]

What would bring about a situation that would call into effect the need for these new prison facilities? A fabricated or natural catastrophe? A major [fabricated] terrorist attack? An earthquake? A catastrophic financial collapse that would cause a panic of such dimensions to cause nationwide panic?

Once a major disaster occurs (whether it is a real event or manufactured event does not matter) Martial Law is hurriedly put in place and we are all in the hands of the government agencies (FEMA) who thus portray themselves as our protectors. Yet what happens when we question those in authority and how they are taking away all of our freedoms? Will we be the ones detained in these campsites? In addition, whom are they going to round up? Those with guns? Those who ask questions? Those that want to know what is really going on. What about the recently reported massive orders for body bags for the USA?

One of my intelligence friends has gone MIA (Missing in Action); right here in America out in the western part of the US. He simply vanished and I cannot find him. All his professional credentials have expired, phone cut off, no forwarding address and no more web site. I am still asking myself what happened, where he is and is he is danger or deceased. He once worked for the Government but poof! He vanishes!

When first coming across this information, many go into a state of total denial. "How could this be? I believed our country was free, and always felt a sense of comfort in knowing that as long as we didn't hurt others in observing our freedom we were left to ourselves." Ideally, that would be true. Nevertheless, some of the dark forces running this government are far from ideal. The time is fast approaching when we will be the ones asking, "What happened to our freedom? To our free speech? To our right to protect our family and ourselves? To think as an individual? To express ourselves in whatever way we wish?"

Once we challenge that freedom, we find out how free we really are. How many are willing to take up that challenge? Very few indeed, otherwise we would not find ourselves in the situation that we are in now. We would not have let things progress and get out of the hands of the public and into the hands of those that seek to keep us under their control no matter what it takes, and that includes the use of force and detainment for those that ask the wrong questions.

Will asking questions be outlawed next? [It has at airports!] Several instances have recently been reported where those that were asking questions that came too near the untold truth (the cover up) were removed from the press conferences and from the public's ear. In addition, those that wanted to speak to the press were detained and either imprisoned, locked in a psychiatric hospital, slaughtered (through make-believe suicides) or discredited.

It is a hate crime to declare that homosexuality is an abomination in the eyes of God. The Boy Scouts now have to allow Homosexual Scout leaders. Are you tried of the pandering?

You do not think it could happen to you. Obviously, those in NAZI Germany who were rounded up and killed did not think it could happen to them either. How could decent people have witnessed such atrocities and still said nothing? Are we going to do the same here as they cart off one by one those individuals who are taking a stand for the rights of the citizens as they expose the truth happening behind the scenes?

Are we just going to sit there and wonder what happened to this country, until it is too late? Perhaps until we hear that knock on the door?

MORE COVER UP:

When telling the truth about AA Flight 587, I realize I am dealing with a government and media hell-bent on hiding the truth, and a majority of the public that does not want to know the truth, or does not care. Nevertheless, here I go anyway.

Let me just say that there is no doubt in my mind that if Richard Reid, the attempted "shoe bomber" of ANOTHER American Airlines transatlantic flight, had been successful in setting off his shoe bomb, and took down the plane over the ocean, the liars in the shadow government and media, would be telling us that the crash was caused by "catastrophic engine failure", or by a flock of seagulls being sucked into the jet engines. Moreover, no doubt, the American people would be sitting there like idiots, believing every word of it, and it would soon be forgotten, just like flight 587.

When all the media and government spokespersons told us that American Airlines flight 587's crash (November 12, 2001) was "an accident", one need only look at the known facts to know that they were lying.

Consider the facts: The federal government is on record as saying the crash was "an accident" -- "some sort of structural failure" -- long before they had the voice recorder or the flight data recorder. Curious and suspicious to a very high degree as it is highly unscientific and unprofessional. This even though they have no records of previous airplane crashes showing such unusual "separation of parts" prior to accidental crashes, on the same or similar planes, as was seen in this so-called "accident". Instead, they specifically, clearly and IMMEDIATELY released statements that break with investigatory patterns involving conclusive statements pointing to causes of previous crashes.

One engine, and tail section, separated from the plane. Reports from multiple pilots, including one who witnessed the crash and the engine's separation from the plane, say they saw two explosions, coming from where the fuselage meets the wing.

The NTSB's nonsense ignores the fact that experts have NEVER heard of mere engine failure, or turbulence, to make engines and tail fins fly off airplanes -- in this or any other modern aircraft of its type. The facts point to a clear, unmistakable cover-up. [Ed. Note: Much evidence was collected and here is what happened: A chopper was seen firing a "gatling gun" at the plane. The tail was cut off as well as one engine. Later, a citizen photographed the massive pile of spent cartridges, which had fallen into Queens. He called the cops, and emailed the photos to friends. The "wrong cops" came and he, and his family, were taken away in handcuffs, along with their computer! Their house was later sold, and they were never seen again!

The neighbor, who witnessed it all, will now say n-o-t-h-i-n-g! The New World Order is here folks – operating near YOU! The entire story is too long to tell here.]

With fears of travel downturns being realized, and the economic impact of said downturn being felt painfully throughout the industry and thus the nation, another terrorist attack could have literally put a couple of the airlines out of business for good and would have had untold negative economic consequences, none of which would have helped our depressed economy.

The federal government has been exhibiting a lack of trust and faith in the ability of the American people to handle the truth. They do not think you are "mature enough" to handle the truth. Throughout our recent history, a few FBI and BATF agents were clearly cold-blooded murderers of innocent American women and children; anything but the truth was made known, even though what we were told was way beyond preposterous. Ruby Ridge was an example. [Ed Note: The majority of federal agents are hard working civil servants. Understand the great fear now is the thousands of foreign cops/security officers who have been stationed here since as far back as 1988! Yes, in Atlanta since 1988.]

Back to Flt 587: First, they tried the "catastrophic engine failure" story. Then, when all the evidence blatantly pointed away from that, they had to come up with a different lie.

Then they tried out the "turbulence" line. Even though the plane that was supposed to have caused the turbulence was 8 miles away, over 3 miles outside the range that could have any effect on Flight 587.

Your "shadow" government does not trust you, believe in you, have faith in you, respect you or your judgment, and certainly does not believe you can deal with the fact that the plane, for whatever reason, was downed intentionally.

They want you to keep your head in the sand. How do I know they will never admit this was an attack? From the first news reports, they put out their spin that this was an accident, once they start the lie they never look back. Then, suddenly, the whole issue drops off the TV "radar screen"? However, another sensational event is ushered in at 6 PM to keep your mind off what might really be happening in "your neck of the woods".

If your shadow government, and sometimes straight government, doesn't trust you, lies directly to you, hides facts and avoids discussions of known facts while trying to lure more money out of your pocket and safety from your life..., what does that say about their opinion of you? .

What the NTSB cannot explain away or FAA is how or why the tail section with stabilizer, parted company with the aircraft at precisely the point where it joins the fuselage proper.

There are absolutely no dents, scratches, on the leading edge or on the panels. This proves any other object, in turn proving it was the first component to detach from the aircraft, did not strike the vertical stabilizer. *Clearly, this had to be something out of the ordinary. It was!*

However, here is the NTSB, with 265 dead, and God knows how many mourners, giving us this claptrap about the tail falling off mysteriously. "No tail fell off, not before the explosion. I swear to that," said retired firefighter Tom Lynch, who was doing his exercise march along Rockaway Beach Boulevard on Nov. 12. "I had my head up taking in that beautiful, clear day and was staring straight at the plane." It made a bank turn and suddenly there was an explosion, orange and black, on the right-hand side of the fuselage. It was a small explosion, about half the size of a car. "The plane kept on going straight for about two or three seconds as if nothing had happened, then the second, big explosion on the right wing, orange and black." It was only then that the plane fell apart. It was after the explosion and I'm telling you, the tail was there until the second explosion." [Ed note: The "explosions" were the 6,000 rounds per minute of gunfire striking the plane.]

Lynch, who lives near the crash site in Belle Harbor, claims he has 13 people who saw the plane on fire before the breakup. Until the explosion, the tail was intact. He contacted the FBI, NTSB, Rep. Anthony Weiner, and Senators. Chuck Schumer and Hillary Clinton. "I got no response from anyone," said Lynch, "Sabotage? That is for other people to decide. At first, we hear there were seagulls in the engine, the plane was caught in a jet stream, and the tail fell off. No damn tail fell off until after the second explosion."

Jim Conrad, who retired last month as a police lieutenant after 34 years, accidentally met Lynch in a dentist's office one week after the crash. "I saw exactly what Tom saw. I was near a stop light at the Marine Parkway Bridge. First, the small explosion. The plane kept on going, tail intact, and then the big explosion and the plane nose-dived. For the NTSB to seriously speculate that the bloody tail fell off in the face of so much evidence that it didn't happen is arrogant and treating us all like a bunch of morons.

However, NTSB spokesperson Ted Lopatkiewicz still has the nerve to say: "We don't have any evidence of an explosion [after searching] the wreckage or from the cockpit recorder. It doesn't mean it didn't happen." [Ed Note: As I said, it was gunfire, and as one witness said, "*It sounded like a chain saw*". That is just how a "gatling 20mm gun" sounds.]

With the American government frantically trying to halt the slide in the airline industry and stock market brought on by the September 11 attacks, the last thing they would admit is that this was a terrorist attack.

Source: Internet

Chapter 8

EMERGENCY PREPARATION

When all the hype for the predicted chaos of Y2K proved to be untrue, many gave up the idea of preparing for disaster. However, disaster will almost surely come upon this nation someday soon, and as we have seen with the events of 9-11-01, it can come suddenly. It also can occur on a more personal level, as the people at Waco, and as many crime victims will tell you. What we advocate you do, is prepare for disaster. Stockpile food. It does not take much money to do that. You could probably buy a years supply of rice and pasta for under a $100 at your local supermarket. In addition, it is virtually imperishable. You could keep them in storage for 25 years, and they would still be good. A portable wood stove would be a good idea for cooking and heat. For water, it would be a smart idea to have your own well, or at least live near a stream, river, or lake. Filtering through coffee filters and boiling should do the trick.

Stockpile weapons. (Legally Of Course, Even if you cannot get a gun, at least stock up on pepper spray, clubs, and blackjacks. An old sock with a roll of nickels inside makes a neat little weapon. Bulletproof vests and army surplus steel helmets may be a good idea.

It is always important to remember, BRING YOUR WEAPONS WITH YOU WHEN YOU GO OUT! No weapons in the world will do you any good if you do not have them when you need them. Remember, America is now teaming with people who have no souls. They would kill you for a dime, and laugh about it. These types of people are the products of our educational and so-called justice system. The people behind the scenes to terrorize the population into wanting a more overbearing and intrusive government to protect us from the animals they have created create them.

If you do not already live in a remote area, you may want to move to one, for your own safety. Just look at the attacks of September 11. They were all centered in the major cities. If a biological, nuclear, or chemical attack occurs, you can be sure it will take place in the cities. If martial law is declared, where will it be most strictly enforced? The cities.

If you already do live in a remote area, think about security. Low visibility is a big advantage. Lots of pine trees blocking the view of your house from the road is a good idea. Many thorns around the perimeter of your house will help make unwanted entry more difficult. Heavy steel doors and bulletproof Lucite instead of glass windows might be a good idea. Of course, fireproofing your exterior is a smart idea.

Motion detectors and emergency floodlights are excellent. Of course, gas masks could be helpful. A good guard dog may be useful.

Do you know why the Government wants you to remove lead based paint? Is it because it is not good for you to eat? Eating any paint is not good for you, is it!

Is it because it is not good for you to breathe it? Breathing paint fumes is not good for you! No kidding! Is it because it' is bad for the environment? WRONG! Do you think they care! Is it because long-term exposure is bad for you? Use your head! It is a control thing! To prove the point further, I had the pleasure of going to the Pediatricians office with my baby and at the well visit; I was hit with the following questions:

1. Do you own a gun? 2. Do you keep it loaded? Do you lock it up? Do you have lead based paint on your house or on any house, the child visits? Do they really care or is there a hidden agenda? Only God knows the answer to that. [Ed Note: At the time of the end, two of eleven were to have "swords", as per in Luke 22:36. You must determine if the Lord would have you be one of the two or one of the "swordless" nine. Do not get the decision wrong! Furthermore, let the wise read, understand, and hearken, because "two" out of eleven will be "enough" until the Lord returns.]

The Government cannot [easily] track your movements through lead based paint. The Government's infrared scanners CAN see your image in your house. The Government's helicopters cannot see into your house if the ceiling is painted with lead based paint. The Government's motion detectors cannot see into your house through lead based paint. The Government's listening devices cannot eavesdrop through lead based paint. [Ed Note: New and developing technology may make it almost impossible to hide behind any substance except three feet of dirt/rock/cement.]

You may also want to map out routes of escape, and even consider emergency tunnels, just in case. For emergency power backup, you could either use a diesel generator or hook up a duel battery system in your car. Then run a power inverter off your car battery. For heat, a small wood stove will be fine. Stockpile candles and matches. All this might seem a little extreme, but considering all the forces that are at work in our society, following my advice might save your life.

WHO IS THIS GUY, AL CUPPETT?

Most of us following the MARTIAL LAW scenario are well aware of the RED LIST arrests immediately preceding martial law declaration. They have to remove the voices who are warning and waking up people, the leaders of the Patriot community, people who will not willingly surrender their guns to the government, people who believe in individual liberties, and other "threats to the state".

Al Cuppett is a distinguished, retired military member, and a retired GM-14 [Geneva Convention Card-identified as a "*Field grade officer*"], winner of the Bronze Star [for Meritorious Service in a combat zone] and the Purple Heart. He is also a Department of Defense veteran, who spent six of 31-plus years in the service of his country as an *Action Officer* with the Joint Chiefs of Staff. He has been warning us since 1994 about the plans for MARTIAL LAW in America. He briefed the Virginia State Police Superintendent in April 1994 for 80 minutes, that among other things, all our troops would [eventually] be deployed overseas!

Cuppett has documentation that the U.S. Constitution can be now suspended without notice. He wants to expose horrific Executive Orders in the federal registry, which authorize government to ignore the Bill of Rights, round up politically incorrect civilians for incarceration in labor camps and impose military dictatorship with the help of foreign troops. A simple document called an Executive Order. Email me and I will send it to you. RayHope@americasoldout.com

The Federal Emergency Management Agency (FEMA) and its military adjunct under guise of disaster preparedness have created the framework of a totalitarian government. In 1994, Clinton signed E.O. 12919, which authorizes FEMA and the National Security Council to seize control of the nation under a state of emergency during which Americans could be stripped of both their rights and their property.

FEMA itself is a creature of executive order. Trilateral Commission member James Earl "Jimmy" Carter, through E.O.12148, created it in the 1970. The premise for FEMA is disaster relief. Cuppett says that disaster assistance is only a front. In fact, a Congressional investigation revealed that only about ten percent of FEMA personnel are engaged in disaster relief projects. According to Cuppett, FEMA is part of the framework of a sinister governing apparatus created to supplant the Constitution during a real or contrived crisis. That is, to run the US "regionally", forgetting state governors, etc., under the illegal "Continuity of Government" plan. [Ed Note: Why would "flood and mud" people have/need Top Secret-Code Word clearances? THEY ARE HIDING SOMETHING FROM THE AMERICAN PEOPLE! Moreover, you are reading ALL about it in this book!]

Cuppett says that there are heavily fortified FEMA bases all over the country. He says that forty years ago the U.S. State Department published a master plan for an authoritarian dictatorship. Published as official government policy, State Department Publication 7277 is Titled, Freedom from War -- The United States Program for General, and Complete Disarmament in a Peaceful World. This document states that the United Nations is slated to become an "unchallengeable" military force. It states that as the U.N. builds a global military machine capable of enforcing the "peace" on all mankind:

-- the U.S. military must be completely dismantled
-- all U.S. citizens must be disarmed

-- all U.S. weapons must be surrendered to the U.N. military apparatus
-- an armed internal police apparatus, subservient to the U.N., must keep the "peace" in the USA.

Once consummated, the plan outlined by State Department Publication 7277 will put a drastic end to the sovereign Republic established by our Founders two hundred years ago. It terminates the Constitution, supplants our system of checks, and balances with a fearsome military dictatorship to be operated by nameless, faceless, non-elected international bureaucrats.

Cuppett says that elements of 7277 are rapidly being implemented. Under an unchallengeable United Nations dictatorship envisioned by 7277, FEMA is apparently slated to become the brains of America's radical transformation. According to Cuppett, military forces comprised of aliens troops, and professional assassins, may well provide the brawn. Cuppett noted that a military police state in USA would be possible only with the help of foreigners willing to fire on the American people if so ordered by U.N. overlords. [Ed Note: The "entire volume" of this book, will prove this was exactly what was ordered and what happened at Waco, 19 April 1993!]

This is why, he says, our government is quietly authorizing the positioning of NATO, Russian, Chinese, and Warsaw Pact troops throughout the U.S. He says that as Americans are gradually conditioned to accept the skeletal framework of an alien-troop system, "troop fill" will be the final step. The cadre has been in place for years! He anticipates that our government will eventually have imported sufficient foreign troops under various exchange programs to keep the masses intimidated, jailed, and terminated! The *Final Solution*.

Cuppett notes that bridges are being fortified across America to accommodate such heavy military equipment as tanks. He says that many police and sheriffs' departments are being sent police dogs that will respond to commands in foreign languages. He has slides of signs being posted across USA that will direct foreign troops. He has slides of communications facilities erected to direct foreign pilots who might be involved in covert operations during the imposition of martial law.

He says that until all command and control installations are completed, and until sufficient troops are in place, all preparations for martial law must be kept ABOVE Top Secret; hence, FEMA's Code Word clearances! This is why, he notes, most low-level government officials and bureaucrats have no idea what is going on.

Cuppett warns that any emergency could trigger a FEMA declaration of martial law and the imposition of the kind of dictatorship outlined by 7277. He said that agent's provocateurs are hard at work trying to stir up civil unrest and armed confrontations between various groups in America. According to Cuppett, in order to precipitate martial law and effect mandatory gun confiscation as mandated by 7277, we must have a crisis. Terrorist attacks, sniper attacks, and so forth are a tremendous psychological lever for ushering in a police state. (The blackout of 2003 was to have triggered this major event but God stopped it by sending his perfect peace over the affected cities.)

He says that individuals and factions of the U.S. military, which disapprove of the demonic plan for America's impending police state, are being terminated. He says 3000 military brass/retired officers have died of heart attacks, or suicides, in the last few years, indicating that chemically induced heart failure may be one way of eliminating loyal troops that might stand in the way of the plan for martial law.

Cuppett says that, for instance, in 1996, TWA flight 800 shot down over the Atlantic was undoubtedly an assassination episode. He claims that a Black Hawk helicopter launched the missile attack. The Black Hawk units are normally part of Special Forces networks working with FEMA. These helicopters have radar spoofing equipment that prevent them from being seen on radar, which is why the TWA 800's attacking copter did not appear on radar screens during the operation; just the missile's "blip". [Ed Note: However, it is sure that it was a foreign-flown Black Hawk, not American pilots, which fired the CR missile.]

He says it is not unusual for the UN's shadow government to sabotage a plane before takeoff if that plane is carrying persons slated for "neutralization". To wit, most all of the "killing" crashes have originated from JFK! Cuppett has documented an example of a military plane C-21 which recently [before departing Andrews AFB to _OKC, on_ _18 April 1995_,] had its fuel system sabotaged, thus crashing in Alabama, killing a military investigative team, including an Under Secretary of Defense; who were going to Will Rogers Airport investigate the Federal [_prisoner_] Transfer Center. That was the day before the OKC bombing!

Cuppett has pictures of various penal facilities apparently being readied to house civilian detainees arrested under martial law. He has seen a slide of an Amtrak facility with enclosed walkways that would allow trainloads of detainees to be off-loaded under cover. He has proof of penal institutions throughout the U.S., which are now empty and awaiting political prisoners of the future.

He charges that the "war on drugs" is an excuse for building a nationwide network of detainment camps to be utilized during a national crisis. He says it was "reported" that Virginia has built 27 prisons in the last 5 years. He says several prisons in California are nearly empty and maintain only a few guards and inmates as a front until the buildings are needed for a national crisis. He says one such empty prison has 4,100 beds. He has the clipping to prove it!

Cuppett says his contacts have obtained copies of two hit lists being maintained by U.S. Intelligence. The lists are color-coded as Red and Blue. These lists contain the names of people who might be rounded up when the time is right. He says, as of 1996, there were 6.2 million Americans on the Red/Blue lists alone. He noted that many upstanding citizens have been shocked to find their names on the one list that was intercepted by "straight", legal, US agents! And now, with Iraq, and terrorist attacks being used as an excuse to propel us into a full blown martial law/state of emergency status, it looks like this might be that season when they begin to TAKE OUT PEOPLE LIKE Al Cuppett! Moreover, we have been told THEY WILL TAKE OUT ENTIRE FAMILIES so that no one will be left behind to talk. They have attempted to break into his home. However, thanks to Al Cuppett's eye-opening message, concerned citizens of America now have a clearer understanding:

1. Why our national military apparatus is gradually being dismantled and our defensive bases closed. Moreover, why the press is continually bashing our military and police forces!

2. Why our troops and National Guard forces are continually being shipped abroad and kept involved in foreign quagmires.

3. Why U.S. troops now serve under foreign commanders and wear the insignia of the United Nations.

4. Why heavily fortified FEMA bases with underground control centers are being built and upgraded at a feverish pace all over the country.

5. Why America is filling up with foreign troops and military equipment.

6. Why the Communist Chinese government is working to obtain control of a former military installations.

7. Why Special Forces exercising with FEMA and Homeland Security, are continually conducting urban assault exercises in towns and cities across the nation, signaling a future crackdown on civilian populations. Folks, these exercises are desensitizing Americans to the real thing, which, when actually executed, will be run by UN troops!

8. Why, under numerous pretexts, a massive campaign is underway to disarm American civilians.

9. How the phony war on drugs and "illegals" are being used to build penal facilities that may be used as future detainment centers.

10. Why the media keeps harping on the dangers of terrorist attacks to enlist popular support for authoritarian Executive Orders and emergency actions.

11. Ed Note: Why the press, for the past 14 years, in the public eye, has taken great pains to "puff up", and therefore purposely demonize military members, caught in various compromising scenarios. Reason: In the subconscious mind of the US citizen, this makes UN troops appear not to be such a bad "alternative". This is why you have seen generals, officers, including Sergeant Major of the Army, demonized!

If you look at the events that have taken place since the August 1992 outrage at Ruby Ridge, you can see why I believe this event was the turning point for America. Shortly after this event, you had the election of Bill Clinton, possibly the most corrupt individual to ever slither into the White House. That was followed by the atrocities at Waco, the OKC bombing, school and office massacres on scales unseen before, and now the huge wake up call of 9-11. Yes, God has been lifting his protective blessing off this nation in more noticeable ways than ever, and I believe it all began right around the time of Ruby Ridge.

One of federal police agencies' favorite activities is spying on radical political organizations. They do not care for being hindered by such things as the Bill of Rights; Congress has censured the FBI several times for illegal investigations. In the late 1980's, the FBI and BATF wanted to infiltrate white supremacist groups. In 1989, the BATF sent informant Kenneth Fadeley to pose as a gun dealer to spy on groups such as the Aryan Nations in Idaho.

The BATF targeted white separatist Randy Weaver to be one of their moles. Fadeley claims that Weaver approached him with the offer to sell sawed-off shotguns in October 1989. Weaver claims he was entrapped, and in fact, he was acquitted of weapons charges when tried in court.

The BATF set up a sting in order to blackmail Weaver into doing their bidding: "an undercover agent of the Bureau of Alcohol, Tobacco, and Firearms approached Mr. Weaver and pressured the mountain man to sell him sawed-off shotguns. Mr. Weaver at first refused, but the agent was persistent and Mr. Weaver eventually sold him two shotguns -- thereby violating federal firearms law." They were 1/4th of an inch too short!

Weaver refused to cooperate with federal agents. To justify a militaristic retaliation, BATF agents lied to the U.S. attorney's office. BATF agents claimed that Weaver had a criminal record and that he was a suspect in several bank robberies.

Both charges were fabrications, even according to BATF Director John Magaw, who admitted the accusations were "inexcusable" in testimony before Congress. The U.S. attorney's office indicted Weaver on weapons charges in May 1990. Weaver was arraigned in January 1991. After missing his February 1991 court date, Weaver was indicted in March 1991 on charges of refusing to appear in court. When federal agents set up Randy Weaver on minor weapons violations, Weaver refused to show up in court for the charge, instead holing up with his wife and four children in his mountain cabin on Ruby Ridge, forty miles south of the Canadian border.

A Justice Department attorney got an arrest warrant for Weaver, despite knowing that a court official notified Weaver of an incorrect court date. (Weaver was not going to show up anyway.) For the charge of refusing to appear in court for a minor weapons violation, the government conducted a military siege of Ruby Ridge worthy of a small war. As reported by James Bovard in the January 10, 1995 Wall Street Journal, after Weaver's February 1991 missed court appearance, Federal agents then launched an elaborate 18-month surveillance of Mr. Weaver's cabin and land.

David Niven, a defense lawyer involved in the subsequent court case, noted later, "The U.S. marshals called in military aerial reconnaissance and had photos studied by the Defense Mapping Agency. ... They had psychological profiles performed and installed $130,000 worth of solar-powered long-range spy cameras. Weaver was a former Army Special Forces Green Beret who knew too much. By the way, in SF, they teach you to be a little paranoid; it just might save your life. In Randy's case it probably did.

They intercepted the Weavers' mail. They even knew the menstrual cycle of Weaver's teenage daughter, and planned an arrest scenario around it." On August 21, 1992, the siege began in earnest. Six U.S. marshals, armed and camouflaged, went onto Weaver's property to conduct undercover surveillance.

When Weaver's dogs started barking, they shot one of them. Weaver's 25-year-old friend Kevin Harris and 14-year-old son Sammy saw the dog die. Sammy Weaver fired his gun towards the agents as his dad yelled for him to come back to the cabin.

"I'm coming, Dad," were Sammy Weaver's last words before he was shot in the back and killed by a U.S. Marshal. Kevin Harris, witnessing the agents' killing of the dog and child, fired at the agents in self-defense, killing one of them. After the initial shootout, the Weavers and Harris retreated into their cabin, and a small army surrounded the area. Says Bovard, "the commander of the FBI's Hostage Rescue Team was called in, and ordered federal agents to shoot any armed adult outside the Weaver cabin, regardless of whether that person was doing anything to threaten or menace federal agents. (Thanks to the surveillance, federal officials knew that the Weavers always carried guns when outside their cabin.)"

Against a handful of rural Idahoans with shotguns, the U.S. arrayed four hundred federal agents with automatic weapons, sniper rifles, and night vision scopes.

On August 22, 1992, Randy Weaver went to see his son's body in the shack where it lay. He was shot and wounded from behind by FBI sniper Lon Horiuchi. As Weaver struggled back to his house, Horiuchi assassinated his wife Vicki as she stood in the doorway, holding their 10-month-old baby.

Although the feds later claimed Vicki Weaver's killing was an accident, the New York Times reported in 1993 that an internal FBI report justified the killing by saying she put herself in danger.

Everything about the federal government's actions in this case is sickening, but possibly the worst was their taunting of the Weaver family after Vicki Weaver's murder: "Good morning, Mrs. Weaver. We had pancakes for breakfast. What did you have?" That was one of the FBI's tactics revealed in court records, reported by Jerry Seper in the Washington Times in September 1993.

After the initial shootout, the only shots fired were by federal agents. Eleven days after the shootout Randy Weaver surrendered. Former Green Beret Colonel Bo Gritz mediated the standoff, which led to Weaver's surrender.

In July 1993, a jury acquitted Randy Weaver of weapons and murder charges resulting from his set-up and the subsequent siege of his mountain cabin home by federal agents. Weaver's friend, Kevin Harris, was also found innocent. Harris, witnessing the agents' killing of Randy Weaver's dog and son during the siege, fired at the agents in self-defense. Harris killed one of the agents. At the trial, the prosecution claimed Harris fired first; the defense produced evidence that the agent had fired seven shots before he was shot himself.

The federal government argued that sniper FBI Lon Horiuchi accidentally killed Weaver's wife Vicki. At the trial, however, Horiuchi testified that he was an accurate shot at 200 yards.

A jury found Weaver innocent of all serious charges, convicting him only on the original weapons charge. The jury also found Harris innocent, ruling his shooting of the marshal to be self-defense.

9-11 was one terrorist attack that the government could not cover up. TWA flight 800 however, was a different story. In July 1996, even after dozens of witnesses came forward to testify that they saw a missile rise from [near] the surface of the Atlantic and intercept flight 800 in mid air government investigators were still able to fabricate a conclusion completely at odds with the evidence. However, to do that, they had to get Boeing, Inc, to take the fall. [Ed Note: It has been reported that Boeing is secretly paying off relatives of the TWA 800 victims. Why? If brought to court Boeing, or the airline (which is now defunct), could bring expert testimony that kerosene fumes cannot explode, thus destroy the current government "crash theory".

Boeing, thus, is complicit in New World Order operations! Otherwise, would they be paying off the relatives? This will also lead us to "links" to the 9-11 "attacks"; which did not happen the way you saw them on TV! All the 9-11 planes were Boeing-made and equipped!

Envision the CEO of Boeing sitting in his office when Bill Clinton's task force of federal "investigators" came to see him. "We all know" they explained", what would happen if we let the public know that one of our planes was shot down by a terrorist. Clinton would lose re-election, the economy would be ruined, airline traffic would drop, new plane orders would dry up, and

Boeing would lose billions in new sales. Obviously, it is in everyone's best interest that we come up with an alternate explanation. Therefore, that is when the "spark in the fuel tank" lie was born.

Source: Internet and Al Cuppett

(General Ben Partin confirmed it had to have been a CR-type missile. JP-4 jet fuel fumes will not explode! Space does permit a full explanation of this crash! However, it kept Bill Clinton in office. He had to be kept in office at all costs because his "shadow Govt" operated by Hillary, and her 16 member "cabinet", was bringing in all the troops and equipment. That is why they were not allowed to convict him of the impeachment. Are you beginning to get the picture yet! You have to read "*Unlimited Access: an FBI Agent in the Clinton White House*", to understand that Hillary was given control of "Domestic Policy" for the USA! That was her "reward" for his escapades in Arkansas. Folks, it is too big to put in any one book!

Chapter 9

Conspiracy Nut?

The evidence that a missile downed flight 800 is overwhelming, contrary to what the government and friends in the media are telling us. First, there were the photos taken by [Linda Cabot] and other people on Long Island. The photos are available by sending us an email requesting them. Our email address is at the back of the book. (The FBI was "shadow Govt" ordered to take Cabot's photo from her!

Photos clearly show a missile heading for the plane, just before the explosion. Not those fuzzy, unclear photos the media showed us, but clear photos of a missile heading for the plane. Numerous credible witnesses can back this up.

Take the case of United Airlines pilot Richard Russell. He was hired to investigate Flight 800, and learned via inside connections that a navy missile in the course of test firings hit TWA 800. However, he and anyone else who believes this are viciously smeared and labeled mentally unbalanced by the government and media. Russell's report states the fact that there was a navy guided missile carrier in the area of the crash. [The closest Navy missile frigate was in Virginia! The missile would have flamed out 5 miles out of Norfolk! There is no way the US Navy would fire a missile anywhere near NYC!]

Many witnesses saw a missile shoot up from the [near] ocean and initiate the explosion. Sven Faret, who was piloting a plane nearby, clearly saw a rocket launch shoot down the plane. (There you are folks... it was a chopper! The "ship-launch", if believed, would get the New World Order off the hook on the "chopper". If the chopper-launch was discovered it would divulge, to some extent, the "black operations" capabilities based in the US! Think folks!

Over 100 highly credible witnesses saw a rocket streaking toward flight 800 just before the explosion, yet the F.B.I. says there is no evidence to support the missile theory. At first, the media was reporting the missile theory as a distinct possibility. However, within a couple of days they received orders from the shadow government to get their very efficient lie making machine into high gear, and promote the idea that the missile story was a hoax. At first, the media accurately reported that radar had detected a blip merging with the jet just before the explosion. Satellite images from CIA data system 2 satellites prove clearly that a sophisticated guided missile tracked and hit flight 800. [Ed Note: The satellites, which "saw" the missiles, were probably IR satellites, and spotted the heat of the exhausts.]

Radar and satellite evidence remains concealed to this day. When congressional representative James Traficant asked to see some of this evidence, the FBI refused, sitting the privacy act. The media says nothing more about it; the government says nothing more about it. Why should they? There are so many new outrages to lie about. Of course, they locked up Traficant but he is still talking but he has been so demonized, who is going to believe him? He is guilty of a bad haircut for sure! Traficant was a thorn in their side, thus, they got him "on charges" later. They are efficient! [Ed Note: The Miami Herald was reported [by at least 3 people] to have stated that there were two of Clinton's bodyguards (retired) who were on TWA 800. They were going to Paris to expose his escapades in the "LeMonde" magazine. This would have endangered the Administration's tenure, so the bodyguards did not make it. Nor did 228 more people.

On June 11 2001, Timothy McVeigh was put to death. Perhaps, the rush to dispose of Tim McVeigh was an effort to keep him quiet. Considering how the federal government convicted and executed the man, even after it was widely known that critical pieces of evidence, and witnesses, were not allowed to be presented for the defense, we would have to conclude that they wanted him silenced.

This would be necessary to conceal their guilt, or at least incompetence. It was reported by some in the Intelligence community that Mc Veigh was not executed at all but simply placed in a secret witness program for having served his country under the Clinton Administration. This however is pure speculation and not the opinion of most insiders. [Ed Note: One thing is for sure, "Brother" John Ashcroft knows that an ANFO bomb will not cut reinforced concrete past 23 feet. Thus, he let Tim McVeigh die without the whole story ever being told.]

This is just the tip of the iceberg. If the whole story behind it ever surfaces, it would probably shock even hard-core conspiracy theorists. For instance, Tiffany Bible was a paramedic called to the Murrah Building following the bombing. Her affidavit reports three important facts.

1. The ATF were not in the building.

2. That the ATF was already putting out a story that the Murrah Building was bombed "because of Waco" only a few hours after the actual blast and before Tim McVeigh was even arrested.

3. That an unexploded bomb was found attached to a gas line inside the building. A FEMA memo also reports at least two additional bombs were found in the Murrah Building. (Alex Jones has a video, "911, the Road to Tyranny", which plainly has Governor Keating saying, on tape, "We have found two more bombs". Get the video!)

Confirmation of at least two additional bombs found in the Murrah Building. Joe Harp, based on his military explosives experience, refutes the ANFO claim and identifies the additional bombs he sees removed from the building as being military in nature.

This statement by survivor Jane Graham tells of three men she saw in the Murrah Building Garage the week prior to the bombing, and the FBI's obvious disinterest in the matter. Note that the reports of additional bombs are confirmed by the fire department. The suggestion that the bombs found in the Murrah Building were just practice bombs requires that the trained experts of the police and fire department bomb squads be too stupid to know real explosives from fake.

The trained experts of the police and fire department bomb squads used trained explosives sniffing dogs to locate those additional bombs, so not only did the devices found in the Murrah Building have to look enough like real bombs to fool the bomb squad, they had to SMELL LIKE REAL EXPLOSIVES TO THE BOMB SNIFFING DOGS. Virgil Steele, an elevator inspector at the scene also saw two additional bombs being removed from the building.

While I am no fan, nor believer in Psychics, one actually faxed the FBI office and the Murrah Building with a warning to the detonation.

This person calls himself Sollog. Do not be caught up with people like this but I will tell you whomever this person is, they were unfortunately correct, and have also made other predictions, which were correct. Satan works that way, so beware of what you read.

Twenty miles away from the blast, seismographs at the University of Oklahoma recorded not one, but two explosive "events" just after 9:00 a.m. on April 19, within ten seconds of each other. The Omniplex Science Center in Oklahoma City recorded the same dual disturbance, the second one stronger than the first. Dr. Charles Mankin, director of the University of Oklahoma Geological Survey, held a press conference shortly after the bombing and told an assembly of journalists that the seismograph readings CLEARLY indicated two explosions. As Mankin put it to the fourth estate, "even the news media reported two bomb blasts initially, but later changed their story".

Video of Tim McVeigh from a security camera at McDonald's in Junction City cited as proof that McVeigh did not rent the Ryder Truck. "McVeigh had been filmed by a security camera at a nearby McDonald's 24 minutes before the time stamped on the rental agreement, wearing clothes that did not match either of the men seen at Elliott's. There is also no plausible explanation of how he traveled the mile and a quarter from McDonald's to the rental agency, car less and alone as he claims, without getting soaked in the rain. The three people interviewed agreed John Does 1 and 2 were dry.

According to Stephen Jones, McVeigh's former attorney, who has seen the interview transcripts, it took 44 days for the FBI to convince the car rental agency that John Doe 1 was Timothy McVeigh. And in the end they did not dare put him on the witness stand, for fear of what might happen under cross-examination." This might explain why the initial description of John Doe I circulated by the FBI referred to a man with "pock-marked skin, fairly stocky" who stood about 5'10", whereas McVeigh is about 6' 3" tall, thin as a rail (160 lbs) and has a smooth complexion."

McVeigh attorney Jones, who worked on this case for years, believed McVeigh was just a part of a greater conspiracy. Why would McVeigh deny a conspiracy? Supposedly, McVeigh hated the government. If there were others involved, the last thing he would do is turn over information on co-conspirators to those he despised.

In addition, [the party line is] McVeigh saw himself as someone who fired the first shot that would start a revolution against a government capable of atrocities such as Ruby Ridge and Waco. He wanted to take full credit for the bombing, and did not want to share it with anyone. In his view, this would make him a mythic figure, a martyr for the revolution. The other view is that McVeigh was part of a sting operation against Nichols and the militia. Nevertheless, the foreign operatives put some real stuff in the truck, but not fertilizer! McVeigh was probably supposed to be vaporized, but he went to get the Mercury. Thus, he had to be the patsy!

The Murrah Building in Oklahoma City was where all of the records of the Waco Siege were being kept. That alone should raise a few eyebrows. In addition, at the time of the OKC bombing, the militia movement was rapidly becoming popular in America. With the outrages committed at Ruby Ridge and Waco, more and more [conservative] people were beginning to see just what our government was capable of.

Along with that you had militia talk shows on shortwave gaining popularity, and there were some in government that were concerned this movement was becoming too popular. I remember just before the bombing, there was talk about mass raids and arrests of militia groups. However, the possibility of it being a "sting" gone "UN-bad", to demonize militias is the best bet.

When it became well known among militia groups what the government had planned, they had to cancel their dirty little scheme.

Now keeping in mind what we know our government is capable of, let us suppose they decided a more effective way to deal with the militia movement was to demonize it in an extreme way. It is well known that the government had people on the inside in these militia groups. What if they were given orders to encourage and assist some terrorist act, like the OKC bombing? McVeigh was seen with several unidentified individuals in the weeks leading up to the bombing. At the trial, these sightings were never allowed in as evidence.

The morning of the bombing, the ATF office, located inside the Murrah building, was conveniently empty. A bomb disposal truck was seen outside the Murrah building just before the blast. Coincidences? The more closely you look at the McVeigh case, the more something stinks.

Gore Vidal, whom McVeigh asked to witness his execution in June after the pair corresponded for three years, insisted McVeigh did not actually carry out the bombing, and hinted he was now close to revealing the names of those who did. "I am about to drop another shoe. I have been working with a researcher who knows at least five of the people involved in the making of the bomb and its detonation. It may well be that McVeigh did not do it. Nevertheless, when he found out he was going to be the patsy, he did something psychologically very strange. He decided to grab all credit for it himself, because he had no fear of death." Vidal maintained this was because "McVeigh saw himself as John Brown of Kansas", the anti-slavery campaigner who was executed after leading a raid into the south which sparked the American civil war.

Vidal alleged that the FBI not only knew about the plot, it was involved in it. Having infiltrated the rightwing militia group that planned it, it did nothing because it wanted to pressure President Clinton into pushing through draconian anti-terrorist legislation he was refusing to sign. "Within a week of the bombing, Clinton signed it for `the protection of the state and of persons', using the exact language that Adolf Hitler used after the Reichstag fire of 1933."

To the few who might be able to see beyond the headlines and think outside the paradigm, Gore Vidal is approaching the truth here. Vidal understands that we are already living under fascism, and is one of the few people who ever uses this word (the real "F" word) on television. McVeigh was a patsy, but not a hero. He is one of their Special Forces, trained and debriefed. I kept asking myself why was he confessing to the crime, or willing to die. Vidal thinks he was just indifferent to death, I think, strangely enough, he may have been promised he would not. Do we really know if he died there? Vidal said the former soldier decorated for bravery in the Gulf war wanted to send out a warning that the government had been bought by corporate America and "its secret police, the FBI, BATF, CIA, etc, were out of control.

What McVeigh was saying was, `The Feds are coming, and the Feds are coming'." In his strongest statements yet about the man who confessed to blowing up the Federal Building in Oklahoma City in 1995, killing 168 people in retaliation for the FBI's slaughter at Waco, Vidal described him as a "Kipling hero" with an "overdeveloped sense of justice" who did what he did because he was inflamed by the massacre, the FBI's subsequent cover-up, and the way it "had shredded the bill of rights and the constitution. However, he saved his greatest venom for Janet Reno, the attorney general during the 52-day Waco siege, for persecuting a perfectly harmless bunch of religious people and for presiding over the "lies and cover-up" that followed it. "Her mother was a very famous alligator wrestler in Florida, a family profession she herself should have pursued."

(Ed Note: It would take two hours to just verbally cover the info Al Cuppett has discovered about this OKC blast! That includes the fact that Secret Service Agent Paul Wichter was "transferred" from the White House "by Hillary" [Remember, she was the "domestic policy boss. He had been discovered allowing unauthorized "tapping" on the Clinton staff's computers. He died talking to his wife!] Most of the "incidents from 1993 until 2001 were of "domestic policy" origin. Sony Bono too! All except Ron Brown.]

Financial:

The PPT, PLUNGE PROTECTION TEAM is on the job. In fact, had they not been in place during 9-11, the stock market would still not be open. They actually kept it up while everyone tried to figure out what to do. The PPT kept the market closed only 4 days during 9-11. During the crash of 1929, the market was closed for a lesser period. Ever notice how stocks rally fast? You can thank the PPT for that.

Chapter 10

THE HIT PARADE

Susan Coleman: Rumors were circulating in Arkansas of an affair with Bill Clinton. She was found dead with a gunshot wound to the head at 7 1/2 months pregnant. Death was an apparent suicide.

Larry Guerrin: Was killed in February 1987 while investigating the INSLAW case.

Kevin Ives & Don Henry: Initial cause of death was reported to be the result of falling asleep on a railroad track in Arkansas on August 23, 1987. This ruling was reported by the State medical examiner Fahmy Malak. Later it was determined that Kevin died from a crushed skull prior to being placed on the tracks. Don had been stabbed in the back. Rumors indicate that they might have stumbled upon a Mena drug operation.

Keith Coney: Keith had information on the Ives/Henry deaths. Died in a motorcycle accident in July 1988 with unconfirmed reports of a high-speed car chase.

Keith McKaskle: McKaskle has information on the Ives/Henry deaths. He was stabbed to death in November 1988.

Gregory Collins: Greg had information on the Ives/Henry deaths. He died from a gunshot wound to the face in January 1989.

Jeff Rhodes: He had information on the deaths of Ives, Henry & McKaskle. His burned body was found in a trash dump in April 1989. He died of a gunshot wound to the head and there was some body mutilation, leading to the probably speculation that he was tortured prior to being killed.

James Milam: Milam had information on the Ives & Henry deaths. He was decapitated. The state Medical examiner, Fahmy Malak, initially ruled death due to natural causes.

Richard Winters: Winters was a suspect in the deaths of Ives & Henry. He was killed in a "robbery" in July 1989, which was subsequently proven a setup.

Jordan Kettleson: Kettleson had information on the Ives & Henry deaths. He was found shot to death in the front seat of his pickup in June 1990.

Alan Standorf: An employee of the National Security Agency in electronic intelligence. Standorf was a source of information for Danny Casalaro who was investigating INSLAW, BCCI, etc. Standorf's body was found in the backseat of a car at Washington National Airport on Jan 31, 1991.

Dennis Eisman: An attorney with information on INSLAW. Eisman was found shot to death on April 5, 1991.

Danny Casalaro: Danny was a free-lance reporter and writer who were investigating the "October Surprise", INSLAW, and BCCI. Danny was found dead in a bathtub in a Sheraton Hotel room in Martinsburg, West Virginia. Danny was staying at the hotel while keeping appointments in the

DC area pertinent to his investigation. He was found with his wrists slashed. At least one, and possibly both of his wrists were cut 10 times. All of his research materials were missing and have never been recovered.

Victor Raiser: The National Finance Co-Chair for "Clinton for President". He died in an airplane crash on July 30, 1992.

R. Montgomery Raiser: Also involved in the Clinton presidential campaign. He died in the same plane crash as Victor.

Paul Tully: Tulley was on the Democratic National Committee. He was found dead of unknown causes in his hotel room on September 24, 1992. No autopsy was ever allowed.

Ian Spiro: Spiro had supporting documentation for grand jury proceedings on the INSLAW case. His wife and three children were found murdered on November 1, 1992 in their home. They all died of gunshot wounds to the head. Ian's body was found several days later in a parked car in the Borego Desert. Cause of death? The ingestion of cyanide. FBI report indicated that Ian had murdered his family and then committed suicide.

Paula Gober: A Clinton speechwriter. She died in a car accident on December 9, 1992 with no known witnesses.

Jim Wilhite: Wilhite was an associate of Mack McClarty's former firm. Wilhite died in a skiing accident on December 21, 1992. He also had extensive ties to Clinton with whom he visited by telephone just hours before his death.

Steve Willis, Robert Williams, and Todd McKeahan & Conway LeBleu: Died February 28, 1993 by gunfire at Waco. All four were examined by a pathologist and died from identical wounds to the left temple. All four had been bodyguards for Bill Clinton, three while campaigning for President and when he was Governor of Arkansas. They also were the ONLY 4 BATF agents killed at Waco.

Sgt. Brian Haney, Sgt. Tim Sabel, Maj. William Barkley, Capt. Scott Reynolds: Died: May 19, 1993 - All four men died when their helicopter crashed in the woods near Quantico, Va. - Reporters were barred from the site, and the head of the fire department responding to the crash described it by saying, "Security was tight," with "lots of Marines with guns." The Marines seized a videotape made by a firefighter. All four men had escorted Clinton on his flight to the carrier Roosevelt shortly before their deaths.

John Crawford: An attorney with information on INSLAW. He died from a heart attack in Tacoma in April of 1993.

The Branch Davidians in Waco Texas: Who were tormented and harassed by FBI for nearly 2 months, under orders from Clinton and Reno, were incinerated on April 19, 1993. [Ed Note: Task Force Six, a UN PfP outfit, did the dirty deed. The FBI was backed off two days before the 19th. An FBI HRT team member, at the Quantico KD Range told that info in July 1993!

John Wilson: Found dead from an apparent hanging suicide on May 18, 1993. He was a former Washington DC council member and claimed to have Whitewater information.

Paul Wilcher: A lawyer-investigating drug running out of Mena, Arkansas and who sought to expose the "October Surprise", BCCI, and INSLAW. He was found in his Washington DC apartment dead of unknown causes on June 22, 1993.

Vincent Foster: A White House deputy counsel and long-time friend of Bill and Hillary's. Found on July 20, 1993, dead of a gunshot wound to the mouth -- a death ruled suicide. There is enough criminal activity surrounding his death to write a book about. It was "suspicious". ICE BULLET, A WAD CUTTER, same as Ron brown?

Jon Parnell Walker: An investigator for the RTC who was looking into the linkage between the Whitewater and Madison S&L bankruptcy. Walker "fell" from the top of the Lincoln Towers Building.

Stanley Heard & Steven Dickson: They were members of the Clinton health care advisory committee. They died in a plane crash on September 10, 1993.

Jerry Luther Parks: Parks was the Chief of Security for Clinton's national campaign headquarters in Little Rock. Gunned down in his car on September 26, 1993 near the intersection of Chenal Parkway and Highway 10 west of Little Rock. Parks was shot through the rear window of his car. The assailant pulled around to the driver's side of Park's car and shot him three more times with a 9mm pistol. His family reported that shortly before his death, unknown persons were following them, and their home had been broken into (despite a top quality alarm system). Parks had been compiling a dossier on Clinton's illicit activities. The dossier was stolen.

Ed Willey: A Clinton fundraiser. He died of a self-inflicted gunshot wound on November 30, 1993. His death came the same day his wife, Kathleen, was allegedly sexually assaulted in the White House by Bill Clinton.

Gandy Baugh: Baugh was Lasater's attorney and committed suicide on January 8, 1994. Baugh's partner committed suicide exactly one month later on February 8, 1994.

Herschell Friday: A member of the presidential campaign finance committee. He died in an airplane explosion on March 1, 1994.

Ronald Rogers: Rogers died on March 3, 1994 just prior to releasing sensitive information to a London newspaper. Cause of death? Undetermined.

Kathy Furguson: A 38-year-old hospital worker whose ex-husband is a co- defendant in the Paula Jones sexual harassment lawsuit. She had information supporting Paula Jones's allegations. She died of an apparent suicide on May 11, 1994 from a gunshot wound to the head

Bill Shelton: Shelton was an Arkansas police officer and was found dead as an apparent suicide on Kathy Ferguson's grave (Kathy was his girl friend), on June 12, 1994. This "suicide" was the result of a gunshot wound to the back of the head.

Stanley Huggins: Huggins, 46, was a principal in a Memphis law firm which headed a 1987 investigation into the loan practices of Madison Guaranty S&L. Stanley died in Delaware in July 1994 -- reported cause of death was viral pneumonia.

Paul Olson: A Federal witness in investigations to drug money corruption in Chicago politics, Paul had just finished 2 days of FBI interviews when his plane ride home crashed, killing Paul and 130 others on Sept 8 1994. The Sept. 15, 1994 Tempe Tribune newspaper reported that the FBI suspected that a bomb had brought down the airplane.

Calvin Walraven: 24 year on Walraven was a key witness against Jocelyn Elder's son's drug case. Walraven was found dead in his apartment with a gunshot wound to the head. Tim Hover, a Little Rock police spokesperson says no foul play is suspected.

Alan G. Whicher: Oversaw Clinton's Secret Service detail. In October 1994, Whicher was transferred to the Secret Service field office in the Murrah Building in Oklahoma City. Whatever warning was given to the BATF agents in that building did not reach Alan Whicher, who died in the bomb blast of April 19 1995.

Duane Garrett: Died July 26, 1995-A lawyer and a talk show host for KGO-AM in San Francisco, Duane was the campaign finance chairman for Diane Feinstein's run for the senate, and was a friend and fundraiser for Al Gore. Garrett was under investigation for defrauding investors in Garrett's failed sports memorabilia venture. There was talk of a deal to evade prosecution. On July 26, Garrett canceled an afternoon meeting with his lawyer because he had to meet some people at the San Francisco airport. Three hours later he was found floating in the bay under the Golden Gate Bridge.

Ron Brown: The Commerce Secretary died on April 3, 1996, in an Air Force jet carrying Brown and 34 others, including 14 business executives on a trade mission to Croatia, crashed into a mountainside. Charles Meissner died also:

Following Ron Brown's death, John Huang was working on a Commerce Department contract that allowed him to retain his security clearance. Shortly thereafter, Meissner died in the crash of a small plane. He was an Assistant Secretary of Commerce for International Economic Policy.

William Colby: Retired CIA director was found dead on May 6, 1996 after his wife reported him missing on April 27, 1996. Apparently, Colby decided to go on an impromptu canoeing excursion and never returned. Colby, who had just started writing for Strategic Investment newsletter, worried many in the intelligence community. Colby's past history of divulging CIA secrets in the past were well known.

Admiral Jeremy Boorda: Died on May 16, 1996 after he went home for lunch and decided to "shoot" himself in the chest (by one report, twice) rather than be interviewed by Newsweek magazine that afternoon. Explanations for Boorda's suicide focused on a claim that he was embarrassed over two "V-Devices" [V for valor] he was not authorized to wear. [See earlier explanation above too. However, ADM Boorda also knew that Clinton had taken the missile launch "devices" from SSBN sub-commanders and that there was now concrete [for ballast] in SSBN missile tubes. He also knew that Clinton had turned off the undersea [Soviet sub detection] listening devices (See Tom Clancy's books). He knew Clinton was committing Marxist-style treason, and as stated before, wanted to try him before a military tribunal. While in Russia, Boorda was also asked to bring Chinese "peace keepers" to Hawaii and the West Coast in US Navy ships! He refused! He, a Jew, gave his life for his country. The other Service Chiefs have only one country to give for their lives!]

Lance Herndon: Herndon a 41-year-old computer specialist and a prominent entrepreneur who received a presidential appointment in 1995 died August 10, 1996 under suspicious circumstances. He appeared to have died from a blow to the head. Police said no weapons were found at his mansion, adding that Mr. Herndon had not been shot or stabbed and there was no evidence of forced entry or theft.

Neil Moody: Died -August 25, 1996 following Vincent Foster's murder, Lisa Foster married James Moody, a judge in Arkansas, on Jan 1, 1996. Near the time Susan McDougal first went to jail for contempt, Judge Moor's son, Neil died in a car crash. There were other reports that Neil Moody had discovered something very unsettling among his stepmother's private papers and was threatening to go public with it just prior to the beginning of the Democratic National Convention. He was alleged to have been talking to Bob Woodward of the Washington Post about a blockbuster story. Witnesses said they saw Neil Moody sitting in his car arguing with another person just prior to His car suddenly speeding off out of control and hitting a brick wall.

Lume report issued in June of 1996, confirmed its initial judgment that the crash resulted from pilot errors and faulty navigation equipment at the time of Brown's death, Independent Counsel Daniel Pearson was seeking to determine whether Brown had engaged in several sham financial transactions with longtime business partner Nolanda Hill shortly before he became secretary of commerce.

Barbara Wise: Wise a 14-year Commerce Department employee found dead and partially naked in her office following a long weekend. She worked in the same section as John Huang. Officially, she is said to have died of natural causes.

Doug Adams: Died January 7, 1997- A lawyer in Arkansas who got involved trying to help the people being swindled out of their life savings. Adams was found in his vehicle with a gunshot wound to his head in a Springfield Mo. hospital parking lot.

Mary C. Mahoney: 25, murdered at the Georgetown Starbuck's coffee bar over July 4, '97 weekend. She was a former White House intern who worked with John Huang. Apparently, she knew Monica Lewinsky and her sexual encounters with Bill Clinton. Although not verified, it has been said that Lewinsky told Linda Tripp that she did not want to end up like Mahoney.

Ronald Miller: Suddenly took ill on October 3, 1997 and steadily worsened until his death 9 days later. (This pattern fits Ricin poisoning.) Owing to the strangeness of the illness, doctors at the Integris Baptist Medical Center referred the matter to the Oklahoma State Medical Examiner's Office. The Oklahoma State Medical Examiner's Office promptly ran tests on samples of Ron Miller's blood, but has refused to release the results or even to confirm that the tests were ever completed. Had been investigated by authorities over the sale of his company, Gage Corp. to Dynamic Energy Resources, Inc. was the man who tape recorded Gene and Nora Lum and turned those tapes (and other records) over to congressional oversight investigators. The Lums were sentenced to prison for campaign finance violations, using "straw donors" to conceal the size of their contributions to various candidates. Indeed, Dynamic Energy Resources, Inc. had hired Ron Brown's son Michael solely for funneling $60,000 through him to the Commerce Secretary, according to Nolanda Hill's testimony.

Sandy Hume: On Sunday, February 22, 1998, Sandy Hume, the 28-year-old son of Fox News Journalist, Britt Hume. Sandy was reportedly found dead in his Arlington, Virginia home. Aside from the statement that this was an "apparent" suicide, there remains in place a total media blackout on this story, possibly out of concern that the facts will not withstand public scrutiny. Worked for Hill magazine. I believe the elder Mr. Hume may very well know who did it.

Jim McDougal: Bill and Hillary Clinton friend, banker, and political ally, sent to prison for eighteen felony convictions. A key whitewater witness dies suspiciously of a heart attack on March 8 1998 at a Federal Prison in Fort Worth, Texas.

Charles Wilbourne Miller: 63, was found dead of a gunshot wound to the head on November 17, 1998 in a shallow pit about 300 yards from his ranch house near Little Rock. Police found a .410 gauge shotgun near Miller's body and a Ruger .357-caliber revolver submerged in water. Investigators concluded the Ruger was the weapon used by Miller to kill him. Yet, two rounds in the handgun's cylinder had been spent. He had long served as executive vice president and member of the board of directors for a company called Alltel and was deeply involved in his own software engineering company until the day he died. Alltel is the successor to Jackson Stephens' Systematic, the company that provided the software for the White House's "Big Brother" data base system and that was behind the administration's plan to develop the secret computer "Clipper" chip to bug every phone, fax and email transmission in America.

Carlos Ghigliotti: 42, was found dead in his home just outside of Washington D.C. on April 28, 2000. There was no sign of a break-in or struggle at the firm of Infrared Technology where the badly decomposed body of Ghigliotti was found. Ghigliotti had not been seen for several weeks. Ghigliotti, a thermal imaging analyst hired by the House Government Reform Committee to review tape of the siege, said he determined the FBI fired shots on April 19, 1993. The FBI has explained the light bursts on infrared footage as reflections of sunrays on shards of glass or other debris that littered the scene. "I conclude this based on the ground view videotapes taken from several different angles simultaneously and based on the overhead thermal tape," Ghigliotti told The Washington Post last October. "The gunfire from the ground is there, without a doubt." Mark Corallo, a representative for the congressional committee chaired by Rep. Dan Burton, R-In., said that police found the business card of a committee investigator in Ghigliotti's office. [Ed Note: The "tanks and machinegun fire" had to be hidden at all costs! Otherwise, the presence of the in-country UN forces who executed the Branch Davidians would be revealed.]

Johnny Lawhon: 29, died March 29, 1998- The Arkansas transmission specialist who discovered a pile of Whitewater documents in the trunk of an abandoned car on his property and turned them over to Starr, was killed in a car wreck two weeks after the McDougal death.. Details of the "accident" have been sketchy -- even from the local Little Rock newspaper.

Tony Moser: 41, was killed as he crossed a street in Pine Bluff, Ark on June 10, 2000. Killed 10 days after being named a columnist for the Democrat-Gazette newspaper and two days after penning a stinging indictment of political corruption in Little Rock. Police filed no charges against the unnamed driver of the 1995 Chevrolet pickup, which hit Moser as he was allegedly walking alone in the middle of unlit Rhinehart Road about 10:10 p.m.

Barbra Olson: Had just recently finished writing a tell all book about Clinton's last days in office, Barbra Olson's book "The Final Days" is one place to learn the truth about Clinton. Read it and you will learn why Hillary tried desperately to stop it from being published. Olson was, more than coincidentally (?), on the plane that crashed into the Pentagon on September 11, 2001.

Chandra Levy: Chandra worked as an intern for the Bureau of Prisons. She, a very smart Jewess, and all Jews are smart, discovered "certain" [politically jailed] prisoners were disappearing from federal prisons without proper paper work. This could have brought Clinton down also. They killed her, blamed Rep. Gary Condit for a while, and then when her body was found, it was declared "a homicide". Moreover, the sheeple bought it all!

Bill McDougal: The old Clinton crony was in jail and was a chief witness for Kenneth Starr. He did not die of a heart attack, but was given a fatal shot "to induce urinating" so he could have a "drug test". A black chopper landed outside the prison and delivered the "dose" just before he died!

Sony Bono: This is too long a story to reveal here, however, briefly, I spoke with a relative of the Deputy Sheriff who co-investigated the Lake Tahoe "tree" incident. He stated that there was no "tree" in the report, but rather, such was the cause of Michael Kennedy's death the week before. Folks, Bono was "*taken out*", and the fearful demeanor of Rep. Mary Bono's Capitol Hill Staff, later on, confirmed it to me! To wit, Bono was anti-Clinton, pro-gun, anti-gay, anti-IRS, and anti-EPA! He was made to be an "example". Why else did they, a [shadow government] "blackmailed" Senate, fail to impeach Clinton? One, they are complicit in the conspiracy to turn the US over to Satan's New World order, and two, they were afraid of getting "Bono-ed" or "Boorda-ed"! Moreover, Rep. Maxine Waters spoke with me, personally, in December 1997, for an hour or more about this, vowing to "do something". After Bono died, she was silent! *ABC*.

You see, some Administrations, including "co-Presidents", on the command of Brussels, would take out an entire planeload of people to get their intended target. This included any act or deed, from 1993-2001, necessary to keep Bill Clinton and Company, in office! Folks, They" were the channels, elected to public office, who were instrumental in/to the import of the troops, equipment, guns, etc. Remember Chapter 6?

Source: Internet and Al Cuppett

Did you know that the plane of the late Payne Stewart, former US Open Champion and PGA Tour player could have been terrorism? We watched helplessly as the media showed us minute by minute. Those on board that ill fated flight did die quickly and the plane did fly itself for hours but what was not told is who fixed the plane so it would malfunction. This is another story.

Chapter 11

Chemtrails: Been feeling bad lately?

Have you ever gone out on a clear day and look up to notice an unusual number of chemtrails streaking from behind aircraft? Normal jet exhaust will simply vanish within a minute or so. However, more now than ever, I have seen, and am getting reports of, chemtrails that linger for hours, spread out and cover the entire sky. These incidents are often followed by, and can be directly linked to mysterious skin rashes, and other strange illnesses.

To ignore chemtrails is to pretend that the DOD would never test its chemical and biological weapons on unsuspecting people. Most people living on earth want only life, liberty, peace and the pursuit of happiness. In grisly contrast, America's military-industrial complex harbors an introverted and pathological fixation with war games and death technology. In its inexorable quest for absolute power -- that evolutionary state of decay warned about by President Eisenhower so many years ago -- the complex has unleashed a terrifying array of secretive and dangerous experiments. These include weather modification, earthquake induction and numerous chemical-biological tests on unwitting subjects.

Every aspect of our physical environment is now being manipulated for war games. Jets spraying chemical aerosols continuously pollute discolored skies. Bizarre and unpredictable weather is often military-made. Electromagnetic abnormalities -- including artificial lightning -- are generated by HAARP-like installations in sundry places. People are becoming increasingly ill and immune-compromised from such ecological tampering. In an expose on Henry Kissinger's momentous war crimes, author Christopher Hitchens writes in Harper's magazine that during the Vietnam War, a U.S. helicopter unit posted the slogan, "Death is our business, and business is good". This arrogant paradigm is perfect for the grotesque network of over 100 laboratories on campuses and industrial parks across the nation where military and contract personnel develop new technologies and strategies for killing human beings in the name of national security.

The widespread flu-like and Alzheimer's symptoms have been mere side effects of the sprayed chemicals, and not the direct purpose of the sprayings. The extensive use of aluminum oxide, found as the primary component of these reflective clouds, does have serious medical side effects and may well explain the upsurge in Alzheimer's disease in the US--which is reaching epidemic proportions. I think it is also clear that the government has been experimenting with different types and mixes of chemicals, which explains why the observations and effects differ over time. Several years ago, there were many sightings of sticky droplets falling from the sky, trailing spider-web-like strands behind. Upon contact, they made people very ill. Later chemical analysis has shown many aluminum oxide and micro fibers, also composed of barium and aluminum. People living under these spray patterns have developed Alzheimer's-like symptoms.

As expected, the US continues to deny any spraying as well as any experimentation in weather modification. The media is very complicit in this cover-up as well. The allegations have been widespread over the internet for years. Thousands of inquiries have gone out to the media over the years and not once has the major media ever done a story on this issue. The health consequences are huge. Even the politically correct environmental movement has had no luck in pressing the media for coverage. There is no way to explain the Medias refusal to investigate or give coverage to this story except that they are fully aware of it and are under bogus "national security" orders to spike the story.

From the military's own abstract of a workshop on "Chemical Lethality Predictions" we learn that when planes spray deadly chemicals in the form of rain or mist, it is possible to calculate how much of those killer agents can be deposited on each person on the ground. The calculations are so precise that "...ten large VX drops that fall over a populated area have the chance to kill up to 9 out of 10 people." What business has the military to be spraying "populated areas" with lethal toxins? This is not defense at all. This is genocide. So far some of the chemicals that have been collected from the chemtrails spray and lab tested are: 1. Bacilli & Molds, 2. Pseudomonas Aeruginosa, 3. Pseudomonas Florescens, 4. Bacilli Amyloliquefaciens, 5. Streptomyces, 6. Enterobacteriaceae, 7. Serratia Marcscens, 8. Human White Blood Cells, 9. A restrictor enzyme used in research labs to snip and combine DNA, 10.

Enterobacteria Cloacae, 11. Other bacilli and other toxic molds capable of producing heart disease and meningitis, as well as acute upper respiratory and gastrointestinal distress.

Many Americans have reported seeing or feeling chemical mists fall from the sky during chemtrails spray episodes. Chemtrails investigator Will Thomas reports that people hit by these mists usually become gravely ill within 48 hours. Thomas tells of hiker Joe Burton in Tennessee who, in 1998, was sprayed by a plane leaving a heavy toxic fog at treetop level. Burton contracted symptoms similar to Gulf War Illness. Strange chemicals had entered his lungs, attacking his liver, gallbladder, and kidneys. He was also found to have a very rare flu-like virus that was tracked to Geneva, Switzerland, home of the World Health Organization.

Congressional hearings of 1975, 1977, and 1994 confirm in nauseating detail that our illustrious Department of Defense has used the American population as hapless guinea pigs since WWII. Rutgers professor Leonard Cole collected from US military records a horrifying list of biological and chemical agents furtively tested on American and Canadian civilian populations. In 1999, Jonathan Moreno of Clinton's Committee on Human Radiation Experiments, also confirmed in his book Undue Risk decades of murderous military-intelligence experimentation on civilians without their knowledge or consent. In 1953, an odious series of 36 tests was conducted on citizens of Winnipeg in Canada. Our government lied to the Winnipeg mayor, assuring him that the tests were nontoxic and defense-necessary. The actual purpose of these CIA-designed tests was to see how large a percentage of the population could be given chemical-induced cancer.

Our spray planes and spray trucks saturated the people of Winnipeg with the carcinogen zinc cadmium sulfide, the same chemical sprayed on many American cities. By calculating the number of people who subsequently came into medical clinics complaining of sore throats, bronchial problems and ringing ears, the test-masters determined that had the chemical not been watered down, they could have induced cancer in one-third of the Winnipeg population. In 1994, Dr. Cole testified before a Senate committee that he feared the military might develop new and genetically engineered pathogens. He could not have known then that our government had been working on such heinous pathogens since the 1960s, when it initiated a special virus cancer program in order to create contagious cancers for biowarfare.

By 1996, Dr. Leonard Horowitz confirmed in his book Emerging Viruses that both AIDS and the Marburg-Ebola complex were manufactured monstrosities hatched out of America's biowarfare labs. Still today, the military continues with open air testing in populated areas across the United States, using dangerous live stimulants to test biowarfare detection gadgets.

These open-air tests involve the spraying of dangerous germs from backpack canisters and vehicles. Because these germs can cause everything from meningitis to heart disease, the personnel who conduct the tests are always protected with gas masks and body suits.

People in the communities being sprayed are given no protection at all. Captain Joyce Riley stood before a group of government officials last year in Louisiana where the military was determined to conduct open-air germ tests, against the vociferous will of the people. She boldly told them that our own government has perpetrated the only acts of terrorism ever conducted on American soil. Our government's hypocritical warnings about domestic terrorism are ludicrous since a criminal element of the Clinton administration masterminded the 1995 bombing of the Murrah Building in Oklahoma City.

Former Oklahoma Congressman Charles Key and his fact-finding committee have documented the federal government's prior knowledge of the bombing, its complicity in wiring columns inside the building with explosives and its heinous cover-up of the facts. The Oklahoma bombing, which killed 180 people including children in daycare, qualifies the shadow federal government itself as a premier terrorist organization. Meantime, US officials deliberately exaggerate the threat of terrorism from Third World malcontents. Even the General Accounting Office admits foreign terrorists would not likely use bio-weapons because they would have to overcome "significant technical and operational challenges". Yet, as the mainstream media reported two years ago, the terrorist racket is a huge growth industry for hungry corporations that interface with the Department of Defense and lust for $10 billion set aside for terrorism prevention.

In 1994, after Dr. Cole testified before the Senate, the Rockefeller Committee issued a report confirming 50 years of secret government testing on both civilians and military personnel. Perversely -- while all of this lip service was going on -- the military was simultaneously conducting a series of hideous biological warfare tests on the people of Oakville, Washington. During the summer of 1994, US military aircraft began dropping a gel substance on the tiny town of Oakville near the Pacific coast. Everybody in town came down with flu and pneumonia-like symptoms. Some people were hospitalized and remained ill for months. Pets and barnyard animals died. The police chief was patrolling the town one morning at 3 a.m. when a deluge of sticky stuff coated the windshield of his patrol car. He cleaned the goop with rubber gloves but just breathing it made him deathly ill. By afternoon, he had major trouble breathing. The gel material was tested by a number of government and private labs, which found human blood cells and nasty bacteria, including a modified version of pseudomonas fluorescens, cited in over 160 military papers as experimental biowarfare bacteria.

Unsolved Mysteries aired the story on national television in May 1997. Several Oakville citizens reported bizarre encounters with FEMA officials and intelligence personnel from Fort Hood Texas -- home of the Black Hawk unit. These spooks made repeated visits to Oakville, probing people about their health and reportedly intimidating those who had been interviewed on television. Also in 1997, rancher William Wallace was plowing his fields near Kettle Falls, Washington when a US Navy Intruder swooped down and sprayed him with a fine mist. He became so deathly sick he could not lift his arm above his head for days. He lost his job because of his illness. His cat's face became paralyzed and actually began to dissolve until it died.

Wallace went to the CBS affiliate in Spokane with his story. Two days later, a turbo prop aircraft dived over his house spraying something that made him and his family ill again. Wallace told chemtrails investigator Will Thomas he felt this was a warning to "shut up". The CBS affiliate in Spokane finally did a two-part news interview with Wallace in the spring of 1999. Again, in

1997, in Southern Idaho near the town of Caldwell, seven healthy people died in their sleep when their lungs collapsed. All were in perfect health. An article in the Arizona Republic noted that people had suspicions that officials might be covering something up. Two years later an eyewitness report was filed about a dark fibrous material falling on Caldwell homes, cars and lawns shortly before the mysterious deaths occurred. Residents said the material looked like feces.

Medical journalist Ermina Cassani has investigated nationwide reports of such biological waste being dropped on neighborhoods from low-flying planes. Cassani investigated over 30 different drops during the years 1998 and 1999. In 1998, she obtained a sample that looked like dried blood from a Michigan house. Examining this material, a University of Michigan lab found pseudonomas fluorescens, the same bug used on Oakville. It can cause horrible human infections including fatal shock, and because of its glowing properties, it allows the military to track its path.

There were also other ugly pathogens, including staph and several fungi, which can cause lung disease. Consider the high fungi content of this sample in the context of the mysterious fungus that infected Kentucky horses last spring. Could not furtive aerial drops provide a convenient mode of economic sabotage? Cassani also reported 29 biological "drops" in the state of Utah. HAZMAT teams in biochemical hazard gear cleaned up the feces with chlorine. Utah is home to the infamous Dugway Proving Grounds, a chemical-biological test center where hundreds of former workers have contracted Gulf-War like symptoms, according to a 1997 testimony before a government committee. During numerous chemtrails spray episodes, the small town of Sallisaw in Eastern Oklahoma area was saturated with a web-like material in which lab techs discovered unusually large enterobacteria. The critter was a mutant of E. coli, salmonella and anthrax; undoubtedly, one of the military's designer bugs. Sallisaw resident Patrick Edgar has reported on the internet that the entire town was made extremely ill by the spraying and that the town now has epidemic rates of both lupus and cancer.

Biological weapons encapsulated in protective coatings like synthetic webbing would explain why so many people who see web-like filaments drifting down from the skies report illness after touching the webs. When the webbing is closely examined, it is proven fabricated filaments of the type developed by both industrial and military entities.

Last year, South Africans reported web-like filaments falling from aircraft that formed a blanket-like appearance across vegetation, telephone poles, and fences. When the cattle ate it they developed large bumps on their hides, became listless and went blind. Informed people everywhere are now wary of "web looking" materials. (Hope recently collected this material after massive spraying in a state he was in and these samples are undergoing lab tests at this time) Email: RAYHOPE@AMERICASOLDOUT.COM for the results.)

This year, using both electrostatic precipitation devices and HEPA air filters to collect outdoor atmospheric samples, chemtrails researcher Clifford Carnicom and his associates have documented desiccated blood cells floating in the atmosphere in both New Mexico and Colorado. With so many atmospheric samples containing biological components, Carnicom has concluded, "crimes of the highest order are being perpetrated against citizens without their knowledge or consent."

Al Cuppett has had too-numerous-to-mention Soviet and US-made, unmarked, choppers and spray planes directly over his house. He is a licensed pilot and knows they have no business operating in the mountains in worse-than-IFR weather. Both he and his wife have come down sick after some of these over flights. Fortunately, a prophet of God spoke to him in 1988, after he had returned from his fourth [scary] trip to "assist" Jimmy Swaggart, "No weapon that is formed against thee shall proper".

Moreover, a Federal Firearms Licensee, and gun dealer, near Al's, had a MI-17 "Hip" chopper, with a magnetometer panel on the bottom, fly directly over his business at 70 feet. Al had a picture of it. Not to mention other photos of other aircraft over his own house.

These choppers are operating out of an old [deactivated] "camp" at Quantico Marine Base. Marine Corps Air Station personnel have attested to these operations. They also operate out of the Peter's Mountain FEMA base near Cismont, VA.

Ed Note: See the *General Jumper Letter* exhibit in the Appendix.

Source: http://www.geocities.com/northstarzone/index.html#top Al Cuppett

Here are a few articles reprinted with permission you may find interesting:

FBI, Military Have Rehearsed for SEIZURE of Nation' Food Supply

Date: March 18, 2003
By: Pam Schuffert

Several years ago, I received a report from Tennessee about the FBI/military SPEC OPS rehearsing in the seizure of national food distribution warehouses.

FBI were present, many FBI white vans, and military SPEC OPS FORCES from Fort Bragg, Fort Knox and Fort Campbell were all present. Local employees were deliberately locked out. These gov/military forces were rehearsing for the future government/military seizure of national food distribution warehouses under coming MARTIAL LAW.

Under coming MARTIAL LAW, our Constitutional will be abolished, and in its place will be the PRESIDENTIAL EXECUTIVE ORDERS, effectively turning America into a police state.

One of these executive orders states that the government can then seize ALL FOOD SUPPLIES, PRIVATE and PUBLICLY OWNED. This means that they can seize the nation's NATIONAL FOOD DISTRIBUTION WAREHOUSES. These warehouses provide all the food that is shipped out to your local grocery stores. Should these warehouses be seized, YOUR LOCAL GROCERY STORE SHELVES WILL BE STRIPPED BARE IN A MATTER OF A FEW DAYS!

In addition, FAMINE WILL LOOM ACROSS THIS NATION as never before... EVEN as the NWO planners have designed, in order to paralyze the nation's resistance to NWO takeover by creating a lack of food, and creating CHAOS as well through rampaging looters breaking into homes and stores in search of coveted FOOD.

Learn to READ BETWEEN THE LINES in your local newspaper!

The article I am now reading states that "...The Homeland Security PLAN includes more Border Patrol officers, stepped up patrols at...airports..., and INCREASED SAFEGUARDS OVER THE NATION'S FOOD SUPPLIES..."

Which being interpreted, means THEY ARE PREPARING TO SEIZE THE NATION'S FOOD SUPPLIES IN ORDER TO "PROVIDE SAFEGUARDS!"

They know that a nation paralyzed by hunger cannot effectively resist the NEW WORLD ORDER agenda under martial law, can they?

Moreover, LACK OF FOOD becomes an effective thumbscrew with which the government can persuade otherwise-resistant Patriotic Americans to "jump through the hoop" of government compliance: COMPLY OR DIE!

Are YOUR food supplies adequate for you and your family? Are they secure? Are they long-term?

BE PREPARED!

-Pam Schuffert

The Coming Persecution of the Church in America

By: Pam Schuffert

Perhaps several years ago, many Christians would not give heed to such a message as this. Only in recent months are many Christians suddenly waking up to the sobering reality that we may be facing end time persecution in our nation as never before. Terrorist events never thought possible to occur on our soil have happened. Now, on the wings of public outcry over the twin tragedies of September 11, 2001, draconian laws are being raced through Congress, supposedly in the effort to help curb terrorism, but suspiciously beginning to sound as if we are slowly being turned into a police state.

Many groups and civil liberties organizations are alarmed at what is unfolding in our nation. Are our liberties being sacrificed for "security?" In addition, who can prove that surrendering vital liberties has EVER brought forth "security" or "protection? Some of the harshest dictatorships with the most stringent and oppressive laws in place have provided no genuine security for its citizens, only oppression and greater controls over the people.

The emerging government/intelligence community definition of "terrorist" is vague, but perhaps quite deliberately. What IS the definition of a "terrorist?" Great penalties are now being dictated against both "terrorists" and those who "harbor terrorists." "Suspected terrorists" can now be detained indefinitely, without a warrant. The term "potential terrorist" is also being used as well.

Nevertheless, what is a "potential terrorist?" You would be concerned to know that under the Clinton Administration, Louis Freeh (former director of the FBI) and Janet Reno (former U.S. Attorney General) put forth the Justice Department's latest definition of a "potential terrorist", which still stands. A copy of this disturbing report was smuggled out of the Justice Department during the Clinton Administration. Read the following carefully and decide if YOU might fit into their category of a "potential terrorist":

US Attorney General Janet Reno has sent a confidential memo to the U.S. attorneys that an investigation would take place against "right wing and fundamentalist Christians".

It states that investigation and surveillance of right wing political groups and fundamentalists, religious organizations and individuals will take place in certain states. Dossiers on targeted individuals are to be compiled and retained in the Washington, D.C. in the Justice Department.

In the event of a wide spread uprising (as in martial law or a national disaster) these individuals must be viewed as "potential terrorists".
-Janet Reno, former U.S. Attorney General

Now are you alarmed? With our nation in this present state of national disaster and increasing turmoil as biological warfare agents are being mailed out and reports of new threats surface continually, can you see that the above document refers to the period we are in?

Do you begin to understand the sobering implications of the term "potential terrorist?" Many Americans could nod their heads in agreement over the harsh new laws being enacted against "potential terrorists," naively thinking that the government's definition of such terrorists might be "wild eyed Moslem religious fanatics" intent on inflicting terror and pain on "the great Satan," America. Now you know there is a much broader definition of "terrorist" that the government

89

has in mind! And that broader definition includes" right wing political groups, fundamentalist Christians, religious organizations, and individuals".

NOW that you realize this, can you nod your head in agreement over these draconian laws being passed...when you realize they can be used against YOU? Against your Church? Against your Pastor? Against your religious organization?

Right wing groups also include America's militias as well, not surprisingly. Moreover, note how they are now being targeted WITHOUT SUBSTANTIATION as "potential sources" for the anthrax scare! Today it is both Moslem extremists and America's militias being targeted: tomorrow will it be America's Christians and other "potential terrorists"?

I was greatly disturbed when I began to hear government sources being interviewed on national television following September 11, who constantly used this term "potential terrorists". For most fellow Americans, the hidden meaning was veiled. However, for researchers like me, the term "police state" began to register in my mind. In addition, with it, the indication of end time persecution that will accompany it for the Church in America. All that I have been hearing recently in various news reports tends to confirm what CIA and other government insiders have painstakingly revealed to me regarding the hidden government agenda of intense persecution of the Church in America to come. In addition, how such persecution would be activated under the great national disasters anticipated to come to our nation (and tragically welcomed or actually encouraged by those elements that have long planned to use such circumstances to bring this persecution into operation and the New World Order into power.)

In light of Louis Freeh /Janet Reno's previous declaration of exactly WHO are perceived by the government to be "potential terrorists" under this present national crisis, the following information is most timely.

Those who study Bible prophecy have long known that great persecution of Bible believers shall come to every nation, especially in the end times prior to Jesus Christ's return. Matthew 24 makes this abundantly clear.

Matthew 24:3-And as He sat upon the Mount of Olives, the disciples came to Him privately and saying, "Tell us, when shall these things be? And what shall be the sign of Thy coming, and of the end of the world?" (Note carefully the period they are speaking of, and realize that He is speaking especially of this end-time period prior to His return.)

Jesus begins to explain to them many things. He warns of false Christ's, wars and rumors of wars, of nation rising against nation. He warns them of famines and pestilences and earthquakes in many different places. But then He states," All these are the beginning of sorrows."

He then begins to expound on the coming reality of end-time persecution.
Matthew 24:9-"Then shall they deliver you up to be afflicted, and shall kill you, and YE SHALL BE HATED OF ALL NATIONS for My name's sake. And THEN shall many be offended, and shall betray one another, and shall hate one another."

Jesus speaks of false prophets arising and deceiving many. (Matthew 24:11)
He reveals that iniquity, or sin, will abound, and the love of many shall grow cold as a result. (Matthew 24:12) (We know we are witnessing that hour in which sin is abounding and even glorified, both in America and throughout the world. Acts of sin which people were formerly

ashamed of are now being paraded openly in public and glorified on televisions and movies and rock music.)

He concludes this passage describing the nature of end-time persecution before His return by stating, "But HE THAT SHALL ENDURE UNTO THE END, THE SAME SHALL BE SAVED." (Matthew 24:13)

Note carefully that He did NOT say, "But he that is RAPTURED, the same shall be saved," but rather "He that shall ENDURE UNTO THE END, the same shall be saved." This is speaking of overcoming persecution and temptation and remaining faithful to Jesus Christ even unto death, and it is speaking clearly in the context of end-time persecution.

Only under a coming ONE WORLD GOVERNMENT that is against God and His Christ (the "New World Order" as it is often referred to today) can believers in Jesus Christ be simultaneously hated in every nation. Jesus declares that ALL NATIONS shall hate His followers in the end times prior to His return, and deliver them up to be afflicted (persecution) and to ultimately be put to death.

Moreover, when Jesus states, "ALL NATIONS", He means "all nations". All nations must then include the United States of America, in order to fulfill His prophetic word, which cannot be broken.

Many Christians have lived under the present delusion that serious persecution unto imprisonment and martyrdom can NEVER take place in America.

They point to America's God-fearing founders, the Constitution, First Amendment rights, etc., and many other factors to insist that end-time persecution of this nature cannot happen on American soil. Alternatively, they insist that before such persecution could ever take place, the "Rapture" will occur (even before they can "suffer the loss of a hangnail" for Jesus' sake) and they will be taken out from end-time persecution before it can come.

Both of these doctrines are deceptions. They have no foundation in the Word of God and in the words of Jesus Christ (Who IS the Word of God.)

Jesus Christ declared firmly that end time persecution would come to His followers in ALL NATIONS. And that he that ENDURES TO THE END would be saved. (NOT he that is "Raptured!") In fact, He even warned that there would be times (undoubtedly of severe persecution) in which His disciples would long to see the hour of His coming, but that it would not necessarily occur at that desired time to rescue them.

Jesus spoke these words to give a foundation of understanding to His people, and to His believers who would face these tribulations in the end-times as well. He wants His people prepared for the things that they are called to suffer for His name's sake, so that no one might be overcome of evil or unprepared to face such testing. He warns His people, so that they might begin to prepare themselves spiritually to endure and overcome what they are to face for His sake.

As I have traveled across America with my well-researched book, PREMONITIONS OF AN AMERICAN HOLOCAUST, which documents the coming persecution of the Church in America and it's well laid infrastructure by the enemies of the Gospel, I have been saddened and disappointed by the response of many pastors and many Christians to this pertinent information. They have turned aside from the truth embodied in end-time prophecy, in order to embrace the doctrine of "the Rapture" or have said that "... because of America's Godly heritage in its beginning, such incidents of persecution could NEVER happen in America."

I have repeatedly heard pastors lead their congregations to believe that before end-time persecution can come upon the Church in America, the Rapture will come! Yet, this has not proven to be the reality in many nations in recent decades for Christians. We know that millions died in Russia and the former Soviet Union for their faith and unwavering testimony of Jesus Christ. How many have died in China for their faith? How many in the Sudan? Indonesia? Nepal? Cuba? Africa?
For such persecuted Christians, there was no Rapture to save them from end-time persecution. Rather, the Words of Jesus Christ held true: "He that endureth unto the end, the same shall be saved."

Did you know that America is filled with unknown martyrs? Although we will never know the names of many of them except in eternity, Christians have been dying for their faith in America for many years. How?

In the ten years that I have investigated organized, hard-core Satanism in America, I have been factually informed of the reality of both children and adults targeted and abducted for sacrifice BECAUSE they were Christian (or from Christian homes) and taken away to be brutally tortured and sacrificed. Moreover, just because you may have never heard of this means nothing!

The news media in America IS CIA/Illuminati /government controlled, and they make sure that their people are in place throughout our nation to ensure blackout of such information to the average American. America's Satanists are very well organized and operate under a high level of covertness to protect their names, reputations, and legally. In my reports from SATANISM IN AMERICA TODAY, I have documented many accounts from former high level Satanists of people being targeted BECAUSE they were Christians. They were stalked, abducted, and sacrificed for their faith. As one friend admitted to me,

"Satan was demanding Christians for sacrifice, and by golly, we obliged him. They were targeted, stalked, and sacrificed like all the rest..." (From a former CIA assassin, Satanist leader in one state, now Christian lecturer exposing the occult.)

One eyewitness account from the mountains of NC admitted that, as a Satanist, she participated in the abduction of a well-known Christian witness/intercessor in that region that the local Satanists hated.

She was abducted while walking home on a rural road at dusk. Their van pulled up next to her, men jumped out and seized her, and she was thrown into the back of the van. Her mouth, hands, and feet were then duct-taped and she was injected with a knockout drug. When she revived, she found herself chained naked to a Satanic altar deep in the heart of the Great Smoky Mountains, in a massive cave known to all Satanists in that region.

She was then tempted to deny Jesus Christ as they offered to let her live IF she would work for them to infiltrate churches, spy on Christians, etc. According to this former Satanist' account, she refused. Her only reply was "I cannot...I AM A CHRISTIAN!" Moreover, they then proceeded to torture her most brutally, until she finally died. My former Satanist friend never forgot this. In addition, her father, who participated in the martyrdom of this young woman, eventually became a Christian as well.

Other eyewitness accounts include Christians being abducted and nailed to literal crosses and tortured to death. One abducted pastor pleaded with his Satanist persecutors to repent and accept Jesus Christ as Savior, even after he was nailed to such a cross.
Finally wearying of his Christian witness, one Satanist took a knife and slashed his throat to silence him. He died on that cross for the testimony of Jesus Christ...in the heart of those mountains known as "the Bible Belt". (Oh, Church, how little you know about true persecution in America!)

From Indiana, we have the testimony of former high priestess Elaine, now a Christian exposing Satanism. Elaine's daughter Claudia, also being trained at one time to become a high priestess like her mother, admitted: "We Satanists in Indiana even invented a cross that would separate in the middle after the victim was crucified. We also designed wooden spikes instead of metal nails, because it would inflict more pain on the victim. After the victim was nailed to the cross, they were then torn to pieces as we separated the cross into two sections..." Christians were frequently their victims, both adult and child.

Friends, how many times has this scene been repeated throughout the centuries, beginning with the early Church? When Christians were brought before Roman tribunals and questioned about their faith, they had a choice. Throw a pinch of incense on the altar to Caesar and declare him to be "divine" ("Caesar is lord") OR to boldly declare "Christian (a) sum" (Latin for "I am a Christian.") And for their confession of "I am a Christian" and refusal to bow the knee to Caesar, history records that they were brutally tortured and killed, not even young believers being spared.

Throughout the centuries such persecutions have been repeated worldwide...YET the Church has survived, overcome, and even grown during such times. We Christians in America have this great potential to both overcome and to grow, even during the coming season of great persecution. For we, too, are called to be FAITHFUL UNTO DEATH and to be over comers in the midst of tribulation.

The people of God are not being prepared realistically in America for end-time persecution and martyrdom to come in America by their pastors. Most Christians are NOT being prepared to "contend earnestly for the faith". In fact, many have compromised their witness and testimony of Jesus Christ even under normal circumstances.

Often, when threatened to "leave your Christianity out of the workplace", they have consented and refused to be the witnesses for Christ God's Word calls them to be. Often compromise with the Gospel can begin quite slowly and subtly, but eventually lead to a tragic denial of Jesus Christ in the end. Of this, we must beware.

So many are sitting back and hoping in a "Rapture" to take them out before they could ever face end time persecution and martyrdom for His name's sake. Yet they have NOT ONE SCRIPTURE TO STAND ON that conclusively declares this expected scenario to be fulfilled!

NOT ONE SCRIPTURE! In fact, they have just the opposite, as revealed in Matthew 24. Nevertheless, they have hearkened to the voices of false prophets from behind many pulpits, who have prophesied to them falsely that such end time persecution will not overtake them, and they shall escape by the "Rapture".

By the way, are we living in the time close to the second coming of Jesus Christ? Of course! Many end-times Bible prophecies being fulfilled in this generation make plain we are living in the end-time period near to His return.

Again, since Jesus plainly declared that NO ONE knows the day nor the hour, again it is presumptuous for North American Christians to believe that the "Rapture" will be based upon their desire to escape end-time persecution and hence avoid testing and refining. We are given no such promise that He will return just in time to escape prophesied end-time persecution.

Hear what happened to Chinese Christians , prior to communist takeover in China, who were told by their pastors, "...you have nothing to worry about...before the communists can take over and persecute you, we will be raptured!" Yes, this was commonly taught in China in the churches at that time, as Christians became uneasy over the rise of communism to power. Yet...there was NO "Rapture" to take out the Chinese Christians when communism came to power. They instead found themselves arrested, imprisoned, tortured for their faith, and martyred. Moreover, their persecutions and martyrdoms continue to this day. Moreover, reports began to come out of China of Christians cursing their pastors and becoming angry with God because of this!

"Pastor! How could this happen! You said we would be raptured before we would ever be arrested and persecuted! How could you have failed to prepare us! How could God fail us?"

Moreover, the reality was, God did not fail them. His Word plainly revealed what would come under end time persecution to His people. God fails no one! Nevertheless, sadly, often His pastors DO. In addition, such Pastors then become false prophets to His people. Moreover, tragically, God's people often PREFER false prophets in the pulpits of their Churches, whenever the truth is too hard to bear and is something their flesh does not want!

Pastors often revealed to me that they could never reveal such truth as contained in my website or book to their congregations, because they might then frighten and lose members (hence lose money through loss of tithes). Yes, 501-C-3 compromised Pastors have proven many times they love numbers and money MORE than the truth and more than the Souls of their congregations.

I hear the members of these congregations, falsely taught that "peace and plenty" was what the future held for America. They would be "Raptured" out of all persecution to come, even now cursing their Pastors and becoming angry with God as everything God's Word (and the contents of my book) warned of begins to be fulfilled...this time on American soil.

(Friends, do not even bother to curse such Pastors: they are already under the curse and wrath of God for failing to prepare His people for this hour of testing! And the blood of those who fall away as a result of their false teachings will be upon the hands of such Pastors, who have prophesied falsely to them of "peace and prosperity" when God's Word revealed something quite different.)

Since the double tragedy that destroyed so many lives in New York City and Washington, DC, we now see a foretaste of the persecution coming that is coming to this nation now surfacing in the form of new, draconian laws that already are threatening the civil liberties of all Americans. In fact, recently an FBI officer confronted researcher Al Martin (a man whose work is similar to mine in exposing the government corruption and the New World Order, etc.) He was warned that within a year, he could be arrested for "seditious talk" for making such statements formerly protected under the First Amendment rights.

Could Pastors and evangelists also be arrested for "seditious talk" under the new laws to be enacted? Could Christian witnessing in public or broadcasting on Christian radio be labeled by THEIR definition to be "seditious talk?" Consider it a great possibility. However, does this mean that we are to stop our Christian witness? NEVER!

Remember: your Christian liberties did NOT originate nor come from the US government! They come from Almighty God. God Himself has given you this marvelous Christian liberty through faith in Jesus Christ. The state did not give it to you, and the state cannot take it away. Now, we know it is a spiritual liberty, which we have been set free from the power of sin through faith in Jesus Christ.

What we experience in the spiritual must also be manifested into the physical realm as well, for it to be true liberty in the fullest sense.

"If the Son therefore shall make you free, ye shall be free indeed." (John 8:36)"For, brethren, ye have been called unto liberty..." (Galatians 5:13)In addition, the command to confess Jesus Christ before men and to preach the Gospel to every creature comes directly from God Himself. We are not excused from this great commission just because wicked men, alienated from God and His commands, tell us to disobey Him!

When my Christian Pilgrim ancestors (John and Priscilla Alden) landed on this soil in 1620, it was to found a nation upon the Word of the Living God. They came to establish a nation that would be free from the tyranny of those who would oppress their Biblical religious convictions. Moreover, they were determined to never again come under the yoke of tyranny or oppression from such foreign powers ever again.

My famed ancestor Levi Redfield fought in the Connecticut Militia alongside many other courageous men who were willing to give their lives for LIBERTY! They fought with a Bible in one hand, and in the other hand a weapon of justifiable physical defense against those who sought to bring them under bondage once again. In addition, BOTH were necessary to obtain America's freedom! "Stand fast therefore in the LIBERTY wherewith Christ has made us free, and be not entangled again in the yoke of bondage." (Galatians 5:1)

Oh Church in America, will you not realistically prepare your hearts for the coming hour of the cup of testing, persecution and martyrdom that even the Church America must drink of for Bible prophecy to be fulfilled? Moreover, will you not prepare yours hearts to RISE UP in FAITH AND VICTORY to OVERCOME THE ENEMY in this hour?

Your hidden persecutors are many, and they extend into the White House and the highest levels of our government and our military. Justice Department investigators have already defined you Bible-believing Christians as "resisters of the New World Order" and secretly condemned you to be arrested and put to death, your churches, and homes to be seized by FEMA and foreign troops and confiscated, and decreed persecution for all those who would offer resistance.

The concentration camps throughout America are many and the thousands of boxcars with shackles are waiting to transport countless souls to these camps to be persecuted and terminated for their faith and resistance to Satan's agenda for this nation. FEMA officials have boasted openly to various Pastors that, upon declaration of martial law in America, they will seize their churches (all quite "legally") and turn them into command posts for their bases of operation! The foreign troops (Russian, German, Chinese, and others) trained to arrest you (even at many of our own military bases such as Fort Polk, LA) and transport you to these detention camps number well over $2,000,000.00

German Bundeswehr/Luftwaffe (Army/Air Force) soldiers are present in America and Canada by the thousands and are stationed in over one hundred bases and facilities, and have boasted to me openly, in both Germany and America that they are in America for the hour of martial law. They have admitted to me that they will NOT have a problem performing what they have been sent to do: arresting and firing upon American citizens! In addition, AWACS from Germany are now present in America, to patrol our airspace in anticipation of widespread uprising under coming martial law.

The military has admitted to us they will deploy chem-bio weapons to help weaken the resolve of the American Patriot to resist the UN/NATO New World Order takeover of our nation. My CIA insiders have admitted to me that many of these detention camps are also termination camps, and the Church in America is one of the major targets of removal and elimination under martial law.

It is not inconceivable that, in the future, you will see uncompromised Christians arrested, transported to boxcars filled with shackles, to be transported to one of the many documented gassing/crematory facilities to be persecuted and slain for their unwavering confession of their faith and refusal to compromise God's Word.

It is also conceivable that you will witness them being dragged before the many modern guillotines imported from overseas for the mass public executions anticipated of those deemed "resisters of the New World Order." (Revelation 20:4) In addition, if you deem yourself to be a committed Christian, Constitutionalist, Patriot, etc. it is truly possible to find yourself among them. I believe there is coming an hour in which the blood of the martyrs of Jesus Christ will flow in the streets and detention camps of America.

I believe that there is coming a time in which the skies above designated detention/ termination camps will be blackened with the smoke of cremated bodies of those end-time saints who will refuse to bow the knee to Satan and his New World Order, who will remain faithful unto God and Jesus Christ even unto death.

And that such smoke will arise as sweet incense into the nostrils of the Lord of Sabbath, as a true testimony of those who gave their lives for the Gospel and the testimony of Jesus Christ and "loved not their lives even unto the death." Moreover, it is not inconceivable that you may be among them!

Hear the testimony of Doc Marquis, former Illuminist, regarding this:

"As a former high level Illuminati planner for the New World Order, I was brought to the site of the future FEMA death camp in the Mojave. I knew exactly what it would be used for: the termination of Christian resisters of our 'PLAN' to seize this nation under martial law for our New World Order. My reaction when I stood within its deadly confines when a Satanist? Sheer joy! I rejoiced over the thought of Christians being terminated in this place." (Testimony from Doc Marquis, former high level Illuminati, now Christian and director of CHRISTIANS EXPOSING THE OCCULT.)

I believe that there is coming a time throughout America for many Christians in whom there will be no other option BUT to confess Jesus Christ is Lord before men and to die for that testimony. (Revelation 12:11)

This should be cause for great concern and an awakening of the people of God in America! I have documented the information contained in this website in the firm belief that an INFORMED people are an ALERTED PEOPLE and an ACTIVATED PEOPLE!

Now that our nation is indeed and irrevocably in the ominous beginning stages of martial law, how long will you hide behind denial and refuse to seek the Lord NOW for the grace to remain faithful throughout the testing that is to follow. NOW is the time to prepare your hearts to seek the Lord. If there is unconfessed sins, REPENT and get right with Him. You will not have the confidence in the Lord that you shall need to stand fast and to overcome, if your heart is not right with God. Obey the Word of God. Be certain that you are right with God, that your sins are forgiven, and your name inscribed in the Lamb's Book of Life, through repenting of your sins and receiving JESUS CHRIST as your Lord and Savior. (John 3:16)

REFUSE to allow fear to fill your heart, and choose instead to RESPOND WITH FAITH. God has NOT given us a spirit of fear, but of POWER (Acts: 1-8), of LOVE (John 16:27), and a SOUND MIND...the MIND OF CHRIST, to be exact. (I Corinthians 2:16) (II Timothy 1:7; Hebrews 13:6; I John 4:18)

Be FILLED WITH THE [HOLY] SPIRIT. (Ephesians 5:18)

Put on the WHOLE ARMOR OF GOD. (Ephesians 6:11, 13)

MEDITATE on God's Word day and night. (Psalm 1:2)

PRAY without ceasing. (I Thessalonians 5:17)

Be CONFIDENT that what God has promised, that He shall also perform. (Romans 4:20, 21; Hebrews 10:23)

REALIZE that IN ALL THESE THINGS, we are MORE THAN CONQUERORS through Him that loved us. (Romans 8:37)

And, that nothing can separate us from the love of God in Christ Jesus our Lord. (Romans 8:35-39)

Through Faith in Jesus Christ...

-YOU were redeemed to become CONQUERORS, not those conquered.
-YOU were redeemed to become VICTORS...not the victims!
-YOU were redeemed to be OVERCOMERS...not those overcome.

"And this is the VICTORY that overcomes the world, EVEN OUR FAITH!"(1 John 5:4-b)

- CRITICAL ADMONITION: Get back to the King James Bible ONLY! Go back to the "old paths". Stop the praise and worship choruses and get back to the old hymns. You dare not enter into the throne room of God with first having your soul and spirit cleansed by "the washing of the word".

America, your days of liberty and freedom may be numbered. Make the most of your freedoms while you can. In addition, determine in your heart now that you will continue to stand up for the Word of God and Liberty...even when a corrupt government declares our days of freedom are finished.

I am writing from the perspective of being a Christian for 30 years now. I have been to Bible College, attending numerous Christian training schools. I have worked with a Christian television ministry and performed missionary work in many places.

I have traveled thousands of miles and fellowshipped in many different churches. Therefore, I am in a position to make the following statements to the Church and Christians in America. If I sound harsh, it is because the following must be said to a sleeping, naive Church in America who is the major target under coming martial law...and has been a target anyhow.

Satanist hate crimes are rampant throughout our nation. Satanist and Jesuit infiltration into Christian churches and ministries is widespread. Up to one million victims are dying annually across North America on Satanist altars. The Satanist/Illuminist subculture has successfully infiltrated America's schools, Universities, law enforcement, government, judicial and in fact penetrated every level of our society. They are networking furiously together to bring forth their New World Order / Luciferian based agenda. Moreover, they are destroying countless innocent lives in the process, and will destroy millions more in their bloody pursuit. Satanist recruitment into covens is at an all time high...recruiters even go out on Friday nights in college towns or cities and recruit kids on the streets, dressed fully in black robes!

And where is the Church? God has commissioned His people, born again Christians unto whom he has entrusted power and authority in Christ Jesus, to wage mighty spiritual warfare against the works of the enemy. The Bible declares, "Jesus Christ was manifested to DESTROY THE WORKS OF THE DEVIL." He did not commission the police..., the local judge..., or the sheriff's department (they are all infiltrated by Satanists anyhow!) He has commissioned HIS PEOPLE to stand in the gap, to wage war against the enemy who is destroying countless lives across our nation continually.

Because God has not given us a spirit of FEAR, but of POWER, LOVE, and a SOUND MIND, and has continually instructed us to FEAR NOT, we are to therefore march boldly forward with the power of God and CRUSH THE WORKS OF THE ENEMY.

I remain ashamed of the pastors who have admitted to me they are too afraid to deal with Satanism in their city...too afraid to help the Satanists who want out and come to them for prayer and support BUT FIND NONE...and then commit suicide as an exit because the CHURCH WOULD NOT BE THE LOVING SUPPORT GROUP THEY NEEDED in their hour of crisis. [Ed Note: Warning - You cannot exorcise the devil/his angels with the NIV bible; or any new translation! They laugh at the words found in there modern "Novels of the Holy Land" - Al Cuppett]

Satan has already gotten away with murder unchallenged much too long...and wait until you see what they have in mind for YOU under coming martial law! Please...make the difference.

Chapter 12

Agents Warn Christian-Jewish Speaker

Date: July 21, 2001
By: Al Cuppett

My Jewish Friends take heed here!

I first heard of Barbra Richmond on a tape sent to me entitled "Barbara's Story". It was tremendous, even a "tear jerker" in many aspects: so I went to hear her and Mike Clayton in the fall of 2000.

However, she and Mike were using perverted texts (modern bible) and Mike "changed the word in our ears". That is, he told us the KJV was wrong, and that Paul was "not a tent maker" but a prayer shawl maker. Huh? Friend, that is "despising" (Prov 13:13) God's word! That means every word in "the" Holy Bible can be suspect! Later, I met with Barbara for over an hour and *"expounded unto her the way of God more perfectly"*.

A side note: Be advised that every pastor or minister whom I've warned in the last 17 years to get back to the right bible, and the "old paths", but who refused, has either retired, quit, was fired, his church failed, or he DIED! Barbara's case has a terrible ending. God is tired of slothful shepherds destroying his "sheep" with phony scripture, "correct" Greek and Hebrew, and modern church junk methods, etc. Moreover, that includes Brother Swaggart who was Jesuit-tricked into despising God's word ON NATIONAL TV five days a week! I went there seven times to try to save his ministry.

Moving along: In July of 2001, Barbara called me and told me an intelligence agent had told her she was "targeted". I told her not to panic, because the first time you find them after you, or are over your house, it gets a little scary. A week later Dan B... called and said Barbara had had two FBI agents come to her with some important information.

The told her there was "a plan" afoot deploy UN/international cops in "US international airports" to catch terrorists. Furthermore, the UN cops, after the Muslims riot, would be seizing Jews trying to leave the US.

Here it is explained. Some "straight" US agents had intercepted this UN/shadow Govt "plan". The UN uses our leased communications media, thus it is subject to intercept by loyal US agents. These two agents admitted they "believed" as Barbara *did*. Emphasis on DID; past tense. US Muslims, at some point, will "riot", thus scaring the Jews, causing them to flee to Israel... via the airports! When such happens going through an airport will be a wrong move! In addition, there is a UN plan afoot to offer "free" transport to Jews wanting to go to Israel.

Under no circumstances should a Jew accept such "transport". Whoops, there is that Nazi word "transport" again! (See my letter to Elie Wiesel at the back of this book.)

Later, in August 2001, the UN met at Durban, S.A., and declared Zionism to be "racism", thus, a "crime against humanity". This now means that born again Christians, and all Jews are now UN

99

criminals. Regardless of US Jewish sentiments about Israel, the UN considers them ALL to be "Zionists" by birth. Thus, all Jews and Believers are criminals by the dictates of the UN. The KJV Bible is a Zionist "handbook!"

Since October 2002, I have had reports of Jews being harassed and even arrested at "some US airports". One of the reports came directly from the Interior Dept at the Knesset in Jerusalem. I warned you earlier in this book that the UN cops are "about their business" right now. Their entire police infrastructure is operational! They are setting up "short-term" check points right now (26 Sept 2003)!

Just recently, we have learned that Barbara has renounced her faith in Jesus as the Messiah, subsequently changed her name to Lea Rephaeli, and fled to Israel. She apparently started planning her "exit" in July 2001 just after her "loyal agent warning".

Why? (1) Her faith was diminished by "polluted bread" (Mal 1:7 and Luke 13:20-21) teaching. Without pure, word-inspired faith, fear sets in! (2) She failed to heed my advice. (3) She failed to ask the Lord if Al Cuppett was correct! She "bought the spiritual farm" just like every other preacher I warned who failed to listen. Pray for her, as she is misguided soul, and in a terrible predicament. I have wept for her!

Now you may read what Pam Schuffert wrote about Barbara in July 2001:

I have recently spoken to a friend of mine, a former fellow Bible College student, Barbara Richmond. Barbara is a wonderful Christian lecturer who stands in support of Israel and the Jews, who also lectures all over the world. She also speaks of end time events and present occurrences around the world, which are tied in with Bible prophecy.

Recently, following her lectures, a member of the intelligence community who warned her that she was actively being monitored and followed by certain government agents approached her. WHY would certain government agents monitor her? Are there not enough deadly Satanist hate crime mongers, NWO terrorists, etc., that they must follow and harass peaceful people like Barbara?

A few days after the warning, Barbara was approached by two agents and questioned. One admitted he was assigned to follow her for the past six months to see what kind of information she was disseminating to the public. He admitted one key things was her mentioned that IRAQ WOULD ATTACK AMERICA.

This is absolute fact that I have already brought out in my book, PREMONITIONS OF AN AMERICAN HOLOCAUST. America and Great Britain have been deliberately provoking Iraq through repeated strikes, to generate Iraqi missile strike on American soil.

THIS is designed to deliberately plunge America IRREVOCABLY into MARTIAL LAW, as I have been told from sources in the military and Washington DC. In fact, so certain were American and German military sources in 1998 that America would be plunged into martial law through our strikes on Iraq that German Bundeswehr officers in Alamogordo with Holloman AFB were openly leaking it out when I was interviewing there.

People I interviewed in the Washington DC area during that year admitted they were being told to take precautionary emergency measures (food/water supply, etc.) should this retaliation occur, according to one source whose family member worked with the DOD in missile development programs.

These two agents admitted that they were part of the Christian element, which were standing with people like Barbara. They warned her that MARTIAL LAW WAS INDEED COMING, and gave her some tips and precautionary measures as to what she could do and how to warn people.

For example, knowing she was concerned for the Jews in America, they warned that ONCE MARTIAL LAW CAME DOWN, THE AIRPORTS WOULD BE SEIZED AND US CITIZENS WOULD NOT BE ALLOWED TO FLEE OUT OF THE COUNTRY FOR REFUGE. (I have published this fact and warned people repeatedly.)

When I asked Barbara's friend, Mike, if they indicated martial law might be soon, he indicated THAT THIS WAS A POSSIBILITY. (This is why I have emphasized the urgency of closely watching the California power crisis, deliberately created to bring forth a power crisis leading to martial law, first California and then triggering others states to follow. Moreover, watching closely the Iraq bombings.

Frankly, there are so many warning signals to watch for... the increase in strange or deadly plagues or viruses, etc., that I was warned (through certain CIA) would be deliberately released to help foment a martial law crisis and to weaken the people prior to martial law, and more.) In a previous report, I have warned people of government agent's harassment of Messianic Jews in Israel, even interfering with their freedom of religious gathering in Israel. (Again, does not the FED have enough violent terrorists to deal with in Israel, working jointly with MOSSAD that they have to harass peaceful Messianic Jews there?)

I received word from our Pentagon source, Al Cuppett, that even FBI officers have been finding their names already on shadow government lists (such as FEMA'S infamous "RED and BLUE" list) marked for termination under martial law. [Ed Note: This discovery happened in Virginia in 1996! It was "straight agent" intercepted and was a "Region Three Blue List", and it was keyed on Social Security numbers -- only!]

This follows the government's pattern of the "use and toss" psychology, wherein they will use people for their own agenda and advantages, and then conveniently toss them like so much garbage (into Federal prisons on trumped up charges, or terminate them outright.)

Many of my information sources coming out of the CIA and such have been through the "use and toss" cycle and are blowing the whistle after being burned by the same government they once served so faithfully.

Pray for my friend, Barbara Richmond. Pray for her friends in the FBI who dared to tell her the truth about COMING MARTIAL LAW.

Pam Schuffert reporting from the USA-

DO NOT READ THE FOLLOWING PAGES UNLESS YOU HAVE THE COURAGE.

"ANGELS of DEATH"-Quarantine. Camps
And TERMINATION for Us!

Date: April 6, 2003 By: Pam Schuffert

"The Angels of Death: Or, THE SPECIALLY TRAINED DEATHCAMP TERMINATORS for the NEW WORLD ORDER"

The NWO TERMINATORS who will play a major role in America's "FINAL SOLUTION" for all RESISTERS OF THE NEW WORLD ORDER.

"...She is on the verge of madness because she knows about an approaching AMERICAN HOLOCAUST that can only rival the previous Holocaust..."

The above words were contained in the letter of a woman who has served as a volunteer for the SPCA (Society for the Prevention of Cruelty for Animals) for many years. She wrote these words in reference to a high-level SPCA official (the head of her regional SPCA) who apparently KNOWS the purpose for many SPCA volunteers who have been deliberately hardened emotionally through the "mercy killing" of millions of animals.

In October of 1996, this SPCA volunteer was invited to attend a special seminar to be held for SPCA employees. The speakers would attempt to help the employees deal with the emotional trauma of killing the unwanted animals.

Here are the shocking words of the Christian SPCA volunteer attending this meeting.

"The seminar was held in a lodge in a forest. All the attendees were women. This did not surprise me...most of my office is made up of lesbians. There are a few who aren't, but in our branch, lesbian women control and run all aspects."

"At the seminar, we were told: 'You MUST not feel guilty for helping an animal die painlessly. It is better than having them starve to death. Do not think about the killing: think about the wonderful lives you are giving to the hundreds of animal that are saved...resources are limited. We SELECT THE HEALTHIEST and the most adoptable animals. FOCUS your attention on them. Do not think about the animals that have to be killed. We carefully select the animals that will make it. Those that are vicious will never find homes. It is better for them that they die painlessly before they hurt other animals or people, or themselves. It is HUMANE TO KILL THEM and to end their sufferings. The young and healthy are the perfect examples of ones that can be saved. Dogs that are strong, trainable, and healthy will be easily adoptable...'"

(Note-Keep this reasoning is in mind as your read carefully the rest of this report.)

The Christian SPCA volunteer listened carefully to these words. She also noted that many of the attendees were radical lesbians of feminist background. Their lifestyles stood in stark contrast to her own, as a Christian who is happily married AND aware of the insidious coming NWO agenda for America as well.
She continues in her observations:

"Following the seminar, the attendees all went to dinner together. The woman who is head of my regional SPCA attended the dinner. About 35 years old, she wore a black beret with official looking insignias and pins on it. Her hair was cut short in a man's razor cut. (She looked more like a man than a woman.) She wore a navy blue double-breasted jacket, slacks and black oxfords. She also wore a wedding band and showed us pictures of her son."

"This regional director had attended the meeting to see if there was something that was effective in dealing with the stress of animal termination.
Seeming uncomfortable around other people, she sat down with me
In addition, began to order 'tequila with beer chasers.' After downing four of them, she was drunk but lucid. She kept going back and forth betweens jokes and tears. I moved next to her and asked, 'What's wrong?' She said, 'I've killed millions of animals.'"

"I touched her hands and repeated the sentences just taught in our seminar.
'It's best for them...they will suffer less...'" "She began to cry. Her head was on the table, face down. She did not look much like a feminist butch anymore. She looked like one of my children. Her hat fell on the table. I stroked her curly hair. She turned her face to me, her cheek on the table and face wet with tears... Voice low and full of gut-wrenching sobs, she said, 'You DON'T understand. You DON'T understand!'"

"I said, 'Help me understand.'"

"She was very quiet for a long time...and then in calm, unbroken sentences, she told me the secret horror with which she was living. As I listened, I went from horror to sympathy to compassion and then back to horror."

"The following is a condensation of the words then spoken by this tormented SPCA leader as she poured out her heart to me..."

"In late June or early July, this high level SPCA official attended a NEW WORLD ORDER futurist seminar in Denver, Colorado. She must belong to this group as a part of her job with the SPCA. Many international attendees would be discussing the growing food shortage. Lecturers told this SPCA official that there would be food shortages in the USA. Riots and wars (internal fighting) were predicted. Because of HUNGER, all sorts of diseases would ravage the population. The viruses and bacterial infections that have been killing people in Africa will soon make it to the United States. HUNGER, DISEASE AND DEATH WOULD BE ALL AROUND.
"This SPCA official was further informed that RESOURCES WOULD BE IN SHORT SUPPLY...not everybody could be saved. Only those most likely to survive would be given the precious resources of food and medicine. They explained that those that are healthy, young, or useful in some way would be spared."

("When this SPCA official mentioned hearing this at the meeting, I was reminded of the speaker at the other seminar we had just attended, who taught us how to choose the animals that will be saved.")

"She was told that THE OTHERS WOULD BE ALLOWED TO DIE IN A PAINLESS, HUMANE MANNER. As I listened to her, explain what the international lecturers told them, I was reminded again of the words of the SPCA seminar speaker earlier. I had noted that, in their reasoning, a quick and painless death is better than starving to death or dying a slow and agonizing death from some of the new diseases like Ebola."

"The conference in Colorado told her that 'ANGELS OF DEATH' had to be created in response, and that a program of training these 'Angels of Death' had been going on in the SPCA for over

thirty years. With the rise of SPCA's throughout the nation and the world, HUNDERDS OF THOUSANDS OF THESE 'ANGELS OF DEATH' HAD BEEN TRAINED in this thirty year's period. When the time comes to put them to work KILLING HUMANS, they will be told the same things they were told when killing animals:
'It is better to let them die painlessly than to starve to death...'"

"The startled SPCA official was further informed that research over a thirty year period showed that lesbians without children were actively sought out in certain areas to fulfill their quota of 'Angels.' FOOD RIOTS, they warned, would soon fill the prisons with millions of violent prisoners WHO WOULD HAVE TO BE HELPED TO DIE painlessly, just like the vicious dogs that cannot be rehabilitated.

All this was worded to sound similar to what we had just heard earlier in the seminar, justifying putting animals to death."

"They explained to her and the attendees that SO MANY PEOPLE WOULD BE LABELED A DANGER TO SOCIETY [note-i.e.-Christian resisters, Patriots, gun owners, militias, Constitutionalists, etc.-PS] that MASSIVE HOLDING PENS would have to be created for them. THEY DID NOT CALL THEM CONCENTRATION CAMPS, BUT THAT IS WHAT I IMAGINED THEM TO BE. "

"They told her that ONCE THE CAMPS OPENED, the OLD, the VERY YOUNG, the TERMINALLY ILL, the disabled, the MENTALLY ILL...anyone who CANNOT WORK or bear PERFECT CHILDREN will be helped to HUMANELY DIE."

"This SPCA official who was pouring out her heart it me kept repeating these words: 'The SPCA is hardening our human emotions by forcing us to needlessly kill animals...
THEY ARE MAKING US INTO MONSTERS FAR WORSE THAN ANY IN HITLER'S GERMANY...'"

"Finally, this leader's grim account was over. I said to her, 'You really need to talk to someone...' It was as if I had hit her. She lifted her head off the table and said with fear in her eyes, 'No, I can't! NO ONE CAN KNOW!'"

"Then she moved closer to me and said, 'I go crazy at times...it's the killings...I hope I didn't make a fool out of myself.' She then got up, appeared stone sober, and quickly walked out of the restaurant without saying a word to anyone else. I was the only one who heard her story. Evidently, our regional director has awakened to the New World Order conspiracy, and it has made her sick. Being responsible for the slaughter of millions of animals was hard enough on her, but now she has realized that THE TRAINING SHE AND HER 'ARMY OF ANGELS' RECIEVED FROM THE SPCA WAS JUST 'PHASE 1' OF A LARGER, GLOBAL PLAN FOR REDUCING THE WORLD'S POPULATION." -End

The UNDERGROUND CHURCH About to Emerge In USA/Canada

Date: March 18, 2003
By: Pam Schuffert

With the declaration of WAR WITH IRAQ, and the announced government intentions throughout this nation of bringing forth AMERICAN UNDER THE POLICE STATE (under the pretense of battling "increased terrorist threats")the hour is soon at hand of the emergence of THE UNDERGROUND CHURCH IN AMERICA.

As I have consistently reported, the GREAT PERSECUTION OF THE CHURCH will commence as America comes under MARTIAL LAW (state of national emergency) and the POLICE STATE emerges.

FREEDOM TO PEACEABLY ASSEMBLE, as guaranteed every American citizen under the Constitution, is about to be greatly curtailed and even abolished in many areas soon.

In addition, those who dare to venture out of their homes under red alert/martial law curfew, EVEN TO ATTEMPT TO MEET IN THEIR CHURCHES OR HOUSES OF PRAYER OR SYNAGOGUES, could find themselves SUBJECT TO ARREST, CONFINEMENT, INTERROGATION, and even being sent off TO THE CAMPS as a result.

As former NWO planners, former CIA, and former high level Satanists have all admitted to me, "MARTIAL LAW IS IT"...the hour of the beginning of the persecution in earnest of the Church across America (and Canada.)

With a STATE OF NATIONAL EMERGENCY/MARTIAL LAW being declared, OUR CONSTITUTION IS TO BE ABOLISHED. And with it, OUR RELIGIOUS FREEDOMS and other guaranteed rights and privileges ARE IRREVOCABLY REVOKED.

Our FREEDOM of SPEECH will be abolished.

Our right to PEACEABLY ASSEMBLE will be abolished.

In addition, EVERY Christian church depends on these two rights in order to effectively function. FREEDOM TO FREELY PREACH THE GOSPEL will be effectively abolished, as the above Constitutional rights are abolished. Prayer meetings, Gospel crusades, tent revivals, and the liberty to freely preach the Gospel and speak the truth WILL ALL BE HEAVILY MONITORED, CURTAILED AND EVEN ABOLISHED...IF they can!

With the restriction of FREEDOM TO TRAVEL, how can one attend church?

Furthermore, two FBI sources recently admitted to a fellow lecturer, that WHEN THIS ALL COMES DOWN, the AIRPORTS WILL BE SEIZED AND AMERICANS WILL NOT BE ABLE TO FREELY LEAVE THE COUNTRY. Moreover, everyone who attempts to flee will be subject to major scrutiny, and facing FEMA "RED/BLUE" list arrests and OTHER list arrests, such as JUSTICE DEPARTMENT, military lists, etc. How then can missionaries or evangelists travel to other countries to minister the Gospel?
[Ed Note: Maybe the missionaries should discover the reason the US is so wicked before they go overseas to preach. Otherwise, they risk "exporting" the same "gospel" which has destroyed the US and allowed the "black" powers of antichrist to engulf us! The new perverted bibles and "new ways" are the reason! – Al Cuppett]

I have already informed my readers about just what kinds of people will find themselves on various lists, subject to pick-up and termination under a state of national emergency/red alert/martial law.

"Potential terrorists" can include committed Christian fundamentalists and their Christian organizations, outspoken Christian leaders, outspoken patriot/leaders, militia members, etc. EVERYONE PERCIEVED BY THE NEW WORLD ORDER TO BE THREATS TO THEIR COMING WORLD AGENDA FOR AMERICA IS SUBJECT TO BEING PLACED ON THEIR LISTS AND BEING PICKED UP AND TERMINATED UNDER MARTIAL LAW.

This is precisely how former CIA/NWO planners explained it would operate to me, and how it will happen. As roadblocks begin in earnest, and interstate highways are seized and major roadways as well, cars will be stopped, searched for weapons, and the occupants' names checked against various FEMA/military/government lists of those Americans to be picked up and removed.

Those "resisters of the NEW WORLD ORDER" on the lists will be taken away, never to be seen again in many cases. The camps have been prepared FOR THEM well in advance. I was startled one day to learn from the research of SERGE MONAST of Quebec, Canada, that CHRISTIAN WOMEN IN MINISTRY was also deemed to fall into FEMA RED LIST designation (those to be priority arrested and terminated.)

This is for several reasons. Christian women are highly effective in winning souls to Jesus Christ and in ministry. Nevertheless, the NEW WORLD ORDER is utterly ANTICHRIST and Satanist in nature, and hence filled with hatred for ALL Christians who are effective in spreading the Gospel.

Christian women in ministry are also highly sought after by the Illuminists/Satanists of the NEW WORLD ORDER for prime victims for sacrifice to Satan as well. The NWO Satanists believe that they receive MORE AND MORE POWER FROM SATAN TO BRING FORTH THE NEW WORLD ORDER with EVERY ACT OF HUMAN SACRIFICE THEY OFFER, as they have explained to me personally. [Ed Note: As noted earlier, Christian women are "Category One" on the Red List so they will be "available" for satanic sacrifices. The Fourth Reich will be wicked than the Third!]

Hence, they informed me they plan to count EVERY CHRISTIAN ARRESTED AND TERMINATED UNDER MARTIAL LAW, as simply ONE MORE SACRIFICE TO SATAN to obtain power to bring forth Satan's NEW WORLD ORDER.

In addition, because Satanism teaches that THE MORE HELPLESS, INNOCENT, PURE AND RIGHTEOUS the victim is, the MORE POWER Satan will give them for sacrificing it; they consider Christian women in ministry to be PRIME TARGETS for SACRIFICES.

Fellow Christians, ARE YOU LISTENING? As insane as all this sounds to rational Christians, THESE NEW WORLD ORDER SATANISTS BELIEVE ALL THIS!

In addition, they fully intend to carry out this ruthless and bloody NWO agenda COMPLETELY! In addition, at OUR expense. KNOW THINE ENEMY

(Over 600 modern concentration camps, thousands of prisoner boxcars and shackles, plus millions of modern guillotines in place for the hour of martial law should convince us of their determination to carry this out!)

The hour of the emerging of THE UNDERGROUND CHURCH IN NORTH AMERICA is rapidly approaching. (Ray Hope: There are already a great number of home churches in America also known as small groups. The NWO has no hope of stopping them all because we had the jump on their agenda and in America we still have agents and officials who love their neighbor and love the Lord.)

It is time to prepare to protect our loved ones and those Christians in ministry from the ruthless onslaughts of Satan's murderous supporters of THE NEW WORLD ORDER in the future. The hour of persecution is fast approaching! Are you preparing?

-Pam Schuffert

Chapter 13

Eyewitnesses Describe Boxcars, Guillotines.

Date: June 21, 2003
By: Pam Schuffert

Dear Friends,

BRACE YOURSELF! I just met with some contacts here in Asheville, NC that I have known for ten years, (Asheville is home to the powerful Vanderbilt Illuminati cult which promotes the NWO agenda) and GUESS WHAT?

One has PERSONALLY SEEN (with her son) the PRISONER BOXCARS WITH SHACKLES and GUILLOTINES here! THEY DROVE IN AS CLOSE TO THE BOXCARS AS THEY COULD GET BEFORE BEING BLOCKED WITH BARBED WIRE. Here is what they personally saw:

WHITE PRISONER BOXCARS-they were painted UN WHITE, had no doors on the sides, only on EACH END. NO WINDOWS only small slats at the top with prisoner bars. Interspersed between each PRISONER BOXCAR was a FLATCAR.

In addition, interspersed between each prisoner boxcar WERE FLATCARS, WITH SIX GUILLOTINES ON EACH FLATCAR painted WHITE. They are spaced three guillotines on one side, three guillotines on the other side of the flatcar. The guillotines are positioned side-by-side, in a manner so that the decapitated heads will simply fall over the side of the flatcar when beheaded.

My friends counted AT LEAST FOUR prisoner boxcars and three flatcars with six guillotines each on them...but they suspect there are many more, since the train was parked on a curve they could not see beyond at that time.

These are the very prisoner boxcars and guillotines as described to me by my father's former satanic high priest, who also operated with the Satanists of Asheville, NC as well. (He has since become a Christian and allowed me to interview him at a Christian Retreat in Florida.) In addition, even as he told me they had been placed in BILTMORE VILLAGE area of Asheville, BUT LATER WERE MOVED (after my investigating and reporting publicly on them) to a more remote region where they would be less visible, so my friends who saw them personally admitted they had indeed been moved.

This is the same series of PRISONER BOXCARS WITH SHACKLES AND GUILLOTINES of which my father's previous high priest admitted, "...and we have ONE THING MORE besides guillotines and shackles in these boxcars...SATANIC ALTARS!"

I have repeatedly witnessed to the Body of Christ that EVERY CHRISTIAN ARRESTED UNDER MARTIAL LAW to be TERMINATED, as these NWO Satanists would count a "RESISTER OF THE NEW WORLD ORDER" (Satan's manifest kingdom on earth) as ONE MORE SACRIFICE TO SATAN TO OBTAIN POWER TO BRING FORTH THEIR NEW WORLD ORDER. (Revelation 13: "And men worshipped THE DRAGON, who gave POWER to the BEAST.")

America's Satanists have admitted to me that they are worshipping Satan the Dragon with MORE AND MORE acts of HUMAN SACRIFICE, to obtain power from Satan to bring forth his world government of ANTICHRIST, or THE BEAST.

And here in ASHEVILLE, NC, home to the George Vanderbilt Illuminati Luciferian cult of "the rich, the elite and the powerful" (as these deluded Satanists love to call themselves) they are fully prepared to arrest and SACRIFICE THESE BIBLE BELT CHRISTIANS TO THE DRAGON UNDER MARTIAL LAW. The prisoner boxcars are all in place, the guillotines are all in place, and these brazen Satanists are chortling over their NEXT series of major SACRIFICES TO COME.

And the slumbering church in Asheville, naive and ignorant of such planned horrors to come, deluded into thinking they have a "CHRISTIAN PRESIDENT" and hence nothing of the sort can ever happen HERE) are in for a rude awakening when MARTIAL LAW/RED ALERT IS FINALLY DECLARED HERE IN THEIR REGION.

-Pam Schuffert

Expect Major Conflict between German Troops and Americans

Date: April 8, 2003
By: Pam Schuffert

In the future, expect a MAJOR conflict between the thousands of German troops Prepositioned throughout America and Canada, and the American/Canadian Patriots Fighting for SOVEREIGNTY and LIBERTY under coming MARTIAL LAW/RED ALERT.

The German Bundeswehr (military) and Luftwaffe (air force) that I have interviewed Periodically, both in America and Germany, have made it clear that THEY ARE HERE IN AMERICA FOR THE HOUR OF MARTIAL LAW. They have openly boasted, even to America locals, that they are in America/Canada, to SEIZE YOUR WEAPONS, ARREST YOU, (if you are "ON THE LIST") AND FIRE ON YOU IF YOU OFFER RESISTANCE UNDER MARTIAL LAW.

German Bundeswehr that I have interviewed in Alamogordo, NM and in Germany has Admitted that they are well aware that MARTIAL LAW IS COMING TO AMERICA. And that they have a key role to play under martial law, in subduing America under the Iron heels of the NEW WORLD ORDER/UN world Globalist government.

In fact, Germany is already boasting that they are the HEAD of the EU, the rising world Government in Europe. And few in Europe would dispute that! Moreover, many people I have interviewed in Europe about this are very unsettled over this fact. They remember Germanys grim past all too well.

German troops have trained extensively in former Yugoslavia/Kosovo, under the auspices of the UN/NATO/Partnership for Peace agenda for turning former Yugoslavia into a vassal of the United Nations.

I have personally viewed color photos of German troops, wearing UN Blue berets, operating UN tanks in former Yugoslavia. In their program called OPERATION HARVEST, the program to confiscate and destroy privately owned arms and weapons, these German troops have run their UN tank treads over rows and rows of rifles and arms confiscated from local freedom-fighting groups, each group seeking greater liberties for their particular faction in Yugoslavia.

Moreover, in America under MARTIAL LAW, they will perform essentially the same thing, participating in roadblocks to search cars for weapons or find people ON THE LIST for round up

They will participate in door-to-door SEARCH/SEIZURE/ARREST Operations, looking for firearms to seize and again rounding up everyone ON THE LIST...much as a previous generation of young Nazi soldiers did under Adolph Hitler. They will participate in the operation of the DEATHCAMPS OF AMERICA as well, even as a previous generation of young Nazis did.

And as the German Bundeswehr officer boasted to America locals in Alamogordo, NM, "...your President knows WE GERMANS WON'T HAVE A PROBLEM!" Indeed. I interviewed many people while researching in Germany, who admitted the wounds of WWII, had not healed in many hearts, and that hatred for the Americans had been passed down from father to son. Now many of the young German Bundeswehr military now stationed in America, who are fully aware of the coming MARTIAL LAW, AGENDA and their role, are lusting for the hour of confrontation with the hated Americans.

For many Germans, it is a TIME TO FINALLY EVEN THE SCORE! And to raise Germany to a place of pride and power once again, even as America is trampled under the iron jackboots of the NEW WORLD ORDER. My interviews with the German people and the German military have left no doubt in my heart that a time of great violence and confrontation between two opposing forces is about to occur under martial law in America.

I interviewed a former Bundeswehr soldier, Attilla, in Munich one day. "Tell me, Attilla, is it TRUE that German Bundeswehr will have NO PROBLEM actually firing upon innocent civilians in America under martial law?" He saw how disturbed and saddened I was as I asked him this troubling question. He replied, almost apologetically, "Look, Pam, A SOLDIER IS A SOLDIER! Sure, while they LIKE your American babes, your American booze and rock music in America, a soldier is a soldier. AND WHEN THEY ARE ASKED TO FIRE UPON YOUR AMERICAN PEOPLE, THEY WILL RISK COURT MARTIAL IF THEY DO NOT OBEY THEIR SUPERIORS! They WILL fire upon your people...," he concluded. Yes, I am personally very sad and troubled by all this. I am, after all, part German (my father was full-blooded Aryan German.) My father, in his better years, played a major role in the Allies' BERLIN AIRLIFT that rescued thousands of starving Germans from the Russian blockade of Berlin. He is honored to this day in the ALLIED MUSEUM in Berlin. Moreover, I grew up for several years in Germany.

Do I love the German people? Yes, very much. Moreover, I am extremely troubled over the role that young German soldiers will be asked to play in America under coming MARTIAL LAW. I also love my AMERICAN PEOPLE very much. I am grieved over the thought of German troops firing upon my fellow Americans. I am grieved over the boastings of German troops whom I have interviewed in America, who think it is funny and will not have a problem firing upon Americans...at all. I have prayed and wept much before God, beseeching Him to hold back all violence and future conflicts between German troops in America, and my fellow Americans, under martial law.

I KNOW that future conflict will eventually be inevitable, due to the NOW agenda the German and other UN/NATO/PfP based troops will seek to impose on the freedom-loving American people. Simply be aware. [Ed Note: I met German Bundeswehr officers at Dulles, escorting fully equipped troops, by the hundreds. They all but admitted they were "for peacekeeping operations". I spoke to them in German!]

-Pam Schuffert

Chapter 14

WHAT CAN BE DONE

By now, you have seen enough and are either thinking the author should be locked up or the author knows things that many do not. Your opinion of me is immaterial at this point. However, what matters is what you do with the information.

If you do not know Jesus as Lord and Savior won't you invite him into your heart now? Still not ready? Perhaps you should read the balance of the book but I suggest you accept Jesus now, because today is the day of salvation and we are not guaranteed tomorrow or even a minute from now. Just ask the victims of 9-11 who went to work and expected to go to lunch and then go home.

The Christians in America will say, "Pastor, WHY DIDN'T YOU Warn US OF THESE THINGS TO COME?

Even as they are arrested by foreign troops and marched off to the waiting prisoner boxcars to be taken away to be gassed and cremated, or worse, they will curse their pastors for FAILING TO BE THE FAITHFUL AND HONEST WITNESSES TO GOD'S PEOPLE THAT GOD IS CALLING FOR IN THIS CRITICAL HOUR.

I have spoken to such pastors, and many are familiar with my materials and others'. NEVERTHELESS, THEY HAVE LET ME KNOW HOW AFRAID THEY ARE OF THE CONSEQUENCES OF TELLING GOD'S PEOPLE THE TRUTH!

-Afraid of losing their "501-C-2" tax-exempt status.

-Afraid of losing members.

-Afraid of losing money.

-Afraid of falling out of popularity because they will not jump on the "praise" bandwagon.

-Afraid of persecution from the government. God did not give us the spirit of fear, his word confirms that so why are most of our Pastors going about business as usual. Why are divorces, homosexuality, adultery, and sin rampant in the church?

In addition, the ONE IMPORTANT FEAR THEY HAVE FORGOTTEN IS THE FEAR OF THE LIVING GOD IN THIS HOUR! They will give an account to God for every soul in their congregation who perishes by falling away under persecution to come, because such pastors FAILED TO SOUND THE WARNING CRY of what is to come upon God's people, and should they fail to prepare God's people to face and endure END-TIME PERSECUTION FOR THEIR FAITH.

WHAT THE PROPHETS SAID ABOUT BABYLON

1. Babylon would be an END TIME GREAT NATION (Rev 17, 18; Isaiah3:19.

2. Babylon would have a huge seaport city within its borders (Rev 18:17).

3. The Great City Babylon is the home of a world government attempt (Rev.17:18, Jer.51:44, Gen. 11:1-6, compare Matthew 24:27, implied throughout)

4. The Great City Babylon would be the economic nerve center of the world (Rev 18:3).

5. Babylon would be the center of a one world Luciferian religious movement (Jer 51:44).

6. Babylon would be the center for the move to a global economic order (Rev 13:16).

BABYLON THE NATION

1. Babylon would be the youngest and greatest of the end time nations (Jer 50:12).

2. Babylon would the QUEEN AMONG THE NATIONS (Isa 47:5, 7; Rev 18:7).

3. Babylon would be the most powerful nation in the world (Isa 47, Jer 50, 51, Rev 1.

4. Babylon would be the HAMMER OF THE WHOLE EARTH (Jer 50:23; Rev 18:23).

5. Babylon is called a woman, and has the symbol of the Lady (Isa 47:7-9).

6. Babylon would be the praise of the WHOLE EARTH (Jer 51:41).

7. Babylon is center of world trade (Jer 51:44; Rev 17:18; 18:19).

8. Babylon would grow to be the richest nation in the world (Rev 18:3, 7, 19, and 23).

9. All nations that traded with Babylon would grow rich (Rev 18:3).

10. The merchants of Babylon were the GREAT MEN OF THE EARTH (Rev 18:23).

11. Babylon is a huge nation, with lands, cities, and great wealth (implied throughout).

12. Babylon is nation "peeled", or timbered, a land of open fields (Isa 18:2).

13. Babylon is land quartered by mighty rivers (Isa 18:2).

14. Babylon is a land that is measured out, and populated throughout (Isa 18:2).

15. Babylon destroys her own land, with pollution and waste (Isa 14:20, 18:2, 7).

16. Babylon is a land rich in mineral wealth (Jer 51:13).

17. Babylon is a leading agricultural nation of the world (Jer 50, 51; Rev 1.

18. Babylon is the leading exporting nation in the world (Jer 51:13; Rev 1.

19. Babylon is the leading importing nation of the entire world. (Jer 50, 51; Rev 1.

20. Babylon is a nation filled with warehouses and granaries (Jer 50:26).

21. Babylon is the leading INDUSTRIAL NATION OF THE WORLD (Isa 13, 47, Jer 50, 51; Rev 1.

22. Babylon is noted for her horses (Jer 50:37).

23. Babylon is noted for her cattle, sheep, and other livestock (Jer 50:26, 27; Rev 18:13).

24. Babylon is noted for her fine flour and mill operations (Rev 18:13).

25. Babylon is a nation of farmers and harvests huge crops (Jer 50:16, 26, 27).

26. Babylon is a huge exporter of MUSIC (Rev 18:22).

27. Babylon's musicians are known around the world (Rev 18:22)

28. Babylon has a huge aviation program (Isa 14:13-14; Jer 51:53; Hab 1:6-10).

29. Babylon's skies are filled with the whisper of aircraft wings (Isa 18:1; Jer 51:53).

30. Babylon has a huge space industry, has "mounted up to the heavens" (Jer 51:53).

31. Babylon fortifies her skies with a huge military aviation program (Jer 51:53).

32. Babylon is portrayed as a leading in high tech weapons and abilities (Jer 51:53; Hab 1:6-10; implied throughout).

33. Babylon is a nation filled with warm water seaports (Rev 18:17-19).

34. Babylon is a coastal nation and sits upon MANY WATERS (Jer 51:13).

35. Babylon trades with all who have ships in the sea year round (Rev 18:17-1.

36. Babylon is nation filled with a "mingled" people (Jer 50:37).

37. Babylon is a SINGULAR NATION founded upon OUT OF MANY, ONE (Isa 13, 47, Jer 50, 51, Hab 1).

38. Babylon is a REPUBLIC or a DEMOCRACY; many counsels (Isa 47:13) rule it.

39. Babylon's governmental system breaks down (Isa 47:13).

40. Babylon is bogged down with deliberations and cannot govern properly (Isa 47:13).

41. Babylon's leaders use astrology, seers, and mystics for guidance (Isa 47:13; Rev 18:2).

42. Babylon labored in the occult from her very inception (Isa 47:12).

43. Babylon falls to the occult just before her end by nuclear fire (Rev 18:2)

44. Babylon was born as a CHRISTIAN NATION (Jer 50:11).

45. Babylon turns upon its heritage and destroys it all in the end (Jer 50:11).

46. Babylon's Christian leaders lead their flock astray in prophecy and salvation (Jer 50:6; implied Rev 18:2).

47. Babylon's Christian leaders are "strangers" in the Lord Houses of Worship (Jer 51:51).

48. The people of Babylon are deep into astrology and spiritism (Isa 47:12; Rev 18:2).

49. Babylon becomes the home of all antichrist religions in the world (Rev 18:2).

50. Babylon is a nation of religious confusion (Isa 47:12-13).

51. Babylon turns upon its own people and imprisons and slays them by millions (Jer 50:7, 33; 51:35; 39; Dan 7:25; Rev 13:7; 17:6; 18:24).

52. Babylon sets of detention centers for Jews and Christians and rounds them up for extermination (Jer 50:7, 33; 51:35, 49; Rev 17:6; 18:24).

53. Babylon has a mother nation that remains in existence from her birth to death (Jer 50: 12).

54. The mother of Babylon has the symbol of the LION (Dan7:4; Ezek 38:13; Jer 51:38; Psalms 17:12).

55. The mother of Babylon will rule over her daughter her entire life (Dan 7:4; Jer 50:12).

56. The mother of Babylon will be a state of major decline as the end nears (Jer 50:12).

57. Babylon is considered a lion's whelp (Ezek 38:13; Jer 51:3.

58. Babylon will have the symbol of the EAGLE and builds her nest in the stars (Dan 7:4 EAGLE WINGS; Isa 14:13-14; Jer 51:53).

59. Babylon turns totally antichrist and is the leading antichrist power at the end (Rev 18:2; Isa 14:4-6).

60. THE KING OF BABYLON is called LUCIFER, the ANTICHRIST (Isa 14:4-6).

61. The King of Babylon will rule from THE GREAT CITY BABYLON (Isa 14:4-6; Rev 17: 1.

62. A world government entity will rise up to rule the world from BABYLON THE CITY (Isa 14; Hab 2, Rev 13, 17, 1.

63. This world entity will be a diverse entity, different from all other ruling bodies of the world (Dan 7:7, 23).

64. This entity will be a TREATY POWER ENTITY (Dan 7:7, 23 DIVERSE).

65. This entity will rise up and use the military power of Babylon the nation to RULE THE WORLD (Isa 14:4-6; Hab 1 & 2, Rev 13, 17).

66. Babylon is a huge producer and exporter of automobiles (Jer 50:37; Rev 18:13).

67. Babylon is a nation of CRAFTSMEN, experts in their trade (Jer 50, 51, Rev 18:22).

68. Babylon is noted for her jewelry of gold and silver (Rev 18:22).

69. Babylon is a huge importer and exporter of spices (Rev 18:13).

70. Babylon is a huge exporter of fine marble products (Rev 18:22).

71. Babylon is noted for her iron and steel production (Rev 18:12).

72. Babylon has huge corporations that have bases around the world (Rev 18:23, implied throughout)

73. Babylon is a nation of higher education and learning (Isa 47:10, implied throughout).

74. Babylon is a nation with a GREAT VOICE in world affairs (Jer 51:55)

75. Babylon is a VIRGIN NATION, untouched by major war (Isa 47:1).

76. Babylon has a vast military machine (Jer 50:36; 51:30; Hab 1 & 2, Rev 13:4).

77. Babylon will be instrumental in the setting up of Israel in the Middle East, and is the home of God's people (Jer 50:47; 51:45).

78. Babylon will have a major enemy to her north (Jer 50:3, 9, 41).

79. Babylon's enemy will lie on the opposite side of the world, over the poles (Isa 13:5)

80. The enemy of Babylon will be a FEDERAL OF NATIONS (Jer 50:9).

81. The enemy of Babylon will be largely Moslem in make-up (Jer 50:17; Rev 17:16; Psalms 83:5-12).

82. The enemy of Babylon will have nuclear missiles capable of reaching Babylon (Jer 50:9, 14, Rev 18:8, 1.

83. The enemy of Babylon will be noted for her cruelty (Isa 13, 14, Jer 50, 51, Rev 17, 1.

84. The enemy of Babylon will also have a huge aviation military machine (Jer 50:9, 14, Rev 18:8, 18 implied throughout).

85. The enemy of Babylon will come into Babylon unnoticed (Isa 47:11, Jer 50:24; 51:2, 14).

86. Babylon will be filled with her enemies brought in under the guise of peace (Dan 11:21).

87. Babylon will have all of her borders cut off, and there will be no way of

escape (Jer 50:28; 51:32).

88. Babylon will be destroyed by nuclear fire (Implied throughout)

89. Babylon is land vast land with huge cities, towns, and villages throughout (Implied throughout).

90. Babylon will have been a huge missionary nation for Jesus Christ (Jer 50:11; 51:7).

91. Babylon would be a home to multitudes of Jews who leave (Jer 50:4-6, 8, 51:6, 45)

92. The people of Babylon would not know their true identity (Jer 50:6, implied throughout).

93. The people of Babylon would think they are God's elect and eternal (Isa 47:7-8, Rev 18:7).

94. The people of Babylon would enjoy the highest standard of living in the world (Rev 18:7).

95. The people of Babylon would grow mad upon their idols (Jer 50:2, 38; Hab 2:1.

96. The people of Babylon would go into deep sins of all kinds (Rev 18:5).

97. The nation Babylon dwells carelessly before the Lord (Isa 47:

98. Babylon becomes proud, haughty, and does not consider her end (Isa 47:7- .

99. Babylon deals in the occult, in sorceries and drugs (Isa 47:9, 12; Rev 18:23)

Is America BABYLON? There would likewise be a series of SIGNS that would begin to emerge that would give BIRTH TO, and WATCH THE RISE OF, as well as THE FALL OF AMERICA-BABYLON.

Almighty God REMAINS a
GOD OF MIRACLES

Date: March 22, 2003
By: Pam Schuffert

Friends, REMEMBER that OUR GOD is AN AWESOME GOD as you face into the future. He has been with His people throughout the centuries, worldwide, through many a crisis, war, famine, state of persecution, etc.

HE KNOWS HOW TO KEEP THOSE THAT ARE HIS! In addition, remember that we are always looking forward to THE RESURRECTION...to ANOTHER WORLD...ANOTHER KINGDOM...and that THIS WORLD SHALL BE JUDGED AND PASS AWAY!

Only those who remain faithful unto death, through every trial and test remaining faithful to Jesus Christ and the Living God shall inherit the "world to come" and eternal life. "BUT HE THAT ENDURES TO THE END, THE SAME SHALL BE SAVED."

This world MUST BE JUDGED! Moreover, America, in her sinful and wicked state, MUST BE JUDGED! Moreover, Bible prophecy indicating the great end-time persecution and martyring of end-times saints of Jesus Christ under an antichrist world government controlled by Satan MUST COME TO PASS!

Bible prophecy will never be changed to please our flesh and its whims. "Father, THY WORD IS TRUTH." Rather it is up to US to be changed into the character and nature of Jesus Christ, and to know Him even in his suffering and testings and death...AND RESURRECTION AS WELL!

There is no testing that God permits to come to His saints, through which HE WILL NOT BE WITH THEM TO THE END! And you KNOW that such testing perfects us in many ways. We must be conformed to the image of Jesus Christ, even unto His sufferings and temptations and His death as well.

May we seek to glorify God, through all we are called upon to endure and suffer for His name's sake, and may many unbelievers come to Jesus through our testimony as a result in the times to come.

-Pam Schuffert

The Truth about Enron:

1. Enron's chairman met with the President and the Vice President in the Oval Office.
2. Enron gives $420,000 to the president's party over three years.
3. Enron donated $100,000 to the President's inauguration festivities.
4. The Enron chairman stayed at the White House 11 times.
5. The Enron Corp. had access to the administration at its highest levels and even enlisted the Commerce and State Departments to grease deals for it.
 6. The taxpayer-supported Export-Import Bank subsidized Enron for more than $600 million in just one transaction.

The president under whom all this happened WAS NOT George W. Bush!
It was Bill Clinton!

I urge you to be in prayer in the coming days, weeks, months and Lord willing years and know that if another Clinton goes into Presidential Office, if you are a Christian, gun owner or someone like me who is all the above, you are in serious trouble. We already face nukes aimed by China at Taiwan, The North Koreans want to use a nuke on America, and Muslims want to kill all Americans. Would it help if we donned a fan belt and diaper on our head? Talk about a clandestine and covert operation. We could then rename America Babylon. In a way, America is Babylon.

In the Terrorist Training Manual, it calls for trainees to blend in with the culture of America. That means according to the manual, wearing designer clothes, drinking pop, smoking, looking at pornography, driving a mini van and blending in and being part of the community. At the right time, these people, some of whom you currently work with, will be activated for Jihad or war. Keep your eyes and ears open and your mouth shut.

–Ray Hope

Read on, there are still a few more pages to go!

Chapter 15

The Battle belongs to God

Think Big Brother can't find you?

A Texas school district's 500 buses have been equipped with transmitters that send out radar signals, making drivers with radar detectors within a mile of a bus think that a police officer with a radar gun is searching for speeders nearby.

Texas-based Speed Measurement Laboratories and Cobra, which makes radar detectors, donated the drone transmitters worth $250,000 to the school district in an effort to improve safety and influence other districts to purchase the technology. End--

JetBlue Airways gave 5 million passenger itineraries to a Defense Department contractor that used the information as part of a study seeking ways to identify "high risk" airline customers. The study, produced by Torch Concepts of Huntsville, Ala., was titled "Homeland Security: Airline Passenger Risk Assessment" and was intended to be a proof-of-concept analysis for a project on military base security.

Details of the study and JetBlue's involvement were reported online Thursday by Wired magazine, which credited privacy activist Bill Scannell for bringing attention to the issue on his Web site, Don't Spy On. US. The Transportation Security Administration, the federal agency in charge of airline and airport security, said Friday it was not involved in the study.

The Torch study analyzed the records JetBlue provided in September 2002, as well as other demographic data collected about the passengers, including Social Security numbers and specific information about their finances and families.

The apparent goal of the study presented at a technology conference in February, was to determine the usefulness of combining passengers' travel and personal information in order to create a profiling system that would make air travel safer.

One conclusion of the study was that "data elements have been identified which best distinguish normal JetBlue passengers from past terrorists." End--

We cannot escape Big Brother but Big Brother cannot escape God and his Judgment. So what have we to fear? God!

President Bush has renewed the exemption allowing the military to refuse to provide any information about its operations at Area 51 in Nevada. Bush says it is of "paramount interest" to exempt the Groom Lake facility. I am not a UFO theorist but there is something rotten going on at that location and most people would say it is UFO cover-up but most likely, it is a major staging site to prepare for Martial Law.

Saying it was of "paramount interest" to exempt the Groom Lake facility, Bush signed the order, renewed yearly, since President Clinton first put it in place in 1995, the Associated Press reports. He is our President and we must respect his judgment and authority according to the laws of our land and according to the Law of God. End--

We are being desensitized. For example, drunk driver checks are for making people feel comfortable being stopped along the road at a checkpoint.

Matthew Chapter 10 verse 16: Behold, I send you forth as sheep in the midst of wolves: be ye therefore wise as serpents, and harmless as doves. 17: But beware of men: for "they will deliver you up to the councils, and they will scourge you in their synagogues; 18 And ye shall be brought before governors and kings for my sake, for a testimony against them and the gentiles. 19 But when they deliver you up, take no thought how or what ye shall speak: for it shall be given you in that same hour what ye shall speak. 20 For it is not ye that speak, but the Spirit of your Father which speaketh in you. (This is only valid for those who know Jesus Christ as Lord and Savior)

21 And the brother shall deliver up the brother to death, and the father the child: and children shall rise up against their parents, and cause them to be put to death. 22 And ye shall be hated of all men for my names sake: but he that endureth to the end shall be saved. (We say we love Jesus but are we willing to suffer for him and his namesake?)

23 But when they persecute you in this city, flee ye into another: for verily I say unto you, Ye shall not have gone over the cities of Israel, till the Son of man be come.

24 The disciple is not above his master, nor the servant above his lord.

Verse 26 tells it all: Fear them not therefore: for there is nothing covered, that shall not be revealed; and hid, that shall not be known. 27 What I tell you in darkness, that speak ye in light: and what ye hear in the ear, that preach ye upon the housetops.

Jesus says in verse 30 But the very hairs on your head are all numbered. 32 Whosoever shall confess me before men, him shall I confess also before my Father which is in heaven. 33 But whosoever shall deny me before men, him shall I also deny before my Father which is in heaven.

Matthew chapter 11 verse 28 Come unto me, all ye that labour and are heavy laden, and I will give you rest. 29 Take my yoke upon you, and learn of me; for I am meek and lowly in heart: and ye shall find rest unto your souls. 30 For my yoke is easy, and my burden light.

Matthew 24 verse 21 For then shall be great tribulation, such as was not since the beginning of the world to this time, no, nor ever shall be. 22 And except those days be shortened, there should no flesh be saved: but for the elect's sake those days shall be shortened.

So dear friends, do not be deceived when you hear reports of people saying Jesus is here or there because in the last days, even the very elect shall be deceived if it were possible.

Jesus Christ is King of Kings and Lord of Lords whether anyone likes it or not.

The next page you read is the most important page of the book. Failing to read this will cost you your life. Reading it will save you life.

If you would like to accept Jesus now as your Lord and Savior, he is ready to receive you. Perhaps you may want to rededicate your life to him. He will forgive you your sins and meet you at your point of greatest need. His word promises that HE WILL NEVER LEAVE YOU NOR FORSAKE YOU.

Pray this prayer.

Dear Jesus,

I am a sinner and I have missed the mark. I have sinned against you God but now I humbly come to you and ask you to forgive me. I know that through my own works, I cannot achieve salvation but only through the shed blood on Calvary. Lord, I believe you were crucified and rose from the dead on the third day and are now at the right hand of God The Father and you are coming back to take me home when I die or upon your glorious return. I need something to believe in Lord. The world has failed me; my own plans have left me empty. Save me O God that I might live my remaining days for you. Teach me your ways and I will tell others about your love and how you saved me from my sins.

Thank you Jesus for loving me. Because your Holy Word says that whosoever shall call upon the name of the Lord shall be saved, I am saved!

If you prayed that prayer, let us know and tell a friend or family member.

Email us at RayHope@americasoldout.com

Remember, Jesus just saved you from your past, put it behind you, and live for him. Do not let Satan remind you of what was. When Satan reminds you of your past, you remind him of his future. His future is to be locked away and doomed to eternal Hell in the lake of fire. Read more about that in Revelation.

Your first bible reading should start in Matthew. If you do not have a bible, let us know and we will see you get one.

You may also subscribe to our free Intelligence newsletter by writing us RayHope@americasoldout.com. For media arrangements, please contact us via email.

.For comprehensive planning and briefings, please email us at RayHope@americasoldout.com

God Bless You,

Ray Hope

The End--but for those who know and follow Jesus, it is just the beginning of eternal life!

Reliable sites for information, news, and research:

WWW.NEWSMAX.COM

WWW.WORLDNETDAILY.COM

WWW.DRUDGEREPORT.COM

WWW.LARRYNICHOLS.COM

WWW.AMERICASOLDOUT.COM

WWW.WALLSTREETUNDERGROUND.ORG

WWW.DEBKA.COM

WWW.WORLDTHREATS.COM

WWW.INFOWARS.COM

gallon buckets- these have a variety of uses- waste, water and or food storage.

Battery operated and or solar shortwave radio- available at any Radio Shack ®

First aid supplies.-these come in handy.

Small coins in silver and gold- good for bartering

Toilet paper- I have a friend who literally thinks this will be better than gold. (Catalog stores no longer send you their 500 page catalogs free anymore)

Letter to the Chairman, the Joint Chiefs of Staff by Al Cuppett

Alexander "Al" Cuppett
U.S. Army/The Joint Staff (OJCS), * Retired
RR1 Box 34-T
Madison, VA 22727
10 Feb 2002--25 Feb 2002 (Update #1)

TO: General Richard B. Myers, Chairman, the Joint Chiefs of Staff (JCS)

INFO: GEN Shinseki, CSA; Gen Ryan, CSAF; ADM Clark, CNO; GEN Jones, CMC; ADM Blair, CINCPAC; ADM Fargo, CINCPACFLT; GEN Jumper, ACC; CINCLANT; CINCLANTFLT; CINCCENT; CINCEUR; CG FORSCOM; Senators Allen, Shelby, Miller, and Warner; Congressmen Barr, Paul, Bartlett, Cantor, Goode, and Burton; and Virginia federal and military/police officers/officials

SUBJECT: Soviet (sic) Defeat of the USS Kitty Hawk's Radar Surveillance "Screen" in WESTPAC

It was recently brought to my attention that last year, in the Sea of Japan, a Russian 'Flanker-Fencer" recon sortie, completely surprised a US Navy Battle Group (BG), led by the USS Kitty Hawk. I understand near panic ensued as the BG CO could not identify the sortie until visual ID was confirmed. Moreover, I suspect the Kitty Hawk's radar array is probably the most advanced in our inventory. More recently, I spoke with a contact associated with surface warfare ops, who confirmed the "F&F" over flight did happen! We have a real problem general, as no 'super power" is "super" if their radar(s) can be "spoofed". In the event you did not know how the Soviets were able to acquire the spoofing technology, here is a literal postulation of how they did it; i.e., the Clintons strike again:

Beginning as far back as 1988, US Presidents, principally traitors Bill & Hillary Clinton, on the orders of the New World Order (NWO), headquartered in "Brussels", have allowed the import/debarkation of literally hundreds of thousands of foreign troops, cops, and flat out 'agents-provocateur' into the USA! This has been accomplished under the [illegal and unconstitutional] *Partnership for Peace (PfP), Treaty on Open Skies (TOS), Project Harmony, Community Police*, and *Cops on the Street* programs, ad nauseam. This includes the latest, despicable, and freedom-infringing, *NATO-ETAN AWACS* mission(s) operating over the USA!

Included in the aforementioned cabal of foreign forces were thousands of Soviet/Chinese/UN pilots, flying their own aircraft (a/c), or having learned to fly our "donated" a/c at Westover AFB. All the clandestine missions now being flown are under the [patently illegal] auspices of the *TOS* treaty. Since these missions are "black operations" sorties against patriotic Americans, including myself, it was necessary that the "black ops" a/c be equipped with "radar spoofing" ECM "pods", or be so equipped in some manner. This has precluded them from being seen on FAA radarscopes USA-wide. I've deduced they're "spoofer" equipped as I've studied many missions, including numerous sorties [bio-chemical included!] against US entities, to include TWA Flt 800; and AA Flt 587, it being the most recent. To wit, I faxed General Jumper that he ought to "splash" a few of these bio-chemical murderers! All he, or somebody, did was have "the baldheaded" talk show host, immediately, *within 30 minutes*, [break the program format] and denounce me [people who believe in "chemtrails"]! So much for trying to save the USA.

129

It's now apparent, thanks to "*military-loathing*" Bill Clinton, the first Russian crew to be introduced to/trained on the US equipment, as far back as 1993, immediately dead lined one of the US a/c, detached the radar spoofer "black box", and shipped it, and the Technical and/or Operations Manual, straight to Moscow!

The Russians then reverse-engineered the ECM components, discovering the sensitive algorithm(s), etc, contained therein, and, in the intervening years, produced their own counter-radar/ECM "black box". If you think the Walker's gave away the store, wait until we see/admit what the Clinton's gave away. On the other hand, are the Chiefs afraid to tell us?

Needless to say, general, we are not a "super power" anymore, except in the press; and the Soviets know it! We're nothing but a paper tiger, shipping nearly all of our combat troops overseas to peace keep, while hundreds of thousands of foreign troops prepare to rape and pillage the USA, by executing '"*urban pacification operations*" *when martial law is declared;* subsequent to the UN's current "*terrorism, and the 'soon-to-take-our-rights-away' campaign*" now in progress, since 11 Sept 2001!

General, I've talked to the officers of German/Argentinean "occupation forces" myself, in their own language, as they debarked at Dulles International Airport! They have admitted to my suppositions! I know whereof I speak! Sir, we are D-O-N-E! It is all but over!

Surely, you 'Five Guys', i.e., you, and the Service Chiefs, must know about all or most of this. Then-CNO, and Jewish hero, Admiral Mike Boorda figured it out, unfortunately the "black ops" thugs put three bullets into his noble body, and thus he wasn't able to try Slick Willie before a military tribunal for high treason! You 'Five Guys' got the "*Boorda message*", as did the US Congress, when "Clinton-antagonist" Sonny Bono was taken out! Moreover, in 1999 I spoke with a relative of the sheriff who investigated the Lake Tahoe "accident". To wit, there was no "*tree*" in the sheriff's report! He also stated, "*That tree deal was Michael Kennedy the week before*"! Unfortunately, neither Bono nor Boorda realized the magnitude and power of the pernicious, yet surreptitious, UN/NWO 'black ops' forces now in country. I do, as do many others who are also 'in-the-know'.

In closing, be advised if the Joint Chiefs continue deploying our troops overseas, per the orders of George Bush and Colin Powell, we'll all soon be slaves/dead! And there, sir, you have the scenario in a nutshell. Godspeed general, as we shall all soon need it!
(The attached two memos pertain to the critical scenario we now find ourselves in.)

Very respectfully, with warm regards,
/Signed: *Al Cuppett*/

Bronze Star, Purple Heart, et al, RVN, 1970-1971; *Secretary of Defense Civilian Service Medal & Joint Meritorious Unit Award*, 1990 *31 years svc, including 19 years "joint service" duty (with 2 yrs in then-AF/XOKCR & AF/SITI) to, and for, the United States!

2 Atch

From:
To:
Sent: Saturday, October 04, 2003 9:29 AM
Subject:

Appendix

This is an example of New World Order- Black operations- As noted in Chapter 6.

Be advised, the following two letters explain the deaths of the four military observers who were at Waco in April 1993. This is how the New World order works. They are here folks; indeed, they walk, and kill, among us.

Alexander B. Cuppett
US Army/The Joint Staff (JCS), Retired
RR 1 Box 34-T
Madison, VA 22727
7 September 1999

Honorable Dan Burton
Room 2185 Rayburn Office Bldg
Washington, DC 20515   (This is the letter that got "General" Reno again investigating Waco in mid-Sept 99.)

Subject: The Waco Cover-up, and other "Incidents" since the Clinton Inauguration in 1993

Dear Congressman Burton,

You were correct in your recent assessment of Janet Reno. It is not "incompetent" people working for her; rather, she is covering up the presence of UN troops, and police forces, which did the dirty work at Waco, as well as having participated at Oklahoma City, and in the shoot-down of TWA Flight 800; and in hundreds of other places! These "Partnership for Peace" troops, and "Project Harmony" cops, more accurately referred to as "UN secret police", have been infiltrated, with the full knowledge of the then-in-power Administration(s), into the USA since before 1989. However, most of the forces have come in under Bill and Co-President Hillary Clinton. This can be proven! ---- To wit, I have enclosed a letter I wrote to an FBI agent (Atch 1), which details sufficient pertinent information to unmask the cover-ups at Waco, Oklahoma City, and TWA 800; and at other places/times.

Sub-attachment 1-A details just a portion of the UN secret police infiltration across the USA. Sub-attachment 1-B mentions just a segment of the pernicious chem.-bio spraying now being carried out against the people of the USA by "Treaty on Open Skies" aircraft. Sub-attachment 1-C reflects the "intimidation" sortie against a courageous US sheriff who dared expose the New World Order/United Nations cabal on a national radio program in 1995.
I have enclosed another attachment (Atch 2) which was given to me, from a magazine, which has many data in it. However, regardless of what is/has been published, remember some critical facts: Americans do not incinerate American kids! Moreover, there have been few, if any, on-the-scene rank-and-file federal agents ever allowed to testify as to what actually happened the last couple of days at Waco. In fact former FBI Agent Richard Schwein, who was at Waco, stated truthfully that the, "streams of automatic weapons fire", as shown in the FLIR videotapes, did not come from FBI forces, and that, "..not one round was fired by an FBI agent on that tragic day".

He is correct! The killing machine gun fire was from UN weapons/armor out of sight behind the building. Such was alluded to by one of the HRT agents actually on the scene, who was quoted by a fellow agent in July 1993, at Quantico, as having said, we were "backed off", and somebody else came in there and burned the building down! It was not the FBI, although Ms. Reno said it was. This is the cover-up! Americans will not slaughter Americans in such a manner!

The filmmaker, Mike McNulty, who made the documentary video, mistakenly [misstated or] stated that "federal operatives" were doing the firing, which was visible in the FLIR sequences. This is untrue! He was in no position to say who was firing in the IR filmstrip. It was UN operatives, apparently summoned from Task Force Six, at Ft Hood, who, once the FBI was ordered far back, slipped in behind and did the coup de grace. Moreover, these personnel are here under illegal UN auspices, operating as "Operational Sub Groups (OSG)". Moreover, they are now in the neutralizing/killing business all across the USA!

(See the sub-attachments.)

Furthermore, the documentary video, which was purposely unnamed in the news media, since the Globalist did not want to publicize the damning scenes, was "Waco: Rules of Engagement". However, nowhere, at any venue, has any legislator asked the question, "If the FBI didn't fire/operate armored vehicles from behind Mt Carmel, who did?"
The fact of the matter is this: Operational command and control of all in-country UN forces comes from Brussels, Belgium.

The White House is flat told what the "operation" will be, and is then ordered to "cover" any negative fallout with legal governmental forces, such as the Secret Service, FBI, etc. There is a "basement cabinet", in place, to coordinate any and all "domestic policy" cover up operations! You need to subpoena actual on-the-scene-Waco agents into executive session, without the press! That is, if there are any still alive, or now stationed in the USA!

There are a million more words, which could be written here, but what is enclosed will suffice, if it can be sent to you.

Respectfully,

CC: Congressmen Ron Paul and Bob Barr

Atch a/s

Alexander B. Cuppett
US Army-The Joint Staff (JCS), Retired
RR 1 Box 34-T
Madison, VA 22727

1 October 1999

Subject: Waco's [Delta Force] Observers Killed in/during September 1999

TO: Whomever it may concern [and even those who are not concerned, because they shall be -- very soon!]

Here's a paragraph I put in a letter to Congressman Dan Burton, dated 7 Sep 1999, which was hand-carried to his Capitol Hill office, as well as two other MC's, by a committee staffer on 8 September: Note the last section with double underline. Quote.

The fact of the matter is this: Operational command and control of all in-country UN forces comes from Brussels, Belgium. The White House is flat told what the "operation" will be, and is then ordered to "cover" any negative fallout with legal governmental forces, such as the Secret Service, FBI, etc. There is a "basement cabinet", in place, to coordinate any and all "domestic policy" cover up operations! You need to subpoena actual on-the-scene-Waco agents into executive session, without the press! That is, if there are any still alive, or now stationed in the USA! Unquote.

On about 24 September on Bo Gritz's radio show, I was told, a guy called in from, I think, Ft Bragg, and said that [the] "three military Delta Force officers who were at Waco, observing, are now dead, to include a Special Forces guy, who was there too". Two drowned in some type "underwater cage" exercise, and one was [somehow] shot. The fourth I do not know how his end came. As far as I can tell, it took "them" from the 8th or 9th, until the 15th, to kill the first one of the "on-the-scene" military guys. Somebody should check with the FBI's HRT at Quantico and see if they have "lost" any FBI agents recently; or since Waco.

I called Chaplain/Colonel Jim Ammerman on the 30th, and in the course of the conversation he stated, he had been informed from Ft Bragg that they [Delta Force] had just had 6 guys killed in the last week or so; including the four who were at Waco. That time frame would have been 15-29 September. Colonel Ammerman is much in the know, and even though retired, is still officially "duty-connected" to the US Army.

Why did they kill six, and not just the four? It would have been too obvious to any knowledgeable officer on Bragg, that those four were the ones at Waco. Therefore, they took out two more to make it not so obvious. Just like, they ordered all the appliances, and not just the TV set, taken out of the person's house [across from Attorney Mike Benn's] in Dallas after the chopper shot the two rockets into the [wrong] house. I think I covered that event in my first video. I covered it completely in the second video. -- So... as one, unnamed, four-star general said two years ago -- "They can take out anyone they want at anytime they want".

Furthermore, in the "cover up arena", a federal judge tried to "gag" Retired FBI Agent Ted Gunderson from talking/typing about OKC. Gunderson, who has his own investigative business in California, [probably] just said, "Let him try to gag me... Hey, your honor, bring this to court and we'll surely learn what really happened at OKC". "They" could do nothing against him, as bringing him in for contempt would risk exposing the completely dirty plot and cover-up, which

Gunderson and General Partin, both, had put out on the underground grape vine, or whatever you want to call it.

Prayerfully, in His glad Service,

P.S. Update -- AP news release, October 31, 1999 states: "Military reluctant in Waco Siege, report says". Further, the report states, "...military officials insist that three Delta Force members were present that day as observers only". Moreover, the final relevant statement in the article reads, "No Army official familiar with the situation was available for comment Saturday, said Gerry Gilmore [probably a Clinton(s) appointee], a Pentagon Army spokesman". [No, and guess why they are not available folks? They are all 'dog-tags-in-teeth' dead! Read on!]

The fact of the matter is the three [observing] officers are now dead, along with a fourth military [Special Forces] observer, who was also present; and now two more officers, as noted above. Waco critic Congressman Dan Burton and Reno-appointed 'Waco-investigator' [ex-Senator] Danforth, have both been "dropped out of the press" as they are afraid [and now too late] to proceed, for fear of being "taken out".

All six officers died in strange circumstances within about 10 days of the above-noted letter being delivered to Dan Burton, Ron Paul, and Bob Barrs' offices on 8 Sept 99. Ed note: Waco, OKC, TWA 800, Valuejet, Ron Brown, Bill Colby, Admiral Boorda, Vince Foster, and now Egypt Air 990, to name just a few, are all part of the UN/New World Order "US-takeover" being implemented by the "Clintons and Company" -- And so the cover-up of the UN troops, the Soviet Spetsnaz, etc., including pernicious agents-provocateur, operating in the US, continues unabated and unchecked!

Al Cuppett
US Army-The Joint Staff (JCS), Retired
366 Graves Mill Road
Madison, VA 22727

19 September 1999 [Update-2]

To: True "Believers" and Jewish Citizens of the USA (The Polish concentration camps were built BEFORE the Germans got there!)
Subject: The Coming Holocaust in the United States!

Dear friends, whomever, the following letter was received on this date from the United Kingdom: QUOTE:
[Durham County, UK] Sept 9, 1999
Al Cuppett (sic)

Greetings and blessings to you in Yeshua's name. Please forgive me for not writing sooner to you to thank you for the video [**Straight from the Joint Chiefs] and all the information printed on 11 sheets. Just thank you! Since then you will know the video arrived broken (though a friend fixed it.), but the wrong [type] VCR here. We may still be able to see it if we get a new [compatible] VCR.

However, praise God for the [audio track of the 2 video] tapes Charles sent - we have heard the awesomeness of all that is to happen & yet so few want to know or believe what is being said. It is so much more [easier] to search for blessings and 'gold dust', [i.e., a new, extra-biblical, Satanic "lying wonder" now manifesting itself on duped 'believers'] etc. [than to believe the truth of what is about to happen]. Only God can reveal the truth, [and] if only a few receive, we have the responsibility to share & pray God will open blind eyes.

I am sure the Lord has given you a difficult task, but believe He has given you the strength, power, & protection to continue. It is an awesome task when we think of all of the Jews in the U.S. carrying on as the Jews did in Europe before that catastrophe struck! O' God, help me & all who know to play our part, however small at this time. [Queen] Esther was able to help & preserve her nation (the Jews) when things were desperate! May we now be the Esther's and Mordecai's in these days, O' God!

I told you in Jerusalem at [name omitted] House of Peace what God had shown me when we were in Poland at a concentration camp there last year. A notice on the wall of the 1st hut [barrack] (with pictures) told that all had been prepared & made ready (#)before Sept 3rd, 1939 - On that day in Poland, the Germans swept into Poland & swept 100's [hundreds] into the [#already prepared] camps[!!]. As all this was already there for that day, the Lord spoke to my heart to say - 'Now all is ready & prepared, once again, for the next onslaught!'. - When you spoke in Jerusalem it was confirmation of what the Lord had said. Bless you in all that you are doing in Jesus' Name.

God bless you
yours in Jesus' Name

[Signed] B... [Name withheld by ABC]
UNQUOTE.

Well folks, I hope the additional "witness", above, will persuade all reading this of the gravity of the situation and times in which we now find ourselves. The Lord Himself knows I have tried for 7 years to warn a sleeping, "stiff necked people", regardless of their "faith". –

Moreover, if you do not believe the above is possible, now, in the US, check out the attachment, which, however, does not address FEMA'S [already built!] 142 "dissident/resister" detention camps/prisons in the US! Ed note: The Polish police could not be induced to arrest Polish Jews, due to national/local allegiance, but the Illuminati/others, had the camps built; waiting for "foreigners" to arrive, to first rob, and then jail/kill the Jews! Godspeed, 'cause we are all going to need it!

In the Lord's glad Service, the King of Kings, The Lord Jesus Christ, Al Cuppett Signed: Al Cuppett

Atch a/s (or see reverse side)
** this video, and "Black Ops and Prophecy", are available by calling the Prophecy Club @ 758.266.1112

the world was never told this; thus, there was an international conspiracy, just as there is now! For those reading America Sold Out- See Chapter Six for the Atch Noted above.

U.S. Army/The Joint Staff (JCS), Ret.
RR1 Box 34-T
Madison, VA 22727
18 March 2002

TO: My Jewish Friends everywhere

Subject: Spying on Zion, the USS Liberty Incident, the Bush Dynasty and Applied Judgment

Spying on Zion

For many years my contacts have kept insisting there is a British section. at/operating with the
National Security Agency (NSA) at Ft Meade, MD, which is spying on US citizens; quickly
passing the collected communications intelligence (COMINT) data on to NSA,CIA, and/or UN
operatives in the US!

In this manner the spirit/letter of Fourth Amendment, is not [officially] broken, as it is not
Americans actually tapping the lines. We now know, through intelligence indicators, that
clandestine and illegal trapping, tapping, and monitoring of all private voice, data, and email
traffic, is going on across the US using the high tech, Echelon. In addition, Carnivore systems;
with the blessing of NSA, CIA, and the recently established, National Recon Office have been
given access to intelligence facilities under United Nations mandates and/or agreements, or
worse, by order of the [now-discovered]?shadow government, a.k.a., the Basement Cabinet as I
have called it for years. To wit, Ollie North slipped/identified it as the parallel government.

Now, after reading The Secret War Against the Jews (by Loftus/Aarons) I can safely declare that
US citizens, particularly Jews, now, and in the last 60 years, have been, and are being ruthlessly
spied upon as I write this memo. Here is how it all came about:

According to Loftus and Aarons book, in 1940, the British obtained permission to tap phones to
spy on Americans who were aiding the Nazis. However, it is now clear they were also spying on
Zionists/Zionist supporters within the US, who were advocating a Jewish State! I remember in
1994, when Admiral Bobby Inman, a previous NSA director, withdrew his Slick Willie-
appointment as Secretary of Defense.

The books states that Inman, knew his NSA predecessors had allowed the Brits to tap any
American phone they wanted, and he feared this might be disclosed in a political, partisan witch-
hunt. It is also disconcerting that a military careerist, a flag officer, would be a Marxist president.
choice for Secretary of Defense, unless he had other credentials, leanings, or ALLEGIANCE!

I would hope, had he been confirmed, he would have sent combined arms support, i.e., armor and
artillery units, to Somalia, which military-loathing Clinton and then-Secretary of Defense Les
Aspen, failed to do, thus dooming 18 American boys to be dragged through the streets of
Mogadishu. However, such are the lessons learned with our troops under UN/New World Order
(NWO) commanders! Specialist Mike New was right!

The high tech spying continues today. Therefore, as I have warned Jews across the US, they are
the continuing targets of the United Nations/NWO. This includes born again
Believers/Messianics supportive of Israel! My Jewish friends, you cannot discuss anything
critical ANYWHERE NEAR, or over ANY electronic device, including fax machines.

Remember, your voice can be trapped (recorded) from your cell phone anytime it has its battery installed!

Take heed! Furthermore, the Brits have allowed the US to tap British phones via the intelligence gathering facility at Menwith Hill, UK. Thus, the two government's trade pirated and illegally obtained data, which was collected against UK/US citizens; and can deceitfully; say there are no Americans spying on Americans, and no Brits spying on Brits. As the Brits say, Clever, eh

The USS Liberty Incident

First, unknown to most US citizens, the British have done nothing for the Jewish people since the Balfour Declaration in 1917, which announced British support, in principle, for a Jewish State on the land we now know as Israel. This was done as a favor to Chaim Weizman, the Father of Modern Israel, who had saved British rumps in WWI, when he invented synthetic acetone just in time to save England, which had run out of explosive propellant for artillery/naval shells. That is a fact! Moreover, I suspected way back in 1967, before I became a born again Believer at 0030 hours, on 5 Jan 1969, that there had to be something terribly wrong going on for Israel to have attacked the ship. I was right, but it took me until 2002 to find out the truth!

Unfortunately, since Lord Balfour the Brits have, by and large, been vehemently anti-Semitic, particularly if you consider the ongoing monitoring of US Jewish phone lines, by the Temporary British position [now at NSA HQ], as it is known; therewith, having gained original access to monitor Nazi sympathizers in 1940. To get right to the bottom of this: The book makes it clear that the US Navy, not knowing what was being done with the Intel data which the Black room on the Liberty, was collecting, ended up as the culprit.

The NSA spooks were transmitting the Israeli Order of Battle, to include all Israeli troop/armor movements, based on SIGINT data collected, to a major British intelligence center on Cyprus! The Brits in turn, true to anti-Semitic form, were sending the near-real time Intel data straight to Arab commanders opposing Israel! This was costing Israeli lives by the minute, thus, the Israelis had to stop the spooks from sending the data to the Brits, otherwise they were doomed. To wit, every move the IDF made, within 30 minutes, was relayed to the Arabs!

The Israelis, in true mercy, made the Liberty strike as surgical as they could, as they could have sunk the ship. [Read the book!] Unfortunately, the ships commander did not know what his ship was being used for, and it was mostly Ships Company, not the NSA spooks, who paid for our anti-Semitic actions with their lives! He who blesses the seed of Abraham shall be blessed; those who curse the seed shall be cursed. We reaped what we sowed.

The Bush Dynasty and Applied Judgment?

For the record, in 1990, on 11 Sept, President George H.W. Bush announced a New World Order It was exactly eleven years to the day that the WTC was attacked, and, as the recently gathered, but unpublished facts prove, also sabotaged! I have a ten page write up which confirms that!

In 1991, in September, in a supermarket, I warned that George Bush would be out of office if he did not support Israel. For that comment, an anti-Semitic woman, in Madison VA., turned me in. Subsequently, a loyalist Secret Service agent, (that is one who believes in the US Constitution) investigated me! What I meant is clearly demonstrated as follows:

Ignorant of the word of God, in the first week of December of 1991, then-President George H.W. Bush stated he, [Would not grant four billion dollars in loan guarantees to Israel. Guess what folks? Exactly eleven months later, to the very day, he was voted out of office! Just as I had predicted. In September, should he speak against Israel? I may not be a prophet in some folk eyes, but at least I can read! Moreover, I was right!

For forty years, mathematician and Evangelist Ed Vallowe, researched and counted the Authorized Version (KJV) of The Holy Bible. He discovered a supernatural mathematical code, which I learned of in 1988. The number eleven just happens to be Judgment. (In addition, I have found it can also refer to The Judge with a capital J.)

We find that the WTC attack on 9 Sept 2001, just happened to have FOURTEEN elevens in the combined NYC/PA/Washington scenarios! You can count them yourself from news reports! With that many elevens, if you consider the laws of probability, that should mean the odds of 9-11 NOT being the Judgment of Almighty God, is ONE in about FOUR QUADRILLION! Like one in 4,000,000,000,000,000! I think I got the zeroes right. My ten pages reveal the NWO fraud against the American people; including the NY skyline with the South tower cross hair scoped, on a Justice Department anti-terrorism slide, given to me in May 1998!

Dick Cheney's Home Hospital Room

The neighbors all around the vice president's residence on the grounds of the U.S. Naval Observatory in Washington have been up in arms about underground dynamiting.

Explosions have rocked the neighbors' homes, reports say. The mystery of the explosions, Vanity Fair suggests, is a nuclear proof bunker being built for the vice president and his family.

More goings on at the Cheney residence. A Washington insider close to the FBI tells NewsMax that Cheney has a fully equipped hospital emergency room in his home, just in case of a medical emergency.

While Cheney has been in good health since his last heart attack, suffered just after the 2000 election, he's leaving nothing to chance.

There will be no need for paramedics and screaming ambulance sirens if Cheney gets chest pains again.

Instead, he can go right into the hospital room.

"They can even operate there," a source claimed. The source says they had not seen the room but spoke to people who have.

The 61-year-old Cheney has suffered four heart attacks, the first in 1978.

Now, Cheney goes for regular electro-cardiogram (EKG) exams to measure his heart rhythm.

He also has a "pacemaker plus" implanted in him, which monitors any irregular heartbeat. The device can also work as a defibrillator to slow or quicken his heartbeat.

Ray Hope Comment. It appears The V.P. is not only ready for any heart issues but also insulating himself from what could take place from possible WMD.

Now about our present president: On March 13, 2002, President Bush, the 42nd man in the White House, and the 43rd President of the US, strongly criticized Israel for defending itself, from [planned] Islamic destruction. Furthermore, that was the same day the NWO, somehow, got the Rabbis in Jerusalem to declare a day of fasting and prayer! Research shows that the Illuminists, and the NWO, always do things on the 13th, on full moons, or on other satanic holidays/dates.

Israel is now under NWO control! Therefore, based on the above mathematical facts, just with the numbers. I have set forth, from the KJV bible, I would have you count the [eleven] months until 13 Feb 2003, and see what happens in the Bush Administration. Alternatively, see what happens to the US, since he is our king, if we are still a viable nation on 2-13-03.

In the name of the Messiah of Israel -- Chai Israel ---- F-O-R-E-V-E-R!

Signed: Al Cuppett

P.S. Don't worry friends, The LORD shall save [1/3rd of] Israel. With or without U.S. help -or in spite of it.

Appendix material

This is a photo, with intelligence map of armored personnel carriers hidden at the 4-H Camp in Bittinger, Garrett County, Maryland. A military officer took it in April 2002. These vehicles are for suppression of civilians! Neither the County Sheriff, nor the local National Guard commanders were aware of their presence! This is prepositioned equipment for use by foreign troops during martial law. The Maryland Department of Natural Resources is the cover for this particular operation. This is the type of prepositioned military equipment mentioned in Chapter Six of America Sold Out.

Another Appendix to Chapter Six

Al Cuppett
U.S. Army/The Joint Staff (JCS), Ret.
RR 1 Box 34-T
Madison, VA 22727
28 Sept 2002

Subject: Regional Police stationed in York, PA, [and elsewhere] confirmed to be bad cops.

Recently, upon returning from Texas, I spoke with a woman who lives in York, PA. She commented that the Regional Police in her area are extremely bad cops, and not friendly at all. This confirms what was told to me by a man from York in about 1996, when he saw my photo of a Regional Police car, which I had taken in Jan 1994, on US 30, in York. His comments were the same as the woman's on my trip.

The reason for this abrasive conduct is these police officers are not Americans, rather they are foreigners hired during the Bush-Clinton Administration, under three different programs, the first being Project Harmony. Subsequently, in my 1999 letter, entitled Why the 'Strange' Troops, Police, and Events All Across the USA, and updated through 2002 some 20 times, and also detailed on my 1998 videos, I advised all concerned of their presence; to include various names of foreign cops and [UN] police units now found across the US. The danger of their presence should be obvious: They are [mostly] Soviets, who do not believe in our way of life and Godless Communism, has trained them for over 50 years, to hate the USA. They would not hesitate to arrest you for the smallest reason/infraction. Be advised they are the vanguard of the UN's secret police forces in the US! Unfortunately, they make up only a small percentage of the total UN/Multi-National police forces currently deployed in the US! I keep warning people, but most think its checkout counter expectorates.

Woefully, the International Criminal Court (ICC), which came into being on 1 July 2002, makes their presence here very ominous. To wit, if the ICC judiciary issues a bench warrant for an American citizen through UN or shadow government channels, and not through the Justice Department, you could be arrested and disappear quickly. Not a soul would know where you went, or how. Consequently, with the advent FEMA's Red and Blue Lists in 1996, the presence of these hirelings, which is not a bit different from the British hiring Hessian soldiers in the American Revolution, makes the possibility of a nocturnal trip to a recently-Ashcroft-announced concentration camp a pernicious reality. I warned of these camps in 1998 on both of my videos!

Moreover, such a scenario today, is especially dangerous for Jewish people. Zionists, including those of us back Israel, since the UN has declared Zionism, or support for the State of Israel, a crime against humanity. Folks, one of the original driving tenants of the ICC charter was to try those guilty of crimes against humanity. We have come full circle!

To my Jewish friends: Don't think for a moment that distancing yourselves from Israel, the Jews there, or the PLO-Israel scenario now unfolding, will make you less of a target in the US, or the world. Not a chance! Satan hates the seed of Abraham by the flesh, no matter where you live, and with UN power, are planning a Holocaust in the US, as the world has never seen! This is why, in July 2000, I spoke at the Jewish Hatikva Center with Shifra Hoffman, in a desperate attempt to convince you all to Aliyah to Israel! Can you not see the noose tightening around your Hebraic necks?

Moreover, you are not alone. There are many friends of mine, including myself, who are already listed to be arrested, and summarily executed [this term sounds like very recent G.W. Bush theology], for their pro-Jewish/Israel [or pro-Messiah stand]. I hereby declare that I have done my level best to warn you all. I even put my address, etc, on this letter to further provoke your lagging attention!

Shalom, and Am Israel Chai F O R E V E R!

Al Cuppett
(Aleph Lamed)

Appendix to Chapter Six Al Cuppett
U.S. Army/The Joint Staff (JCS), Ret.
RR1 Box 34-T
Madison, VA 22727
21 October 2002

Subject: Clinton shadow government ordered 700,000 UN peacekeeper side arms into US in 1994!

On 14 Dec 1994 I personally heard a radio news broadcast, wherein the newscaster said, President Clinton has authorized the import of 700,000 Makerov 9mm x 18 pistols from Russia???. Knowing the Soviet Order of Battle dictates the prepositioning of supplies and equipment prior to offensive operations, I immediately suspected these pistols were to be used for operations against the American people; or for suicides, perpetrated against patriotic citizens, since the pistols would have no serial number audit trail. Now remember, the Holy Ghost had spoken to me a year earlier and said, Call unto me, and I will answer thee, and show thee great and mighty things, which thou knowest not; unfortunately, most things were to be unpleasant.

Anyhow, if the above was true, the shadow government, which ordered Clinton to sign the import order, would see to it they were delivered. [Be advised UN/NWO orders are coordinated/sent over a command and control data link from Brussels, Belgium, to every head of state in the world, including the White House.] Therefore, we should look for a delivery, which would be another intelligence indicator. Sure enough, on 21 Dec 1994 there was an article, as I recall, in the Daily Progress, probably AP-generated, recording a secret delivery by a Soviet AN-124 to Redstone Arsenal [Alabama]. The pistols are here, all we have to do is spot them in use.

Subsequently, I mentioned the pistol delivery in my Prophecy Club (PC) video, "Straight from the Joint Chiefs", in February 1998. Be advised in that video I detailed a NGB (National Guard Bureau) letter [April 1994] reflecting that various Soviet Republics would have troops involved in Partnership for Peace (PfP) operations in various states.

The letter dictated that Slovenia would have troops in Colorado. Keep reading!
Later that year in Denver, in May/June, and I covered this point in my second PC video, Black Operations and Prophecy, I met two Makerov-savvy individuals at the Denver PC meeting. One stated he was a police officer, and told me the following:

We have encountered black uniformed cops here, wearing badges, which say International Crimes Enforcement Police. Moreover [as I recall] the lower inscription on their badges reads, Nihil Sede Deo, [Nothing without God]. In addition, these people are driving sedans with SLOV oval stickers on the rear! [SLOV is the international ID for Slovenia.] The sedans also have diplomatic plates of Honorary Pro-Consul and the cops carry some kind of federal or UN ID card! Note: No doubt FEMA or Dept of State-issued!

Now keep in mind this officer had just heard me discuss the Makerov pistol import/delivery. He further stated, But the bottom line is that these cops have Makerov pistols strapped on their hips, and I know a Makerov holster when I see one! Uh, oh!!

So there you have it. Our military loathing Marxist President, Bill Clinton, elected by numbed-down voters, with Ross Perot's help (it was a cooked, steal-the-Electoral-College [TWICE] deal folks!) has purposely committed treason against the United States. Just one more reason why [Jewish hero] Admiral Mike Boorda wanted to have him tried before a military tribunal for treason. Nevertheless, I will dispatch that little puppy, with the horrendous details, later. Pray for me, as I will need it.

This is just one issue in a thousand, which I am well versed. We face imminent peril folks! You Jewish folks had better ALIYAH -Like NOW!

Shalom, in the Name of the Messiah of Israel, the One who showed me all this stuff, by his Holy Spirit,

Al Cuppett   [Aleph Lamed]

A.B. "Al" Cuppett
US Army/The Joint Staff (JCS), Retired
RR 1 Box 34-T
Madison, VA 22727

12 November 2001 (Update 10 Dec 2001)

Chapter 17
WHAT REALLY HAPPENED ON SEPTEMBER 11, 2001?

The following pages reveal a portion of what happened on 11 September 2001, to include excerpts from Waco, Oklahoma City, and the shoot-down of TWA 800, which are set forth here to let you see what, is going on in the USA.

Moreover, it appears that the "crash" of the American Airlines A-300 Airbus today, was also a part of the rapidly encroaching "United Nations Take-over" scenario we all now face.

Have a good time reading the next 8 pages. Your life, and even your soul, depend on finding out what is about to envelop the USA!

Al Cuppett

Bronze Star - Purple Heart Medals, et al, Vietnam, 1970-1971
The Secretary of Defense Civilian Service Medal, 1990

** As a licensed pilot, wide body airliners are not adversely affected by the wake turbulence of other wide body aircraft, no matter how close they are spaced. Thus, tail sections are never at risk; otherwise, as one airline captain put it, the entire US commercial air fleet would have all crashed long ago. Under-strength tail sections ended with the Wright Brothers! Give me a break NTSB and FAA!

12 Dec 2001: reporter Charlie Gibson, for/on one of the big morning shows, interviewed Jackie Power, and her husband, within 30 minutes of the crash. She said the plane passed within 100 yards of a chopper- and the chopper shot the plane. Obviously, she was never heard/seen on any following newscast. -- KONTROL! This shoot down either eliminated someone, or was designed to weaken American Airlines, the strongest air carrier in the business; thus attempting to further demolish the US economy, as well as the global economy!

A. B. "Al" Cuppett
US Army/The Joint Staff (OJCS), Retired
RR 1 Box 34-T
Madison, VA 22727
4 Oct 2001 11Jan 2002 (Update #6)

Subject: Eleven September -- The New World Order (NWO) and the United Nations DECREE: "IN YOUR FACE, UNITED STATES, ISRAEL, BORN AGAIN CHRISTIANS, AND THE WHOLE JEWISH RACE!"

To wit: Ordo Ab Chao... A New World Order [Fourth Reich] out of Created Chaos & GOD'S Judgment Begins!

My dear brother in Canada,

You wanted some information? Here it is. Please note this, if you will, "white paper", will be updated, as appropriate, when the info, and it shall, trickles in.

All wars commence as a result of diabolical conspiracies, all employing a planned "catalytic event", or series of events. They never start by happenstance. To wit, a later-suicidal plantation owner from the James River, VA, was provoked into pulling a cannon lanyard at Ft Sumter, SC, thus starting the US Civil War. A suspicious blast sunk the USS Maine and the US and Spain were at war. An assassination and a suspicious ship sinking brought the UK, and subsequently the US, into WWI. A "rising-3rd-Reich", using an agents-provocateur "attack" on a German, near-the-border radio station, by "Polish" troops, sent Germany into Poland, whereas, 2 years later, a 'suspiciously inept' cabal of US government leaders, failed to prevent the attack on Pearl Harbor.

The two incidents, sequentially employed, propelled the UK and US into WWII. The Korean War was a Russian-Chinese "conspiratorial expedition", provoking actions by a surrogate nation, thus to bring America into another war, on the way to a United Nations-led "New World Order" (NWO)". Later, the USS Turner Joy, and another destroyer, would "supposedly" be attacked by [phantom?] North Vietnamese patrol boats, with the resulting Congressional "Tonkin Gulf Resolution" bringing massive US retaliation by LBJ and the subsequent deaths of 55,000-plus US service personnel. All were ongoing conspirators-instigated conflicts, as the NWO (and the United Nations) marches on towards a establishing a global UN army of "peace keepers" for "world peace". Thus,"...and by peace shall [he, the false Messiah] destroy many." Dan 8:25 KJV-ONLY

Therefore, if we're to believe the Hebrew Bible Code, since it predicted, among many other events, the impact points of thirty-nine Scud missiles in Jerusalem (1991), we must now understand that this same Code has pinpointed the true "global" conspirators in the recent WTC/Pentagon attacks against the USA. To wit, the Bible Code "matrix" implicates a cabal of conspirators, including not only a UN-PL0 cabal, but also even "USA" elements!

Friend, this is no mystery, since most US leaders now in power, as with the Clintons before, aren't only violently anti-Semitic at heart, but vehement haters of true "Believers" [born again Christians] across the USA! Hence, 11 September 2001 was not only a "conflict catalyst? in addition, the Divine Judgment of God against the USA (see Para 4 below), and its wickedness [as I will later prove with Gematrial Biblical Numerics], but the actual beginning of WWIII; and the ultimate march towards, "...a place called in the Hebrew tongue Armageddon", in the "Valley of Jezreel", or the Plain of Esdraelon, just NW of modern-day Megiddo, Israel. Be advised, therefore, the final goal of this Satan-led conflict will be the attempted elimination of all Jews and "born again" Believers on the planet. On 2 October, it was reported that Bush and Powell would demand a Palestinian State with East Jerusalem as its capital.

This shall not "fly" in Israel, or in Heaven! Be forewarned. Prepare for the catastrophe! Understandably, I do want to warn you right here, that you can trust nothing you hear on the TV or read in the press in the US today. For example, Heinrich Mueller, the Third Reich's Gestapo Chief, escaped to Switzerland, with his pilot, and later came to the US. Remarkably, with the help of a collaborator, he bought an estate in Warrenton, VA. Mueller stated, upon being questioned by the OSS in 1947, the he "could bring about a coup in this country". His premise was that if he could get our press/broadcasting hierarchy down to "four major networks in one city", the news could be controlled, and a coup successful. We now have all major networks from one central place, New York City. Watch how they will bring about the implementation of the super secret "Continuity of Govt Plan" (COG), and "regionalize" (divide the USA into 10 FEMA Regions! Hey, what about the 50 state governments?

The UN/NWO is planning to "Backpack-Nuke" those state Govt centers, so the ten "Regents" can rule us from FEMA bases!) Note the term "Regional", e.g., parks, hospitals, etc, springing up recently! Believe little or nothing you see on TV, or see in the current NWO-run US press. Multiply the below-exposed "fertilizer" lie 500 times per month and you will get the idea of the TV-press credibility problem we are fighting!

Several years ago, Tom Brokaw, on NBC, and I saw it myself, broadcast that there'd been, "25 tons" of fertilizer stolen from a Brewston Mills, WV, agriculture COOP. The then-running NWO-UN-Clintonista press "spin", coming just after the OK City blasts, was to further terrorize the US population! Terrorize the people with the lie there was enough "high nitrate fertilizer" in the wrong hands to, in my inflammatory words -- 'blow up half the USA'! Was this Goebbels-style propaganda "news story" the truth? No! Was it ever retracted? NO!

About seven months later, I visited the local agriculture COOP from whence this "fertilizer" was stolen. After showing them my two federal ID cards and my US Army/JCS Badge-adorned "Purple Heart-Combat Wounded" baseball cap, and letting them know that my great uncle Bert's family reunion was held about 10 miles away at "Twin Churches", I queried two different employees about the FBI-Janet Reno "fertilizer heist". The answer: "No fertilizer was ever stolen"! It was a "book keeping error", which brought in the local police, then the FBI... then Tom Brokaw and NBC nationwide at 6:30 PM! All in a clever sequentially choreographed attempt to terrorize the American public to, eventually, give up their rights. The World Trade Center "attacks", along with more soon-coming United Nations-sponsored terror, will serve to destroy our freedoms, as we now know them. All in the name of "peace and security". "For when they say peace and safety; then sudden destruction cometh upon them, as travail [birth pangs] upon a woman with child [it's not tissue!]. 1 Thes 5:3 KJV. That means the destruction will come as labor pains... Like, more frequent and more painful with every terrible, perpetrated event!

Here's another example of recent the "sound bite" lies being forced upon us, regarding The WTC/Pentagon charade:

A press report on 24th reported that the Cockpit Voice Recorder, recovered from Flt 93, reveals the terrorist pilot "spoke to the passengers". However, a 25th press report says that, "All 8 flight/cockpit recorders are too badly damaged to produce reliable data" Why? The terrorists surely conversed in the cockpits, revealing they were not from bin Laden's "camp"; thus, their true bosses, as identified by the Bible Code, must be kept secret from the American people if Bush is to have his "war on terror". Note: This war will be the catalyst to bring Islamic terror to every Jew, and many other "politically incorrect groups" worldwide! (See Para 2 below)

Another "sound bite" report says they found one of the terrorist's passports intact near the WTC crash site in NYC? Give me a break! It is lies and more lies, just like the [me mocking them] 'Great West Virginia Fertilizer Heist' above! The US public will believe anything on the TV news! Just as my wife will believe, only what/anything she reads in the newspaper! ANYTHING! [Note: You will never hear a word about the black boxes again on national TV; unless, after they read this, they go into "damage control mode" to discredit me.)

Legally speaking, based on "Judeo-Christian ethic" and English Common Law, all of which we owe to ancient Hebrew/Jewish people, "In the mouth of two or three witnesses shall every word [or fact] be established". Therefore, let's start here, relating individual reports seen or heard by individuals, or telephoned/written to me since 9-11-01:

Postulation: The WTC buildings were destroyed by a reported "implosion", but in this case, it was actually "timed-sequence incremental" (TSI) charges within the THREE, not just two, buildings. All circumstantial evidence and testimony from on-scene citizens, and reports from the scene, prove it. Moreover, WTC Building Number 7, forty stories high, which was not hit, nor on fire, "collapsed", "live and in full color", before our eyes, exactly as the two others. "Heavy dust" did it. Right! There is more to follow on this issue, however the comments of a career USMC ordnance officer, seeing it live on TV in my residence were: "They just blew those three buildings up!" This ought to awaken somebody! The Lord promised to "set a snare" against the NWO.Will this be it?

27 Sep 2003 Late note: The planes autopilots were seized from the pilots by pirate aircraft, using Global Hawk (Raytheon-built) radio control technology with GPS precision targeting. The so-called Muslim hijackers never got into the cockpits, if they were ever on board. No amateur hijacker could fly a plane from Boston to NYC! What a bunch of bunk! (Ray Hope said" No American pilot would ever intentionally fly his aircraft into civilians, he or she would crash it in manner to inflict the fewest possible casualties.")

The whole cover story was fabricated and fed to the press by the Jesuit-controlled New World Order agents now in the USA! The shadow government, post - 911 identified, is running the whole show right in front of the US populace; as they will believe anything, they see on TV! Long story! In addition, cell calls cannot be made from altitude! The Lets Roll Deal was a NWO programmed charade!

Dan asked Tom Kenney, a FEMA Response Team chief rather on national TV, "What did you guys do? Kenny replied, "Oh, we went up Monday night and were ready to roll on Tuesday morning! Tuesday morning! That is when the planes hit! Rather never said a word! Moreover, the American people probably never caught it.

Furthermore, a Red Cross worker reported a federal agent told him, "Do not deviate from anything other than what's in published news reports". It is TWA Flt 800 all over again! In that case, in order to silence two ex-Arkansas State Troopers, on their way to Paris (this info per the prestigious "Miami Herald") to spill the "Clintonian-Arkansas beans" about Slick Willie, to the "Le Monde Magazine", something had to be done. Nothing could be allowed to jeopardize "The Clinton's" tenure in office, such tenure thereby assuring the ongoing betrayal of the USA to the NWO/UN One World Govt. Therefore, a UN/Soviet-piloted chopper, using a "smart" Soviet-made Continuous Rod (CR) Warhead Missile to "cut the plane in half", with a "**K-Kill", killed the "informers", and keeping Clinton in office.

The rest of the TV/press Flt 800 lies everybody has heard already. For brevity's sake, just a couple of the facts of the shoot down will be covered here. ** (Kinetic energy-driven ("hula hoop-like" and welded) rods, leaving no explosive residue inside the target aircraft. Clever huh?)

Here's another point: Since JP-4 jet fuel fumes, no matter how hot they're heated, will not explode, how was it possible for TWA 800 to be brought down by a "fuel tank fumes" explosion? To wit, what you saw when the B-767 hit the WTC Tower was jet fuel, not exploding, but burning, still moving at about 200-225, not "520", MPH, as the spin doctors would have you to believe. In addition, JP-4 jet fuel kindles far below 2000 [spin doctor-press reported] degrees! The buildings were designed to withstand a Class Four Fire, above 2000 degrees. That the fires were "2000 degrees" is pure hype to support their bogus "collapse" scenario.

Moreover, the TWA 800 disaster was carefully covered up by the Illuminati/Jesuits, with the help of the Chief, New York FBI Field Office. To wit, he was chug-a-luggin' a "few drinks" at the "Friars Club", which isn't a Baptist/Methodist, et al, facility, but a Romanist "watering hole", when notified of the disaster. Moreover, TWA Captain Stacy, then TWA's Assistant Chief Pilot, professionally assisting in the investigation, was arrested after he took a seat cushion cover that had "exotic missile fuel stains" soaked into it. Stacy even wrote a book about it all.

They had to suppress that evidence, as it would prove the UN/Russians were involved, since they are the only ones who have, today, an operational CR missile in their weapons inventory. We now use only HE warheads. Further, the chopper, which launched the missile, was employing a radar "spoofer", thus, was invisible to FAA radar. This same technology is being used by "Treaty on Open Skies" (TOS) aircraft as they spray bio-chemical agents across the USA. (See Para 2(a) below) Moreover, the truth about the UN/Russian helicopter units, now hidden in the US, had to be kept secret at all costs, because there are not supposed to be foreign choppers, on "black operations" missions, killing US citizens! However, they are/will be! How about that?

Subsequently, Mrs. Linda Cabot, who was featured on a national TV talk show, had her high quality photo, of a missile streaking towards the plane, forcefully taken away from her. This was done either by 'Reno-directed' federal agents, or by Clinton-imported-into-the-USA, UN "Cops on the Street, or "Project Harmony" cops, or "Community Police", as ordered by a "Basement Cabinet" member (See below). Note: The entire TWA 800 investigation/cover-up, including Waco and Oklahoma City, and many other "operations", was controlled by "parallel government 'cabinet members'", whom we know to have been operating from Washington from/in the White House/EOB, since at least 1993; with the advent of the Clintons.

This can be circumstantially proven by the specific events centered around the little known, helicopter [two, HE missile] attack on anti-Clinton attorney Mike Benn, in Dallas in 1994. [Note. This expose' of the UN, and its "parallel government" operations out of DC, controlled by the "Beast in Brussels", could be put into a 700 page book, but must be stopped somewhere, if I'm ever to get it on the street.] (See Para 5 below)

1. The "signature" of "Controlled Demolitions", i.e., explosives:

(a) The mother of a member of an "elite" Emergency Med Team, dispatched to NYC to assist, related to me her son's comments; when he returned after only two days due to mental trauma from the horrible spectacle unfolding: "We expected to find many mangled bodies from collapsed buildings, but instead we found inordinate/massive numbers of body parts. In fact, truck loads of body parts". Another "witness" reported the same phenomenon. The body parts are the signature of powerful explosives, and such had to have been generated by the explosive forces noted above.

(b) I personally heard at least one fire fighter interviewed in the first 30 minutes after the "collapse" say, "I heard an explosion and the building started falling down". Moreover, the fire fighters knew there was no danger of collapse, as they'd been in many skyscraper fires, therefore they toiled without fear, not knowing explosives were set to go off; destined specifically to cause maximum terror, horror, and shock within the USA. What the fire fighter heard, and we all saw on TV, was the first small "incremental" explosive charge, one thousands to come, sending out, in a "skyrocket-like" display, concrete chunks.

Each chunk followed by dust particle trails that were the result of concrete having been blown into countless molecules of cement dust. You saw it all, including Building 7, which will never again to be shown on/in the TV or press!

Late comment, 10-30-01: A trucker 1/4th mile away stated that the TV coverage deleted the "tremendous noise" that accompanied the "collapse". Sure, 5000 two-pound charges going off in sequence would make a lot of noise! A cover up and what is here should suffice to "uncover" it all. Prepare for the end, the "four [Apocalyptic] horsemen" ride!

Late notes: 11 Nov 01: (1) It was reported to me that of the many FBI and Secret Service agents assigned to offices in the WTC complex, all but one in each office were absent from their offices on 9-11. [As you continue to read, this point/issue will clarify itself.] (2) On 11/11/01 a militia member vehemently complained/questioned on the Net about why "Mayor Giuliani was banning under threat of arrest, all video/photo taking of the WTC crime scene". Well, if the above 2 items are true, it's the same "cover up mode" as OKC, when they buried all the building debris in a land fill, and put a 24-hour guard on it! (Moreover, that's "1st person" true!)

Now you know why the young lady had a dream (which follows below) about the WTC scenario, and why the Hebrew Bible Code included "USA" involvement in 9-11.

(C) A police officer wrote me a letter as follows: The entire NYPD Bomb Squad was killed in the collapse of the first Tower". This would indicate, if they were there before the plane hit, they must have been called when somebody found suspicious [explosive] devices. Moreover, professionally, it would have been near-criminal to have sent the entire bomb squad to one location to assist in a non-explosive related operation; since there could have been a requirement to have a bomb unit somewhere else in NYC. If, however, the entire squad was there it must have been in response to a critical report of one or more/many discovered explosive devices. The time of the bomb squad's arrival must be checked; and that data must come from the actual lips of the official who dispatched the squad. No other source can be trusted as NWO "press control" is in full operation in NYC.

(d) By personally researching the tactics of the NWO in the last 9 years within the US, I can see through their 'press presented' scenario. I saw the "explosion" the firefighter heard, when the dust and chunks of concrete began to fly ["implode"] from just below the burning section. The generation of massive dust concentrations is the primary signature of "incremental" (TSI) explosives being employed. Human beings hurrying near these explosives would have been cut into pieces, exactly as noted by the EMT Tech in Para 1a.

(e) From two separate reports: One employee and I know the man's best friend's mother, on the 30th floor, states that managers with "bullhorns" were telling people to stay in their offices, as "there is no danger". He took the stairs and is alive. A second report states that another employee heard instructions to go back to work from a "PA system".

Either way, the conspirators, with the help of "parallel government/cabinet" operatives (those terms to be defined below), were striving for a "maximum kill ratio"; thus, bringing more outrage from Americans, goading them into a war that will eventually involve all major powers, and bring about the near-destruction of the USA, via bio-chemical and nuclear attacks! Remember this the day you read this!

(f) Related, but critical-to-the-case, information: The US Congress is now hurriedly passing a bill to pay up our UN debt. Isn't that rather odd, since they had refused for years to pay up? What is up? They got the UN's "WTC message", just as the Senate got the "Sony Bono" message, and the Service Chiefs got the "**ADM Boorda Message." Cooperate with our One World Govt "programs" or else! To wit, Bono was taken out by "operatives", and never hit a tree; while Boorda had three bullets in his body. Both were set on bringing the Clintons down, but by different modes! They were neutralized! You just do not know truth! I have the circumstantial evidence to prove it all! **Understand that Admiral Boorda was a Jewish patriot who gave his life for the USA!

2. The PLO-Islamic "Throw the Jews/Israel to the Wolves" Connection

(a) On 25 Sep, the press reported: (My paraphrase) 'Bin laden says that any US attack on Afghanistan will be a declaration of open season on Americans and Jews worldwide!' This is the "link" from the terrorism in the USA to the Mideast scenario. Although Bush is building an "alliance" with Arab nations, the tide will change drastically just when things, "publicly", are "looking good" for us in the "anti-terror battle". The PLO-IDF conflict soon will "escalate" and we may attempt to help Israel. Then the Islamic-Arab "alliance" will play the "oil card"; that is, "Hey USA, drop Israel [and the Jews] and you can have oil/gas for your 2001 [perverted] lifestyles". Moreover, if we attack any Islamic country the specter of terror will spread across the USA, be it the activities of real Islamic terrorists, or the imported UN/Soviet agents-provocateur in the USA! The likes of which not one American in 10,000 know about. To wit, it will not be Arabs flying the 'press-propaganda' "crop dusters", which are setting us up for bio-chem. horror, but rather, operational "Treaty on Open Skies" UN planes/choppers spraying pathogens on us. See http://www.carnicom.com/contrails.htm for chemtrails info, or run "google.com" for/on "chemtrails"). Note: As soon as Bush strikes any Islamic target, every Jewish Synagogue, Hillel Jewish Center, and yarmulke-wearing Jew, will soon be an Islamic target! So said bin Laden!

(b) 24 Sep: in newspapers, Falwell and Robertson are being characterized as "domestic terrorists", and hate mongers for saying God's judgment is on the USA. Well, friends just check the "elevens" in the "count" below!

3. Gematrial/Scripture Numerics prove God's judgment began in earnest on 11 Sep 2001

A study of the Authorized Version (KJV) will reveal a supernatural numeric code within. It took a mathematician 40 years to prove it, and I have been "watching", not using it, since 1988.

Those of you who have been given a copy of the "code" will note that "Eleven" is, (1) "Judgment", or (2) "The [Divine] Judge". Here is the "count", using the "numbers" that fell out on 9-11-01. Right now, the mathematical probability of the attacks NOT being God Almighty's Judgmental Hand is about one trillion to one. Without a lot of editing here they are:

(1) 11 Sep 2001; (2) $9/11 = 9+1+1 = 11$; Day $254 = 2+5+4 = 11$; (3) Remaining days: 111; (4) The twin WTC towers actually resemble an "11"; (5) Both towers were 110 stories high. Note: Jer 50: 21 says: "Go up against the land of Merathaim" ("im" denotes plurality). This literally might mean, "The land of the 'rebellious plural' or 'twins'" -- Twin towers? (6) Flight 11 hit the first tower. (7) One flight had 92 passengers $= 9+2 = 11$. (8) Flight 77 is a multiple of 11. (9) New York was the 11th state to join the Union. (10) "New York City" has 11 letters; (11) "The Pentagon" has 11 letters. (12) One flight had 65 passengers, $6+5 = 11$. (13) The flag was flown at half-staff for 11 days. (14) The digits in Executive Order 13223, which addressed measures resulting from the attacks, add up to 11 $(1-3-2-2-3 = 11)$. That, at this count, is 11 to the 14th power. Figure the odds. I guess that tops "trillion" and hits one in one quadrillion; i.e., that the attacks were NOT the Judgment of God! In addition, there may be more elevens in the scenario. Note: There shall be more attacks, and worse, until they force Bush to declare martial law. Jews and born again Christians take heed, as you are the soon-coming targets. Note on 11-1-01: If George H.W. Bush declared a NWO on 11 Sept 1990 that is exactly 11 years to the day! THINK!

(4) Hebrew Bible Code input (see the P.P.S at the end) to order this special software, please email rayhope@americasoldout.com order and get special bonuses only available to readers of this

book exclusively.

The Biblical Math analysis above, proves the attack was the judgment of Almighty God on this wicked nation, just as recently prophesied to be coming by "Elijah the Tishbite/Elijah the Prophet", well before this ever happened. The Hebrew Bible Code "matrix plot", ran on the WTC/Pentagon attack, reflects that the UN and the PLO were the prime perpetrators. [Those two groups want, among other things, a scenario in the USA, which will prevent us from helping Israel when the war starts.]

Bin Laden was NOT found in the Code "matrix". Since the Bible Code was able to successfully predict the Gulf War Scud missile strikes on Jerusalem in 1991, it stands to reason it could pinpoint who did, or did not, participate in the WTC attack. It did just that, and it was not Bin Laden. He is just the bogeyman for this "war", and the soon coming martial law scenario. What you are seeing on TV is a very cleverly crafted propaganda campaign.

There are many other "elements" in the "code matrix" which I will try to report on later. However, it was a Satanist-inspired action, and it apparently included a [Code-identified] duped US "elite unit" which, when ordered to do a "counter-security exercise" went in and planted the "exercise-only" [and which they thought were dummy] explosives. (See Para 6 below) There is much info to be revealed, but it comes in bit-by-bit; and takes time to be articulated to "snare" these devils!

5. The plot thickens, or better yet, it has been "thick" for years!

Another "report" stated that the "FBI had been put in charge of WTC building security two weeks prior to the attack" What follows will articulate the "modus operandi" and intrigue of the NWO and, as once Ollie North-identified, the "parallel government" operations that have been on-going in/from Washington and Brussels, at least since the Clintons came to power in 1993.

To understand the complex "choreographed movie set" of what's been recently happening, yea, even for decades, read on: At Waco, an FBI HRT member told his Quantico buddy that "We, and the BATF, were all backed way off on the 49th day, and somebody else came in and machine gunned & burned the place down". However, Butch Reno took the blame for the "suicides", etc. What this little "press-assisted" trick did was pit patriotic (armed) Americans against "federally employed" (armed) Americans, because it was later discovered by an infrared (IR) film, shot during the final attack, that machine guns/tanks were used! Question is, who dunnit?

Subsequently and sadly, Congressman Dan Burton's "Waco-IR" investigator-expert, Carlos Gugliotti, was strangely murdered in Laurel, MD, thus putting an end to the Congressional Waco inquiry. The judge believed the Clintonian-British lie of "sun reflections, not machine gun fire", thus, the machine gun-tank employment issue was covered up by the press, with the help of the UN/NWO, and the Clintons; but not before armed patriots blamed armed FBI/ATF agents for the horrible deed against US citizens! Therefore, the NWO/UN conspirators have cleverly pitted armed Americans against armed Americans! Note: The IR evidence of the machine gun/tank shootout issue had to nip in the bud, because if brought to the fore, some loyalist Congressmen would demand to know WHOSE machine guns and tanks they were! They dare not let people know that thousands of UN troops are in the USA - NOW! Are you getting smart yet! To wit ,, all four SF/Delta Force "Waco observers" are now dead; along with 2 additional "elite force officers" to make it less obvious... just so Congress could not question the Army officers then present that day. For they too, as the FBI already testified, also would have said, "The FBI [US forces] did not fire a single round that day". No, but UN forces did! Read on.

What really happened was that from about the 49th to 51st days, UN combat elements (then, and now in-country) from Task Force Six, at Ft Hood, were Brussels-ordered (via the clandestine White House data link to the "Beast" headquarters in Belgium) to the scene, where they shot/burned the Davidians, and 17 kids to death.

The operation, cleverly covered up by the press, was many fold; with only three discussed here:

One: Demonize, via the press, in all "sheeple American" minds, anyone who believes in weapons as a means of self defense/freedom. Koresh had firearms! Remember, worldwide, the UN always collects weapons when they arrive. They sure did at Waco, and they plan the same here! Note Clinton's anti-gun campaign, and watch for another one to begin here in the USA soon; especially if NWO agent's in country can successfully assassinate a leading popular US political figure, on video tape no less, with a firearm! They are planning it! Ed Note: As of 5 October, it's reported, from VA Beach, VA, that ammo manufacturers are recalling 5.6mm (.223) and NATO 7.63mm (.308) ammo from local US stores. They say the "troops need it", when they are actually keeping it from US citizens, who are planning to defend themselves from the in-country UN/Russian troops!

Two: Again, using the same process, demonize anyone who has a bible. Koresh, though far from being scripturally correct, had bibles! Therefore, at Waco, they successfully demonized firearms and bibles, and anyone associated with either. To wit, spiritual power comes from the bible (a bible, the AV-1611) and physical power comes from a gun barrel. UN in country, now hidden, armed forces plan to take both from us very soon and our freedom as well! The WTC scenario is just part of the "terror and paranoia" generating process. All has been meticulously planned.

Three: Using Waco-like scenarios, to ideologically, early on, pit armed Americans (in-the-know-patriotic citizens) against other armed Americans [employees of the federal Govt], so upon a martial law declaration, and when the subsequent UN hoped-for shoot out goes down, it'll be Americans against Americans. When the pieces stop falling, the black uniformed "national and federal" police, actually USSR/UN troops and cops, will drive out of hiding and pick up the pieces. [No pun intended but the body pieces in NYC are part of the "plan"!]

The same goal was accomplished on the "Night of the Long Knives", midnight, 30 June 1934, when the (armed) SA Storm Troopers killed off all the (armed) loyalist Weimar military colonels and generals; who had the keys to the German weapons armories. They pitted (armed) Germans against (armed) Germans. When the pieces stopped falling the black uniformed SS, hiding in the wings, came in, killed off the SA leaders, and successfully took over the weapons -- and the country! The same method is being used here. It is just a little more difficult as we have a Constitution with a 2nd Amendment. The Germans did not, hence it will be bloodier here.

Before tying in the "FBI security" issue we must discuss OK City, wherein the same task was accomplished by craft and deceit; all of it covered up by the press, the "parallel Govt", and with the help of other NWO ideologues (traitors) in Oklahoma. To wit, just as a starter, the 'parallel Govt" was directed by "Co-President" Hillary and her "16 staffers" for 8 years. She has/had "domestic policy" of the USA.

Do not be stupid and argue, get "Unlimited Access: FBI Agent in the Clinton White House"! Proof: In Feb 96, four of her staffers had to be driven to work, in a 20-inch snow, in Humvee 4x4s. What is she running to require four critical operatives at work? The four staffers supervised the other 12 "Basement Cabinet" members, who were running the domestic side of the Govt for the NWO! Wake the Sam Hill up America, many of you are about to be led to concentration camps you don't even know exist; paid for by your tax dollars!

Back to OK City. First, an ANFO bomb cannot cut reinforced concrete past 23 feet. "Tim's Truck Bomb" was 35 feet from the building. Sadly, the NWO conspiracy has to accomplish "objectives", among other things, in any terror-causing scenario they perpetrate. One goal, as noted, was to pit armed Americans against armed Americans. Check out the meaning of "Hegelian Dialectic", and you will get the 'drift'.

Subsequent to "OKBOMB", as the government called it, the patriotic (armed) community soon found out from General Partin, a Dept of Defense Directed Energy Expert upon retirement, that fertilizer could not do what they saw on TV! Just as the planes and fire did not do to the WTC building what you thought you saw, and were told by Brokaw/Jennings/Rather on TV! However, there was a little known fact that the patriotic (armed) community found out via short wave radio, etc, that you, as a TV-watchin' press-brain-washed citizen did not know: That was the Bureau of Alcohol and Firearms Unit (BATF) in the Murrah Building was NOT in the building on 19 April 1995! The reaction to that by the patriotic community was, knowing that something more than fertilizer did the deed, ".those dirty feds, they put contact charges inside the building for Clinton and blew it up!" That was their reaction, and that is the exact react reaction the UN wants; that is, armed American citizens pitted against armed American Govt employees! Circa Germany in 1934!

6. "WTC-USA" Connection

The Hebrew Bible Code "matrix" reveals the "USA" was also a participant! This was an 'elite unit', which I will not identify. As noted above in Para 4, there was a "counter-security" exercise probably "basement cabinet" ordered against the [reported] "FBI-security". What gives? Order the bible code software by emailing RayHope@Americasoldout.com or by typing this into your browser on your computer http://store.yahoo.com/cgi-bin/clink?biblecodesplus+LHpbWA+index.html

Here is what gives. The (armed) patriotic community is smart enough to know the buildings were blown up. So the "cover" story for their personal consumption, will hinge on the "FBI-Building-security" report. They will immediately, if they do not know about the in-country "agents-provocateur", declare that, "Government agents did it again, just like at Waco and OK City!" The "elite team" probably did put a few, [they thought] "dummy bricks" of explosives into the building. However, the majority of the explosives were planted earlier, possibly even when the building was built.

They even had an architect [all ready and waiting to] "pad" the story for your TV "consumption". NWO ideologues do abound, thanks to the Jesuitic corruption of God's True Word, and the resultant sweep of Evil across the land.

Here's where non-spiritual, "unsaved" people get lost: A report from Nevada reveals that a young lady had a vivid dream about the "towers coming down", and told her daddy, "The man with a white beard and one eye in his head, helped destroy the buildings!" They did not understand what she was talking about until the family walked into a mall and saw a caricature of "Uncle Sam" with a "white beard and a Cyclops-style eye in his forehead". The girl exclaimed, "There he is dad, that's the guy in my dream I saw destroying the buildings in New York!" Thus, the "USA" tie-in by the Hebrew Bible Code. The 'elite unit' was the "USA", identified as "Uncle Sam".

7. Additional info: The now-strange and subversive "Mt Pony Bunker" in Culpepper, VA had prolific chopper activity on 11 Sept! This is replicative of choppers in and out of the FEMA Base atop Peters Mountain the day of the OKC bombing!

This is indicative of massive UN operations in the CONUS, as the FEMA base (and the 33 others too!) is manned/guarded by UN/Russian troops. The Mt Pony facility is supposed to be a "US Archives" facility, so why the choppers? They were flexing the "Continuity of Government" (COG) Plan for take over of the USA, when martial law is declared. I have warned you for eight years! As noted, choppers were operating at the Cismont, VA, (Peter's Mtn) FEMA base the day of the OK City bombing. Why? They were practicing the COG takeover plan! The WTC attack was, in layman's terms, their "cue" to start practicing their "exercise" plan!

Be further advised, that UN "national/federal police", as loyalist federal agents warned us two months ago, are now patrolling US airports! [The Democrats are now demanding Bush fund "federal police" at airports; which will 'legitimize' the UN cops that probably are already stationed there, funded under three foreign police programs under Clinton!] I also have very recent reports from an Illinois police officer that "they", the UN cops, are arresting "wanted" individuals and taking "contraband" out of cars at traffic stops in Illinois and Michigan.

This is also true of busses recently stopped in Oklahoma by these same "black uniformed" cops, with "no insignia" on either their uniforms or their vehicles. In Illinois, the traffic stop was, "set up on Rt 53, North of Wilmington, IL; and another on a road South of Wilmington".. "Those weren't Wilmington IL, police officers. I have seen those guys and they're not that physically big". I warned in the second video I made that "Safe and Sober Stops" by US, constabulary [cops/sheriffs] forces would serve to desensitize the US public to "traffic stops". Thus, the people caught off guard, thinking the cops are "just our cops checking for drunks". It will be too late to run when the Russians pull you out of the car, having checked your SSN and found you on the 'subversive' "Red or Blue List". ---

In The Messiah's Name, Shalom and Am Yisrael Chai! ____

P.S. Two pilots, one a B-767 pilot, say that cell phones WILL NOT work at altitude. On the airport yes, but not high up. Therefore, the reported Lets Roll cell call from Flight 93 was an outright fabrication to make a nice hero for the American people to remember. It also gave everyone a warm fuzzy in the mist of terrible grief. Isn't that nice of the New World Order? Just like all the nice memorials, they build at sites where they have killed scores, if not thousands, to further their agenda.

P.P.S. There is a report that working with/using the Hebrew Bible Code is now a considered a UN "hate crime!" Yeah, they hate TRUTH! The "Code" proves God gave Abraham/the Jews a piece of land - FOREVER!

The author served 21 years with the US Army, on six overseas tours, including 5 consecutive "joint service" tours; then serving nine years as a Joint Staff (OJCS)/Air Staff/Dept of Defense "Action Officer", and "Command and Control Communications-Intelligence Evaluator" in the Pentagon.

He speaks five languages; having traveled/been stationed in over 30 countries, and is probably the only individual in the US who can claim 19 years of "joint service" duty with the Dept of Defense/The Joint Staff. Just a few awards include, not "I love me awards", but only to prove he's

"Been there - and done that!" are: Secretary of Defense Civilian Service Medal, Joint Meritorious Unit Award, 1984-1990, Bronze Star, Purple Heart, et al, Vietnam - 1970-71 -- Copies of citations/awards/decorations available, if requested. Please do not expect them free. Email RayHope@AMERICASOLDOUT.COM for details.

10-11-01: "AWACS" - Five NATO AWACS planes are over the US "helping us". We have 33 of our own. Why NATO? They will not squeal on the "chemtrail spraying" aerial tankers; and they will have our planes shot down, by at least [CONFIRMED!] 24 operational MIG-29s, now in the USA, if we, private or military, fly against the UN "occupation" forces. Once again, clearer: The UN ("TOS") bio-chem-spray planes flying here can "spoof" civil FAA radar! They cannot be radar-seen! Nevertheless, an AWAC's radar cannot be "spoofed" by the foreign planes, so since our USAF guys would discover all these UN planes flying over the US, Bush allowed the NATO/ETAN AWACS overhead. Therefore, "our" military guys will never discover the AWACS spraying us! To wit, the NATO AWACS in Yugoslavia did not tell our SAR (rescue) guys where to look for Ron Brown's down plane; thus, the Soviets got there, killed Brown, and slit Airman Shelly Kelly's femoral artery. The Pentagon knew she was alive! She had witnessed that Brown was alive before they gave him the "dry ice bullet" in the head.

14 Nov 2001: ("USA" involvement in WTC as noted by the Hebrew Bible Code) -- A FEMA "response team" director being interviewed, stated "FEMA was ready" and we even sent a team to NYC on the "10th of Sept"! In addition, on 9-11, President Bush was reading a book to school kids in Florida, when notified by staffers of the WTC "hits". He did not even flinch, but kept on reading the book to the kids. Did the CFR members/leaders in our Govt know? Whatever the case, on 9-11, The President was one cool customer and seemed unshakeable.

21 Nov 2001: Late update: A news piece from - www.thepowerhour.com - from 9 Nov, reveals that fire fighters responding to the 9-11 disaster found (my paraphrase), "no water in the nearby hydrants". When telling superiors, and asking why, they were told, (my paraphrase), 'Be good boys, and don't say anything. We have a (and here it is again) '"national security" issue here"". Yeah, The National Suicide Act of 1950".

Another late item: It was reported to me that of all of the FBI and Secret Service agents having Field Offices in the WTC Buildings, there was only ONE agent on duty in either of the offices when the two buildings were detonated. Was the lone agent "manning the phones" the only Christian/Jew in the two offices)? Again, the parallel Govt strikes once more. Read the OK City/BATF section above. BY the way, the CIA had offices in the Number 7 WTC Building, but managed to scoot out before it also "collapsed". The buildings "collapsed all the way to the 5th basement, all the way to the subway! This is only possible by controlled demolitions! Welcome, USA, to the UN's One World Govt!

10 Dec 2001: Late Item: Radio Liberty (Oct-Nov 2001 issue) reports that the WTC roof doors were locked, preventing trapped people from escaping via helicopters hovering over the buildings. Again, basement cabinet or Brussels-ordered, for maximum kill ratio! Maximum effect to get US citizens to want to send more troops overseas!

14 Dec 2001: Bin Laden, on the G.W. Bush poor quality home video, that no one can really understand, reportedly says he was surprised by the buildings collapse; that is, he could not fathom any collateral damage happening other than that even with, or above, the aircraft impact points/fire zone. Neither did the firefighters expect a collapse either, therefore dying, on the floors below! Controlled demolitions did it! See above paragraphs. None of bin Laden's reported comments can be construed to be anything but just that, comments, as he was watching a newscast.

Late note: The UN is demanding an Intl ID card to fight terrorism; which the Hebrew Bible Code proves they helped perpetrate on 9-11! Ordo Ab Chao all over again! Thesis, antithesis, and synthesis; i.e., the Hegelian Dialectic in practice. READ UP! Bin Laden, as Sadaam was not/will not be caught. They need terror to make you give up your rights! The UN peacekeepers are here to POLICE! By peace will he (the false Messiah) destroy many. Note: Mexico is next to crash, then the USA -- according to David Wilkerson (in 1994), and he has NEVER been wrong!

Al Cuppett
U.S. Army/The Joint Staff (JCS), Ret.
RR1 Box 34-T
Madison, VA 22727

20 August 2002 12 Elul 5762 (Update #3 25 Aug 2002)

Subject: Am Israel Chai versus Global Hawk Or A FRAGMENT OF WHAT REALLY HAPPENED ON 9-11 2001

My dear friends, the Reichstag is burning in the US, the wrong thugs have been blamed, and another Kristalnacht is being planned for the same people who suffered in Europe to include any who would help or hide them in the US in 2002! Read carefully and prayerfully... You must heed the info, which follows. Also, be advised I will update and re-edit this letter as info comes in. Should you see this letter again, it will have a subsequent update number and a revision date, affixed beside the original date.

What does Raytheon's Global Hawk system have to do with Zionism/supporters of Israel? Plenty, but the New World Order (NWO) and the United Nations want to hide the connection at all costs. To wit, many issues in the 9-11 scenarios do not ring true. Here is the biggest of all. By the way, I am a licensed pilot and have close friends who fly Boeing airplanes.

To put it bluntly, the Global Hawk aircraft (a/c) guidance system is the UN/NWO weapon of choice to facilitate pure terror within the United States. Herein, I will, through intelligence indicators, and individual intelligence/citizen reports received since the so-called terrorist attacks on 11 Sep 2001, prove that Global Hawk will be the prime weapon, employed against the American people to include world Jewry. Moreover, you can expect more terrorism via crashed Boeing planes! (Ed note: Recently there was a threat published by the Bush Administration that an airplane would hit the Golden Gate Bridge! How do they know? Keep reading! The public could not stand the truth and the shadow Govt does not want you to know.

Reportedly, in April 2001, a Global Hawk-equipped a/c (Boeing 757, apparently with ferry tanks installed), and slaved to the Global Positioning Satellite System (GPS), demonstrated it was possible to fly without a crew, from California to Australia. However, what would be the purpose of such a capability? There will never be an airline, or a military commander that will permit passengers/troops to fly aboard a no-crew airplane! So what purpose did the April 2001 flight serve? Here it is citizen: It proved you could fly a planeload of people from point A to point B, with an autopilot/GPS capability. . especially if the plane was electronically hijacked/pirated, i.e., control taken from the planes flight crew while in flight!

[Update 22 Aug 2002: Lufthansa PR folks, on a reporters query, denied that the airline replaced the autopilots. But as I said it was reported to me; however, lets ask a Lufthansa avionics tech, NOT the CEO's PR man, about the a/p swap.] It was reported to me that Lufthansa had removed all Boeing-installed autopilot systems from their Boeing a/c. Why? Reportedly, some smart Lufthansa electronic engineers discovered a pirate, radio frequency connected back door to the a/c autopilots, by which control of the target aircraft could be seized [pirated] from the flight crew. To wit, to you laymen, if the a/c autopilot (a/p) cannot be turned off, once activated, or however activated, the flight crew cannot control the a/c. It will then fly where the pirate-Global Hawk is programmed to fly; or go where the remote Global Hawk controller directs it to go. If the pirate inserted a GPS lat-long coordinate in the guidance system, the plane hits the spot! Such was the case on 11 Sept 2001. Can you imagine the horror the pilots experienced as the planes approached the buildings! These Nazis are worse than Hitler's bunch! Welcome to the lies of the Devil, and the New World Order fellow American. Your ignorance, your TV, and your six-pack, will be your demise! No slam on sports but if you continue to spend all those hours in front of the boob tube, addicted to ESPN and other sports channels, you will freak when you are in a concentration camp and have no box scores or sports to watch. Wise Up!

I recently talked to an employee of Raytheon, who advised me, out of school, that the Global Hawk system also utilized mobile vans. What for? Simple, this means they have the capability of steering airplanes, be they recon drones, or Boeing 767's just like the model airplane radio control (RC) advocates do on weekends. If it can be done from the ground, it can be done from an airborne platform near the target a/c. And since Boeing airliners were the only kind that were used in 9-11, and the kind Lufthansa modified, we have a pernicious system about to be exposed for what it is: The hijacking/pirating of commercial airliners in flight; whether the hijack is accomplished by an in-flight platform near the target. A/c or a ground controller in a Global Hawk ground van, pirating the a/c, while in flight, or on final approach, via radio frequency (RF) telemetry! If the a/p cannot be turned off, the plane is doomed. Well, if the a/p cannot be turned off on the center console where the switch is located, how about the a/p circuit breaker? In addition, here comes another revelation!

 Some of a Boeing 757/767's (probably 777's too) circuit breakers ARE located in the basement, that is, forward of the front cargo compartment and CANNOT be accessed by the flight crew in flight! Now isn't that convenient for the Global Hawk system, and the New World Order, if the a/p circuit breakers are out of reach of the flight crew? Does this mean, that if the a/c is seized by a Global Hawk pirate van/aerial platform, and the a/p switch on the console is negated by the back door pirate module; the pilots cannot even get to the circuit breaker! PROBABLY! Want to bet Boeing put the a/p circuit breakers, on purpose, in the basement? [Ed note: Why do you think [allegedly] Boeing is secretly paying off TWA 800 claims out of court? [Allegedly] Boeing knows that a court fight, with expert witnesses testifying for the airline, would reveal that JP-4 jet fuel fumes would NOT explode! Then the Govt would have to admit a cover up, and that it was a missile that hit Flight 800! Moreover, where did that missile come from which many people saw/photographed? A Soviet/UN-crewed chopper fired a Continuous Rod (CR) warhead missile into the plane, cutting it in half! It is known as a k-kill! The chopper also employed a radar-spoofing transponder, which spoofed the FAA civil radar; thus, the chopper was invisible on radar screens! THINK AMERICANS!]

Logical proof: The fact that Boeing would not seek the truth, since it was their 747 airplane that blew up, is very strange. They should be trying to prove it was not JP-4 jet fuel fumes that caused the crash, thus clearing their name! However, they refuse to expose the shadow government jet fuel fumes lie. Why? They must be in league with the New World order, as many CEO's are! It appears they also let their planes be equipped with Global Hawk modules, or some compatible module, so that the planes can be pirated by RF telemetry from an airborne and just maybe a ground platform!

This is not simple folks. Nevertheless, be further advised you have been fooled in the past! To wit, the FBI did not burn down Waco, nor were they nearer the building than half a mile on 19 April 1993! Rather, UN [Partnership for Peace] troops from Ft Hood, TX were Brussels-ordered in to do it! Further, an ANFO bomb will not cut reinforced concrete past 23 feet. Thus, Tim McVeigh's truck bomb, which was 35 feet from the building, DID NOT destroy the Federal Building in OKC!

A flight attendant on Flt 93, which crashed in PA, in addition to the now famous, Lets roll call, called in on an in-flight phone, and advised, (1) we have been hijacked already, and the men are not even in the cockpit. She also stated the seat numbers of two of the hijackers. The names assigned to those seats, when FIRST checked that day, were not Arabic! Moreover, what apparently happened to cause her first report was the captain had told the cabin crew the plane was not under their control, or as the attendant said, hijacked already. [Ed note: Obviously none of this was ever in the national news.] The latest info to date gives this to us: An eyewitness told responding fire/police officials that there was a white, unmarked executive-type jet, which flew low over the crash site immediately after the crash. THIS WAS THE PIRATE PLANE, WHICH SEIZED FLT 93! [Note: I have a report that seven of the so-called hijackers, men with those exact names; have been noted to be alive in the Middle East! Two are pilots and are upset that their names were pirated.]

You would then have to ask, Where did that pirate plane come from, and how, not knowing there are thousands of Soviet/UN planes operating clandestinely in the USA , employing radar spoofing transponders, making them invisible to FAA radar. They operate here under the UN Treaty on Open Skies (TOS). To prove there are illegal planes flying over the US, just search for chemtrails to see the bio-chemical war waged against us by UN planes this very day.

Among many discrepancies in the 9-11 scenario was the absence of at least 6 of the on-board flight/cockpit recorders in the four aircraft. Allegedly, we read in the press only, that family members were allowed to hear the cockpit recorder of Flight 93. However, how much did they actually hear? Hey, I cannot prove that anyone was actually allowed to hear anything. We only have press reports. You must realize the press is controlled. To wit, Tom Brokaw reported several years ago that 25 tons high nitrate fertilizer had been stolen from a Brewston Mills, WVA COOP. That's terror talk Fertilizer! The public is now thinking, oh, no, it is going to be Tim McVeigh all across America! Fertilizer was NOT what brought down the OKC building, nor was there ever any fertilizer stolen! I went to WVA 5 months later and personally had two employees admit NO fertilizer was ever stolen.

It was only a book keeping error that escalated into a terror mongering report. Tom Browkaw never recanted the story that I know of. These are the lies we have to swallow from a controlled press about 50 times a week! Furthermore, Henrich Mueller, the Nazi Gestapo Chief, escaped from Germany, and stated in an OSS interview in Switzerland, that if all news sources were located in ONE city, a coup could be pulled on the American people, just as Hitler and Himmler did in 1933-1934. The coup is being pulled as I type this letter! The evening news is the same four stories you read in the paper the next morning! Check it out!

Therefore, they (the shadow Govt) could never let us hear the cockpit recorders because the captains of all four planes would have revealed, on tape, that they had lost control of the planes. The hijackers were set up, to get on the planes, not knowing they would never be able to control the planes. Global Hawk was set to do the dirty deed, and the US press, and the shadow Govt, would do the cover up. Search the web for Global Hawk to see the truth about this system.

How will Global Hawk affect Jews and the born again Christians who support Israel? One, there are going to be more planes crash, .but Global Hawk will not be blamed, or even admitted to. The terror quotient will go up until there are police officers in every place in the country. The only problem is the American public does not know that Clinton hired, with our tax money, over 250,000 foreign cops, and imported over 900,000 foreign PfP troops during his tenure. [Bush continues this also!] No, this is not tabloid slop seen at the checkout counter! In fact, tabloids were NWO-established in America, for the sole purpose of warping your mind to true reality, so you would not believe what you are reading here. Plain and simple. They have every base covered. Here comes the Jewish connection:

In July 2001, an intelligence agent warned a Jewish personality, she was targeted. A list with her name had been intercepted! [This is obviously the FEMA-maintained Red or Blue Lists] A week later, two FBI loyalist agents warned her, that a [UN] plan had been intercepted, which would , when the when the war gets hot in the Mideast, insure that UN cops would be put in the airports to catch terrorists; but they would be really looking for fleeing Jews. Subsequently, in August 2001, the UN Conference on Racism, declared Zionism to be racist, and as such, a crime against humanity. You can see the plot thickening. Demonize the Jews, and then get their friends and supporters! Same plan as in Nazi Germany. Through planned terror, they got the Dutch Communists, and took over the Govt in 1933. Since their demonization plan worked so well, they then went after the Jews -- and their GOLD!

All that remains is more terror to be committed against the US populace by these in country, agent provocateurs. The easiest way to accomplish this is via the clandestine Global Hawk-connection. To wit, recently, as noted, there was another Bush Administration report of a plane expected to hit the Golden Gate Bridge. Where do they get such intelligence? They do not get it! The shadow Govt, which we just learned about after 911, is being, or will be, Brussels-ordered to commit [or allow operatives in country to commit], and then cover up, with the help of the press, such acts against airliners in flight. Just as Brussels ordered Reno to withdraw the FBI/BATF from the Waco compound, thereby allowing UN troops burn the place down. An FBI sniper admitted to all of this on the Quantico KD range in 1993! That is how it all works. Besides, Americans do not burn up our own kids! Foreigners will!

Consequently, we have another Burn the Reichstag scenario in progress. The people will be further terrorized, via terror incidents, and forced to forfeit their right to life! Planes crashing are the most horrible incidents, as they kill many people. I have not time to cover the whole 911 scenario, therefore, see www.infowars.com, and get the Alex Jones video, 911, The Road to Tyranny, and you will have a second witness to what's happening. Again, search for Global Hawk, and you will get more info regarding remote control of aircraft by this crafty system. (I drafted letter this without any reference to Global Hawk data found on the Internet.)

As the terror progresses, Jews, [and Zionist/Israel supporters] will attempt to flee the US. However, there will soon be a God-ordained calamity executed against the PLO, and Butcher Arafat, to make the PLO and Company, leave Israel. During that short break in time, between the PLO flight and UN-controlled martial law here, US Jews must flee. Like, I have been warning them since1999! The trap is being sprung.

Look folks, I don't have 17 hours to explain what's going on all across the country, or to fully dissect the 911 lie which was foisted upon the US population. You must get smart --- now! ANOTHER KRISTALNACHT IS BEING PLANNED! It will make Hitler's Final Solution look like child's play. Yea, I have warned thee. ALIYAH NOW! Mr. Sharon, get me packing! NOW!

Here is the icing on the cake. In May 1998, In West Palm Beach, where I was speaking while on the Straight from the Joint Chiefs video tour with the Prophecy Club, I was given a set of Govt slides, the subject of which was the Emergency Response to Terrorism. Little did I realize it then, but the cover slide of the Justice Dept/FEMA program to teach the fire chiefs (in 1998) who the terrorists are, it featured the NYC skyline! Trained on the WTC tower, EXACTLY where the first plane hit, THREE YEARS LATER, was a riflescopes cross hairs! If you get the video, Black Operations and Prophecy you can see it for yourself. They, the shadow UN Govt, were, in our face, telling us what they were going to do! [Note: The government's idea of terrorists, per the slide syllabus, was mostly right wing Christians! Ask your fire chief, or get the video! In 1999, they ran the same program to US police chiefs!]. If you are a Jew, or a born again Christian, you had better go to Israel, hide out, pray hard, or prepare to suffer or die!

Back to the Golden Gate Bridge: How could they [our friendly shadow Govt] know a plane might hit the Golden Gate Bridge? First, if the US Govt really had an intelligence source listening, they would NEVER TELL the public, as it would compromise the source, that is, reveal the straight Govt was tracking the terrorists; thus tipping them off that somebody was onto their plans. The terrorists would then cease operations and scoot! THINK AMERICANS!

Nevertheless, the UN squads are, on UN/NWO orders from Brussels, planning to crash some more US planes for terror mongering purposes; thus, the shadow Govt has been UN-ordered to have [actually force] the straight? FBI agents leak the for- public-consumption story about the Golden Gate Bridge. Plain and simple, the UN agents-provocateur is planning to seize a plane electronically, via Global Hawk, and crash it into the bridge! That is how they KNOW and that is how they can put out such a story to the public. If they can scare you enough you will give up all your rights... including your guns... Moreover, that is another issue coming soon! This is how it all works folks.

You see, that is one of the possible reasons why the retired EL AL airlines security chief stated that the new security measures at airports would not decrease terrorists' incidents at all. He knew it has nothing to do with what comes past the X-ray machine! It has everything to do with foreign employees, and NOT about any AMERICAN loyalist employees, working in the airports. But even with American employees pulling security, Global Hawk can still crash the planes; even if everybody aboard, PILOTS AND ALL, are clad in only a bathing suit, and carrying only their purse. If the pirate plane seizes the autopilot they are all D-O-O-M-E-D! Unless the pilots can access the circuit breaker for the autopilot! However, if Boeing put the a/p circuit breaker in the basement where it cannot be reached, it is 9-11 all over again! That is why I sent the emergency message to EL AL today! I am trying to, first off all save Jewish lives, and after all, they have suffered enough! Moreover, I shall do all in my power to save them.

You must realize it takes me 17 hours to explain all this. Three pages won't do justice but they could cost me my life. If you pray, I covet your prayers. Nevertheless, please pray in the name of the Lord Jesus, NOT allah!

Chai Israel   and Baruch Ha Shem

Al Cuppett (Aleph Lamed -- AL)

CHAPTER 18 BONUS:

If you were about to give up hope of ever becoming debt free, you may be in for a shock...I have recently been introduced to a company who terminates all credit card debt, keeps your credit bureau clean in the process and in less than 1 year, eliminates all your credit card and unsecured debt. It sounds too good to be true but it is not. They even have a new program to eliminate your mortgage. I cannot give you details in this book but if you write me at RayHope@AmericaSoldout.com, I will email you free details. You can immediately stop making payments in the process and even if you are facing collections or foreclosure, you can be helped.

This process is founded on the decisions of the United States Supreme Court, as they have ruled repeatedly against the legal authority for banking institutions to lend credit. Federal and state laws allow banks to lend money - not credit. They cannot lend you something they do not have, and they cannot charge you interest on something that does not exist!

$7 trillion of shareholder wealth disappeared between February 2000 and October 2002. We are going to see a total wipeout and I assure you if you have debt on your home, automobile or credit cards, you are guaranteed a free room at a camp near you. In addition, you will be placed in a 12 hour a day work detail. Get out of debt now, time is short. If you need help getting out of debt and you have no way to bail out of your debt....do not file for bankruptcy! Write me at RAYHOPE@AMERICASOLDOUT.COM

Here are some things you need to know about debt

Debt Elimination Q&A

Q: I have never heard of anything like this before. Does complete debt elimination really work?

A: Not only does it work, it works every time! We have processed over 3300 cards and loans for 712 clients eliminating over $22 million in debt. That is a five-year record of accomplishment we can be very proud of.

Q: Don't I owe this money? Isn't wrong for me not to pay it back?

A: Because of our fractional banking system and the lending value of your signature the credit card company never lent you anything. The 1968 Minnesota case of First National Bank of Montgomery v. Jerome Daly, the fact that the banks loan you your own good credit were proven unequivocally. In reality, they "created" the money using your own credit as collateral loaning you what was already yours, the value of your signature. The banks know this and make a LOT of money committing this fraud everyday. In short, the bank/credit card company created an invalid contract tricking you into paying them for your own good credit. Then question then becomes do you really owe the scoundrel that cheated you out of your money?

Q: Is there a guarantee?

A: Absolutely! There is a 100% satisfaction guarantee. First, we hold your funds at our office for 3 days so if for any reason you have second thoughts we can immediately return your check. At any time during the debt elimination process, you may request a full refund.

Q: What types of debt can I legally and lawfully eliminate?

A: Different programs are available that cover all credit cards, including Visa, Master Card, Discover, American Express, lines of credit, bank loans, business debt, and even most student loans can be eliminated. In short, all unsecured lines of credit or loans from a bank or credit card company are covered in one program or another. This excludes mortgages, auto loans, leases, or lines of credit with security attached. You may, however, pay on these secured loans with credit cards and use complete debt elimination to clear the debt.

Q: I would feel more comfortable if I could speak with someone that has gone through the debt elimination process. Is there someone I can call?

A: We understand that is a new concept to many of you. Everyone is familiar with consolidation that stretches out your payments, bankruptcy that ruins your credit, and counseling that leaves you in debt, the idea of totally eliminating your debt, interest and late fees today stopping all payment immediately is hard to believe. Your Advisor has been provided with a list of people you can speak with to help you feel safe and secure.

Q: You say this is not bankruptcy, debt consolidation, or a home mortgage…then what is it?

A: Our legal experts discovered a way to challenge any unsecured debt with a bank. You see, the contracts that the credit card companies make you sign are not legal and they know it! They are simply hoping you never find out. To date, they have been very successful at keeping this information secret from most of America. Five years ago, we discovered their flaw. After testing complete debt elimination with hundreds of banks, we developed a system that delivers every time.

Q: I cannot afford to make any more payments. When will my payment stop to the credit card companies?

A: Immediately! There is no reason to continuing paying on an illegal contract. All interest and late fees will also stop. When the program is complete, you will be debt free on all accounts that were part of the program. Won't that feel good?

Q: I have collection agencies calling me already, can you help?

A: These programs can bring you immediate relief from banks and creditors harassing calls and letters. You need to contact your Advisor immediately and enroll in the program so that we can intercede and eliminate this anxiety for you.

Q: Is there a limit to how much you can eliminate?

A: We have had clients with $100,000, $150,000 and more debt entirely eliminated using these programs.

Q: I have a credit card with a very high credit limit. Will the bank take me to court and get a judgment on my property?

A: Others have had your same concern. No one wants to loose those things they worked so hard for. You see, because the credit cards are unsecured the collectors have <u>no</u> legal grounds for getting any of your property. They would also have to show that you owe them the money and they cannot. The one case out of the 3347 plus credit cards that have been eliminated that did go to court was immediately tossed out. The client walked out owing nothing.

Q: How long will this option be available to me? Will the laws change to stop this in the future?

A: Our legal experts tell us that there is a 14 to 24 month window of opportunity before the laws may change and close this option to us forever. It is important that you consider this seriously when deciding when you should start the debt elimination process.

Q: I am currently enrolled in credit counseling that is consolidating my credit cards into a single payment. Is this going to be a problem?

A: Although consolidation was one of the only options short of bankruptcy, it just is not the best option anymore. Instead of continuing to pay interest for a much longer period of time, 4 or 5 years even, our complete debt elimination programs will stop all payments, interest, and late fees immediately freeing you from the worry and fear that comes with the heavy burden of credit card debt.

Q: Is it best to use debt elimination on all of my cards at once or should I keep one or two?

A: The choice is really yours. You can keep a credit card out of the program for convenience. It is handy to have a credit card for some transactions these days. You do need to be aware that some of the programs may lower the available credit on any card that is not in the program. It is our suggestion that you utilize the available credit you may have to pay for the program and immediately eliminate that debt. In this way, the program costs you nothing!

Q: My spouse is on the credit cards. How will they be affected?

A: No matter which person signs the credit cards or loans the programs will still work for you. There is a small additional fee to include your spouse or other shared account holder in the program. During the process if it is possible to have negative credit entries then all card holders will share those remarks on their credit reports until the program is complete and credit is restored. You should talk this over thoroughly with your spouse before initiating a program.

Q: Will I be able to get more credit cards in the future?

A: Credit will be available to you in abundance. Once the process in complete and your credit restored there are thousands of banks eager to issue cards to you...including Visa and Master Card The banks that you terminated debts with will most likely not be willing to go through that again.

Q: Isn't arbitration required now with all new credit card agreements? Won't I end up there?

A: This is a very frequent question when talking about Debt Elimination. The simple answer is no, the programs are designed to keep you out of arbitration. Banks and collectors have no supporting arguments. If they do insist on perusing arbitration, our team of legal experts is ready and waiting. In some cases, we may even take them to arbitration first! If you prefer not to take part in the arbitration process and have it all handled for you consider our Completely Hands Off upgrade. This solution is designed to make you comfortable and secure in the fact that all of the details are being handled for you.

Q: I have a summons to appear in court for a credit card that has gone to collections. Can you help me?

A: Please get us the documents right away. If it has only been a few days, we may be able to help you with this. It just depends if we have enough time. Do not delay!

Q: I am worried about the harassing phone calls. Will they be stopped?

A: All phone calls to you will be stopped immediately! You should feel comfortable in the fact that the law clearly prohibits creditors and collectors from contacting you by phone. All we do is put them on notice the moment the first call is made. In the unlikely event they choose to ignore the law a simple phone call from our paralegal staff will remind them of their responsibility and the penalty for not following the law. This has worked every time!

Q: My bank says they only do internal collections. Will the program work for me?

A: It is not uncommon for banks to say this. They are experts in this game. The honest answer is they MUST use outside collections in order to write off the debt, collect the insurance, and claim the tax deduction. If you feel that a bank is going to play hardball then your best option is to do get into the same game with one of the other programs such as Express, or Professional. Both of these programs attach the banks straight on and are not dependent on going through the collections process. You can feel comforted in our 18 years of experience dealing with the deceitful practices of lending institutions.

Q: I am planning on buying a home, refinancing, purchasing a car, or making some other major purchase in the near future…what should I do?

A: Major purchases will need to take place either before or after program. During this time, creditors may make negative entries on your credit report that will be completely removed upon completion. If these purchases are in the near future, consider either the Express or the Professional programs that have shorter durations than the complete program. Whichever program you decide to use rest assured that the result will be an AAA credit rating.

Q: Are you registered with the Better Business Bureau?

A: Although we are not registered with the Better Business Bureau at this time, it is important to know that we have had no complaints in our 5-year history.

Q: I have great credit now and do not want to loose it. Will my credit be damaged with this process?

A: We understand your concern and can assure you that all of the programs offered will leave you with an AAA credit rating. Depending on which program you choose credit may or may not be affected during the process. In any case, where a bank or collector steps out of line and places a mark against you it will be removed by simply applying the Fair Credit Reporting Act. You should feel confident that your credit rating would be better than ever!

Q: I would really like to know more about the laws behind this remedy. What reference material do you have for me?

A: There are three things that you should have in your hand a reference to the debt elimination process: the Fair Debt Collection Practices Act (FDCPA) is in Title 15 of the US Code, Section 1962; House Joint Resolution 192 (HJR 192) of 1933; and the Federal Reserve Bank of Chicago's *The Two Faces of Debt*. Each of these pieces is available on the Internet or in hard copy.

Q: Will I need to have a lawyer involved somehow? Won't that get expensive?

A: Sometimes in our lives, it is comforting to get legal council. In the end, it is truly your decision as to whether you spend the money on an attorney or not. It is our experience that clients like you do not need an attorney involved because the laws are very clear and the creditors are simply ignoring them. Our experience as paralegal experts in preparing debt dispute documents and the debt verification process has enabled us to put a system together that is easy to understand and simple to implement.

Q: Call me a pessimist, but what if the founders are run over by a truck? What will happen to me then?

A: The likelihood of all 28 professionals and paralegals in the company suffering a terrible tragedy is unlikely at best. Each one you see is Bank Card trained by the founders in every aspect of complete debt elimination.

Q: I would feel better if I had something in writing. Will that be supplied to me?

A: We understand it is important to make any agreement, including the money back guarantee, clear to everyone involved. Your Advisor has all of the forms, agreements, and documentation in writing for you and will provide them at your request.

Q: Complete debt elimination is what I want to do but I just cannot come up with the money. Can I make payments?

A: This is a common question; you should feel relived that others have needs as you. Payment options are up to the individual Advisors.

Q: Complete debt elimination works only with credit cards and unsecured debts. Can I use my credit cards to pay on my house or car loan then eliminate the debt?

A: You certainly can! This is a common strategy among many clients just like you.

Q: My credit report is less than stellar today and I do not have any room on a credit card. Can I do a Credit Restoration first to get another card and pay for the program that way?

A: Many people like you choose to first clean up their credit in order to pay for the program on a credit card. This is a common practice and should be utilized any time you feel it is necessary. Do remember, however, that the Credit Restoration process can take three or more months to complete. During that time you will need to stay current on all of your payments or the Credit Restoration will be of no effect. If the burden of continued payments for another 90 days seems like to much you should consider other means of payment that will allow you to get immediate relief from those credit card bills.

Q: I am a bit nervous using the Internet to make a payment. How will my payment be confirmed?

A: All of us were nervous the first time we conducted business over the Internet. That is why we are utilizing a service called PayPal to transmit funds electronically. It is the simplest and safest means paying while giving you complete control over the process. Your payment will be confirmed immediately as a receipt in email. If you choose, you can send your payment in by certified mail and a signed receipt will be returned to you through the post office.

Q: I have business expenses on my Bank Card credit cards. Can those debts be eliminated as well?

A: The elimination of unsecured business debt is done on a daily basis with our Professional Program. Many others before you have found relief form those staggering business loans and monthly payments.

Q: Will I have to pay more taxes because of this?

A: The only way taxes would be due is if the credit card company sent you a 1099 at the end of the year reporting it as income. In this case, taxes would be owed, but the taxes will be much less than the original debt. That debt could become burdensome to some. Then consider paying the taxes with a credit card and discharging it later. Ask your Advisor about tax reduction and elimination strategies. They will be happy to share information about these services with you.

Q: What support will there be for me. Is there someone I can call?

A: The Advisor that brought you into the program is there to help whenever you need. Simply get with them regarding your questions or concerns and they will take care of them right away. Standing behind the Advisor is a senior staff member and an entire internal team of debt elimination legal experts to answer every question and concern that may come along.

Q: How will the Debt Elimination affect my credit report? Will I have negative entries? What will show in the end?

A: The program may have a temporary negative impact on credit for 2 to 6 months. Many of our clients never experience even a single negative mark ever. In the end, your report will either show all accounts "Paid as Agreed" or the account will be removed completely. In either case, this will have a positive impact on your credit score!

Q: How long does the process take?

A: The process usually takes about 2 months for your accounts to be discharged. In some cases, it has taken as long as 6 months to get resolution.

FARMERS' & MINERS' BANK et al. v. BLUEFIELD NAT. BANK et al.

No. 2413

Circuit Court of Appeals, Fourth Circuit

11 F.2d 83; 1926 U.S. App. LEXIS 2434

January 12, 1926

PRIOR HISTORY:

In Error to the District Court of the United States for the Southern District of West Virginia, at Bluefield.

CASE SUMMARY

PROCEDURAL POSTURE: Plaintiffs, a bank and its receiver, appealed a judgment from the District Court of the United States for the Southern District of West Virginia in favor of defendants, a bank, and its officer, in plaintiffs' action that sought to recover the sum of two promissory notes upon defendants' alleged oral guaranty.

OVERVIEW: A company sought to open an account with defendant bank with a specified line of credit. Defendant bank was unable to lend the company the entire line of credit, so plaintiffs agreed to carry a portion of the loan. The company executed two promissory notes in favor of plaintiffs. Defendants did not indorse the notes; however, plaintiffs alleged that defendant officer orally guaranteed payment. Plaintiffs discounted the notes, and credited the proceeds to defendant bank. Plaintiffs subsequently sued defendants for the amount of the notes, relying on defendant officer's oral guarantee. The district court entered judgment in favor of defendants. The appellate court affirmed the judgment because plaintiffs failed to prove that defendants intended to make a guarantee and actually did give the guarantee. Further, plaintiffs failed to prove that defendant bank owned the notes or that the proceeds of the notes went to defendant bank's use; therefore, plaintiff was not entitled to recover from defendants.

OUTCOME: The judgment in favor of defendants was affirmed because plaintiffs failed to prove the intent to make or the existence of a guarantee, and plaintiffs failed to prove that defendants owned the notes or used the proceeds of the notes.

CORE TERMS: guaranty, discounted, discount, endorsement, indorsed, contingent liability, conversation, examiners, endorser, rediscounted, guarantor, national bank, board of directors, pecuniary interest, line of credit, correspondence, probability, remembered, contented, borrower, occupied, desired, stood, drew

OPINIONBY: ROSE

OPINION: [*84] Before WADDILL, ROSE, and PARKER, Circuit Judges.

ROSE, Circuit Judge. The parties occupied below the same relative positions as they do here; that is, the Farmers' & Miners' Bank, a Virginia corporation, and H. M. Browning, its receiver, a citizen of that state, were the plaintiffs, and the defendants were the Bluefield National Bank, a national banking association located and doing business in West Virginia, and R. B. Parrish, its active vice president and its chief executive officer, who was a citizen of the latter state. We will refer to them by the positions they occupied below.

The suit was to recover $8,000 and interest, the aggregate amount of two notes for $4,000 each, held by the plaintiff bank. The Tazewell Timber Corporation was the maker of these notes. They were each indorsed by two other corporations, neither of whom are parties to this cause. They are not indorsed by either of the defendants, nor is it contended that either of them ever in writing assumed any liability with reference to the paper in question. The plaintiffs' [**2] claim to recover is based upon what it asserts was an oral guaranty given its then cashier, one Wylie, by the defendant, through Parrish. Wylie testified and gave his version of what happened.

Some time in 1920 and before August 2, he had a conversation with Parrish. He says that the latter then told him the Tazewell Timber Corporation wished to open an account with the defendant bank and desired a line of credit for $50,000. At that time, as both of them knew, the combined capital and surplus of the defendant bank was around $110,000, so that the maximum loan, which the statute permitted it to make to any one borrower, was in the neighborhood of $11,000. In answer to a question in cross-examination, he stated that Parrish said the defendant bank could not grant the credit asked for unless it could get other banks to carry a portion of it. In this connection, the witness testified that he supposes that Parrish asked him if the plaintiff bank could not carry part of the loan for "him" (Parrish), and that he replied that his bank would be glad to do so. Wylie remembered that Parrish talked to him about the financial condition of the Tazewell Timber Corporation and its proposed endorsers, [**3] but he said if Parrish handed him correspondence and financial reports concerning them he (the witness) just glanced at them. At one time he testified that Parrish said he would see that the notes were paid, but that appears to be his understanding of the effect of what was said, for the exact words of Parrish, according to the witness, were: "Whenever the board of directors of the Farmers' & Miners' Bank wanted the notes paid, he would have them taken up." He added that he did not remember whether Parrish said anything about placing them at other banks at that time or not.

Following this conversation, on August 2, 1920, Parrish wrote plaintiff bank a letter in which he said: "Enclosed you will find two notes of Tazewell Timber Corporation of $4,000 each at 90 days. These are the notes that I spoke to you about some time ago. I hope you can use both of them for us and if so please credit our account with the proceeds, $7,878.40." When the notes arrived the plaintiff bank was rather short of funds and could not conveniently handle both of them. It returned one and discounted the other, putting the net proceeds, $3,939.20, to the credit of defendant bank and so advised the latter. [**4] Shortly thereafter witness was again in Bluefield and saw Parrish, whom he told that if he would return the other note it would be discounted also, and this was done; the entries concerning it being of the same kind as those made with reference to the note first discounted. In this second interview with Parrish, the latter said that both notes had been charged by the defendant to the plaintiff bank on August 2, when they were both sent down to it and the matter had since been held in abeyance. The two banks, plaintiff and defendant, had a running account between themselves, the items of which were reconciled from time to time by the transfer of funds through credits in any other bank, as might be desired by the plaintiffs or by defendant. Defendant never drew directly on plaintiff by check or draft, the account being handled by offsetting the entries carried. The defendant never drew a check against the two specific credits given because of the two notes in question. Their maker never had any deposit account in the plaintiff bank, and the notes were not charged or their proceeds credited to it.

Wylie says that the notes were reported by him to the discount committee and directors [**5] of plaintiff bank, and those gentlemen knew that the notes were not indorsed by the defendant bank and that the witness had discounted them at the request of Parrish for the Tazewell Timber Corporation. At one time in his cross-examination and in answer to the question why he had not requested defendant's endorsement, he said, "Well, that is [*85] a question hard for me to answer." At another time, he testified that "he had not asked for an endorsement, because I took Mr. Parrish's word * * * that he would take the paper any time I called on him for doing it." He explained that if the defendant bank had indorsed the notes, it would have been a contingent liability, and "I do not think he" (Parrish) "wanted that." "If they had been indorsed, they would have had to have reported them as a contingent liability." It may be said, and the observation is our own, that the valid guaranty of their payment would equally have created a contingent liability for them; the only practical difference being that they were not as likely to come to the attention of the bank examiners.

For the moment, and for the moment only, let it be assumed that what Wylie testified Parrish said amounted to a [**6] guaranty on behalf of the defendant bank of the payment of the notes. In the federal courts, it is well settled that a national bank has not power to lend its credit to another by becoming surety, endorser, or guarantor for him. Merchants' Bank v. Baird, 160 F. 642, 90 C.C.A. 338, 17 L.R.A. (N.S.) 526. Moreover, it is still clearer that, as we ourselves have said, no officer of the bank, without express authority from its directors, has power to bind it by an accommodation endorsement or guaranty. Wagner v. Central Banking & Security Co., 249 F. 145, 161 C.C.A. 197.

If, then, the transaction was as the plaintiffs' witness Wylie says the directors of the plaintiff bank knew it to be, namely, that he (Wylie) had discounted the notes at the request of Parrish for the Tazewell Timber Corporation, it is clear that the learned judge was right in directing at the close of the plaintiffs' testimony a verdict for the defendants. It is, however, equally well established that a national bank may validly warrant title to the property it conveys, or become liable as an endorser or guarantor of notes or other obligations which it rediscounts or sells, because to do so is incidental to the business [**7] it is authorized to transact and to the disposition of property it has lawfully acquired. People's Bank v. National Bank, 101 U.S. 181, 25 L. Ed. 907. It follows that if there was evidence sufficient to show that the notes in question were ever owned by the defendant bank and that it sold them to the plaintiff bank or rediscounted them with it, plaintiff was entitled to go to the jury, assuming, of course, that what Parrish said amounted in law to a guaranty by the defendant bank.

There is still another contingency by which the plaintiff might have been entitled to a complete or partial recovery. If the defendant bank had never owned the notes, and if the plaintiff bank rediscounted them but had done so on the faith of the guaranty of the defendant bank or of one of its officers, and the proceeds of such discount had gone to the benefit of the defendant bank, the latter would be liable to return the money it had thus received whether its officer was authorized to give the guaranty on its behalf or not, and irrespective of any lack of power there might have been to have conferred such authority, if it had attempted to do so. Aldrich v. Chemical National Bank, 20 S. Ct. 498, 176 [**8] U.S. 618, 44 L. Ed. 611; Citizen's National Bank v. Appleton, 30 S. Ct. 364, 216 U.S. 190, 54 L. Ed. 443; Richmond Guano Co. v. Farmers' Cotton Seed Oil Mill & G. Co., 126 F. 717, 61 C.C.A. 630.

What evidence is there in the record to show that the defendant bank ever owned these notes or ever applied to its own use their proceeds or any part of them? It may be said that, unless the testimony shows that the notes once belonged to the defendant, there is none that it ever received for itself any part of the proceeds of their discount. It is true that when the plaintiff bank discounted them, it put their avails to the credit of the defendant bank and so notified it, but that it equally would have done had the transaction been as defendant says it was, a discount which it, or Parrish, procured for the maker of the notes and in which it had no direct pecuniary interest.

For reasons to be presently stated, the burden of proof rests upon the plaintiffs with more than ordinary weight in this case. If the defendant bank took for itself the money paid by the plaintiff bank on the notes, the means of proving the fact were in plaintiffs' hands and they did not choose to use them. [**9] At their demand, the books of the defendant bank were produced in court and thrown open for their inspection. They contented themselves with proving that when the defendant bank sent the notes to the plaintiff bank, it charged their face less discount to the latter, something, which, as far as we can see, shows nothing material as to any direct pecuniary interest the defendant bank, had in the transaction. If the money truly came into the beneficial possession of the defendant, its books would have established that fact beyond question.

It must be remembered that as far as the testimony goes, there is no reason whatever to suppose that the maker of these notes was already [*86] indebted to the defendant bank. When Wylie had his conversation with Parrish, the transactions between maker and the defendant bank were still in the future. Up to that time, the Tazewell Timber Corporation had apparently not yet opened an account with the defendant bank. Its doing so was dependent upon the latter is being able to secure for it a $50,000 line of credit. Whether that could or could not be accomplished in its turn was contingent upon the defendant bank being successful in it's [**10] efforts to arrange with the plaintiff and others such as were proposed to the plaintiff bank. Of course, if at the time the defendant bank offered the notes to the plaintiff bank they were the property of the former, their proceeds did go to its use, and even if they had not, defendant might well be liable on the guaranty by which it brought about their sale. What is the evidence on this point? Again, plaintiffs failed to use that which was open to them and which if the fact were as they are forced to claim it was, would have revealed it beyond the possibility of doubt or peradventure, for the books and records of defendant bank would necessarily have shown it. No attempt to procure this testimony was made, nor is any explanation of the failure to do so suggested. All that is put in on this point were some letters, which passed between the two banks. They were obviously all written without any attempt to use words with legal precision. [**11] The statements contained in those written on behalf of defendant bank which, if they stood alone, as they do not, might raise an inference that the notes had once been its property, while there are others to be found in the communications from the plaintiff bank which quite as clearly seem to negative any possibility that the plaintiff bank thought the defendant bank was in any wise liable to it. It is not shown that when any of the notes fell due, and before their renewal the plaintiff bank ever charged them to defendant. When the plaintiffs closed their testimony without offering anything more, the learned judge below was right in telling the jury to return a verdict for the defendants.

Let us see how the matter then stood. The plaintiff bank had told the court that it had deliberately refrained from asking for an endorsement of the notes because it knew that the defendant bank by making such endorsement would break the law and provide the means by which it could have been caught in the breach. According to the plaintiff bank's own story, it had contented itself with taking a verbal guaranty which would equally violate the statute; the only difference being that it would [**12] not be so easily possible for the bank examiners to find it out. There are no penalties attached to a breach of this statute, a loan made in violation of it does not thereby become uncollectible, and it may be that even the deliberate participation of the two banks in a scheme to deceive the bank examiners will not justify a refusal to enforce the agreement between them. It has been so held by courts of high authority. Hanover National Bank v. First National

Bank, 109 F. 421, 48 C.C.A. 482; Kendrick State Bank v. First National Bank, 213 F. 10, 130 C.C.A. 202. It is true that in the former case, there was a strong dissent by Judge Caldwell, and there is much of appeal in what Judge Dietrich has recently said in the case of Live Stock Bank v. First National Bank (D.C.) 300 F. 945.

There is no occasion as we see it for us to pass upon that question. Whatever may be ultimately held as to it, there is no doubt the statute is a salutary one. If it were lived up to in letter and in spirit, bank failures would be far rarer than they are.

We think it clear that one who does what plaintiff bank says it did must offer convincing proof of two things: First, that the other party really [**13] intended to give a guaranty which would violate the law; and, second, if he did, and actually gave it, of the existence of some one of the conditions upon which the right to recover upon such a guaranty depends. We have already commented upon the failure of the plaintiffs to offer satisfactory evidence, either that the defendant bank ever owned the notes, or that their proceeds went to its use. All this was upon the assumption that Parrish had the authority from the defendant bank to enter into the arrangement, which plaintiffs say he did and that he in fact did so. Wylie swears that all that Parrish said was that "whenever the board of directors of the Farmers' & Miners' Bank wanted the notes paid, he would have them taken up," and he is not willing to testify that Parrish did not add that, in that event, he would place them in some other bank. Wylie does not say that Parrish said the defendant bank would do anything. Now Wylie may have been right in supposing that Parrish identified the bank with himself as [*87] Louis XIV did the state but that is something which we cannot assume in the absence of proof of which there is none. Moreover, Wylie in one part of his testimony [**14] says that when the matter was fresh in his mind, be told his discount committee and his directors that he had discounted the notes at the request of Parrish for the Tazewell Timber Corporation. If that is a correct version of what he did, of course, the plaintiffs have no case against the bank. If Parrish personally assumed any obligation, it was to answer for the debt or default of another, and as it was not in writing, it is unenforceable against him.

Affirmed.

Here are just a few examples of what the Courts have set as precedent:

"In the federal courts, it is well settled that a national bank has not power to lend its credit to another by becoming surety, endorser, or guarantor for him". Farmers and Miners Bank v. Bluefield Nat'l Bank 11F 2d 83, 271 U.S. 669

"The exercise of powers not expressly granted to national banks is prohibited". First Nat. Bank v. Nat. Exchange Bank, 92 U.S. 122, 128; California Bank v. Kennedy, 167 U.S. 362, 367; Concord Bank v. Hawkins, 174 U.S. 364.

"Checks, drafts, money orders, and bank notes are not lawful money of the United States". State v. Neilon, 73, Pac. 3211, 43 Ore. 168

You send us copies of a recent monthly statement, and if your account is late or in collections, you include any letters, you have received trying to collect on the account. You also send us your signed and notarized Authorization to Send Education. Everything will be sent to you, usually in 3 to 5 working days after you signed up.

A series of letters and replies are sent to the Credit Card Company, banking institution, and/or collections agencies. The letters asks the credit card company or banking institution the following:

1. Do they have the authority to lend you credit?
2. Do they have the authority to create money?
3. If they do not have the authority, then you have been tricked into participating in their fraud.
4. You do not wish to be party to their fraud and they must stop immediately.
5. Since they did not disclose to you the fraud, and since they knew about it when you signed the credit application, the contract is illegal.
6. A contract that is illegal at the time of signing is invalid.
7. We request a $0.00 (zero) balance on the account.
8. Numerous State, Federal, and Unite States Supreme Court decisions on the matter are included.
9. Any evidence of a lawful debt or legal agreement must be presented to you in a timely manner.

They commonly send you a response, stating you signed a contract and you must pay it, or offering you payment counseling, or even reducing the amount you owe and telling you to pay the discounted amount. They may claim to have the proper authority, but they never provide proof.

The following letter(s) sent to the company(s) continues to ask for proof, and place them in default if they do not provide any proof of authority to lend you credit. They also respond to the letters you may have received in response. After a series of letters, you may receive a monthly statement with a $0.00 (zero) balance. You will send us every letter or collection notice that you receive from the credit card company or collection agency. We will educate you on the appropriate responses. The debt MAY be charged off (sold) to a collector. When you receive a letter from the debt collection company, you will then request a validation of the debt, asking them to prove you owe them any money and showing the collector why no claim against you can be maintained. Our program also teaches you how to stop all of the harassing phone calls and nasty collection notices.

This process will help you avoid the invasive nature of bankruptcy and be selective over which accounts you want to terminate. You will save thousands of dollars not possible with a debt consolidation program, credit counseling, or debt negotiation. You are not alone. We have multiple means of communications with our customers including a toll-free telephone number with our Customer Relations Representatives, 9am - 6pm Monday - Friday. We also have a website, conference calls, email newsletters, and automated notices to our customers updating and educating them on the process. We have received a tremendous amount of feedback and compliments on our ability to provide answers and reassurance in a timely manner.

When you entered into a loan or credit contract, you signed a note or contract promising to pay them back, and you agreed to provide collateral that could be seized if you did not repay the loan. This contract supposedly qualified you to receive the money or credit. However, did they provide 'full disclosure' of all of the terms of this agreement? Answer the following questions and decide for yourself if the bank or credit card company was acting in 'good faith,' that you received 'valuable consideration,' and that your 'signature' on that agreement is valid. Were you told that the Federal Reserve Policies and Procedures and the Generally Accepted Accounting Principles

(GAAP) requirements imposed upon all federally insured (FDIC) banks in Title 12 of the United States Code, section 1831, prohibit them from lending their own money from their own assets, or from other depositors? Did anyone tell you where the money was coming from?

Were you told that the contract you signed (your promissory note) was going to be converted into a 'negotiable instrument' by the bank or credit card company and become an asset on their accounting books? Did they tell you that your signature on that note made it 'money,' according to the Uniform Commercial Code (UCC), sections 1-201(24) and 3-104? Were you told that your promissory note (money) would be taken, recorded as an asset, and be sold for cash - without 'valuable consideration' given to obtain your note? Did they give you a deposit slip as a receipt for the money you gave them, just as a bank would normally provide when you make a deposit to the bank?

WHAT IS CREDIT?

"A national bank... cannot lend its credit to another by becoming surety, endorser, or guarantor for him, such an act being ultra vires..." Merchants' Bank v. Baird 160 F. 642 There are many more cases to prove that banks are participating in deceptive banking practices, which is why we request a "zero balance due" statement. Many banking and credit institutions are forced to comply because Fraud is a criminal offense.

Credit is the opposite of money. Money, which is legal tender for the payment of debts, is defined by Congress in 31 USCA Sec 392. This section describes all coins and currency issued by the United States Government as legal tender for all debts, public and private. For purposes of this article, we will call money either coins or currency. In addition, no effort will be made to argue that Federal Reserve notes are unconstitutional; that is beyond the scope of this article.

Now, if you went to a motorcycle dealer to buy a new Harley Davidson with no money down, you would say, "your credit is good." What exactly does that mean? It means that your promise to pay money is good. In other words, they trust you. You sign a loan agreement to pay the motorcycle dealer a certain sum of money with interest, and you sign a security agreement in which you pledge the motorcycle as collateral for the security agreement. Therefore, the motorcycle dealer has accepted your credit, or promise pay a sum of money, in exchange for the motorcycle. Consider how different a bank loan is. When you apply for a bank loan, you sign a loan agreement pledging to pay the bank so many dollars, with interest.

When the bank accepts your promise to pay in exchange for a loan, it means your credit is good. However, the next question is the most interesting.

What does the bank lend you?

The bank will invariably give you a check, which is a promise to pay you so many dollars. In effect, what you and the bank have done is exchange a promise to pay. In other words, you have accepted each other's credit, yet no money has exchanged hands!

Now what do you do with the check? Probably one of two things: either you deposit it into your checking account, or you take it to a merchant for instance, a car dealer. In either case, the check, when deposited goes directly to the bookkeeping department where the numbers are transferred from the check and are added to your account as a bookkeeping entry. Once this entry is made, a bank will say that its deposits have increased.

How can a transfer of numbers increase the deposits? IT CANNOT! This fictional increase is all on the books as there is no increase in the actual amount of money in the bank's vault. All of these bookkeeping entry deposits are called "demand deposits", which means that the customer can literally walk into the bank and demand the deposit. These figures are placed into the bank's liabilities column as money, which the bank owes people.

So, what are the bank's assets? Interestingly, I have just covered part of that. One type of asset is the "deposit" which actually consists of the check you just transferred to your account. It was a loan, an IOU from the bank. Banks will count the small amount of vault cash on hand as a type of asset, also. Nevertheless, most of the bank's "assets" are all the promises to pay. In other words, its loans.

Thus, both the bank's assets and its liabilities are virtually all on paper. In addition, this being the case, the expression from the book Modern Money Mechanics, published by the Federal Reserve Bank of Chicago, that "deposits are merely book entries" is now easier to understand. Now, it is also easier to understand what the electronic transfer of money is all about. All this amounts to be a transfer of numbers, or book entries, from one bank account to another. The same thing happens when you write a check. Numbers called dollars are transferred as a bookkeeping entry from your checking account to someone else's. When a credit card is used, bank credit or book entries are created and transferred to another person simultaneously!

Hence, our money system can be described as a "debt usury" money system. For every dollar of credit that comes into existence, a debt is created to the banks and interest (usury) is charged. Under our present money system, the Federal Government will never be able to balance its budget, and the national debt will continue to grow rapidly. However, every bank loan made in the United States today is also illegal, as all bank loans are based on credit instead of money.

The words "ultra vires" are important words. They mean, "A contract made by a corporation beyond the scope of its corporate powers is unlawful." (See Black's Law Dictionary.) The courts have consistently ruled that banks cannot lend their credit, but can only lend their money, and that all loans of credit are ultra vires.

Because no bank or credit card company charter gives them (all of which are corporations) permission to lend its credit, and Congress never gave them permission to create money, all such loans of credit are ultra wires, or unlawful. By lending credit, they have unjustly enriched themselves. They pay no interest for the use of the credit, but charge their customers the same amount of interest as if they had lent out their own money. It is a racket and con game, to say the least. It is deception and fraud. The collection of interest on credit is in violation of all usury laws. After all, they are collecting interest on money, which does not exist. It is little wonder that as more Americans are beginning to understand this issue they are suing banks on fraud and usury charges.

Now that you have been informed concerning what the United States Supreme Court has stated and the Fraud the banks are committing, you have a decision to make. Do you want to keep supporting FRAUD? If the answer is "NO" than we can help you. Our Debt Elimination Program can be used to eliminate any kind of unsecured debt where credit was extended such as credit cards, personal loans, and certain student loans.

Knowledge is the key to success. This program uses our team of experts to get rid of your debt for you, and take you by the hand, step-by-step, to help you actually get your debt discharged.

You are 100% within the law. You are 100% within your rights...but you need to understand the process. Let me explain.

Debt = Slavery: The Borrower is a Slave to the Lender

How is it possible that the UNITED STATES IS BANKRUPT! Almost 100 years ago, the government agreed to pay the debts of all Americans! They had to do this because they had just outlawed lawful, constitutional money! Years of college will not teach you the truth. Not a single professor I ever met could answer the question: How was the "Federal Reserve Act of 1913" ever passed? It's unconstitutional according to Article 1, Section 8, paragraph 5 of the Constitution, which gives Congress the power "to coin money, regulate the value thereof, and of foreign coin.

Yet the Federal Reserve Banking System does exist. Here is a bit of history and education on banking and money and how it really works.

The government does not manufacture money. Congress says, "We need money, so we approve the borrowing of $10 Billion."

- They go down to the US Treasury Department, who does not have any money either because it has already been spent earlier in the year.
- The treasury department says; go over to the Federal Reserve.
- Therefore, Congress tells the Federal Reserve, "We need $10,000,000,000 and it's been approved".
- The Federal Reserve man or woman says, "Okay, then, issue some treasury bills worth $10 Billion, give them to us and we'll loan you $10 Billion".
- Therefore, the Federal Reserve writes the US Government a check for $10 Billion.
- In addition, the Federal Reserve authorizes about $1.5 Billion in new bills...
- Moreover, the government deposits that $10,000,000,000 and can now spend $10 Billion to pay its employees and such.

Now, where did the $10 Billion come from? Get ready for the answer because it is amazing: The answer is that the $10 Billion was created out of thin air. Nothing even backs our money any more, so there does not have to be anything backing the money any more. The money was created out of a debt obligation. The debt obligation now belongs to the people of the US. In addition, over 99% of the money created in the US is created by debt obligation.

In other words, darn near all money is created out of debt obligation.

Now, since HJR 192 of 1933, outlawed real, lawful money, i.e. money backed by gold or silver, banks do not have any money to loan. Here is how it works out:

- You go to the bank, thinking they can loan you some money, say $100,000.
- The bank says, "Do you have any collateral worth over $100,000?"
- You say, "Yes, the house itself."
- They say, "Okay, let's monetize that collateral that you provided".
- They then loan you $100,000 after you sign a piece of paper saying you will pay it back with interest - a promissory note - a mortgage.

The money did not exist until you signed the piece of paper.

- You sign and *poof* the money is suddenly created out of thin air. You provided the signature on the promissory note and thereby funded the "loan" to yourself.
- The bank now owns your home. Moreover, you get to live in it and pay the taxes on it. In addition, pay back the money you created in the first place, with interest.
- Deal closed.

That is a simplified version, but in essence, any bank auditor can prove beyond any doubt that it was your promissory note that funded the loan. It has been proven repeatedly in various courts.

Therefore, the bank never really made a loan to you. You provided the value. The bank monetized it through your signature.

THE BANK WAS NEVER AT RISK FOR ANYTHING!

However, this is not popular information to spread around and I am sure you can see why.

How it Works...

According to UCC Article 3, Section 603, if you make an offer to pay off your debt obligation and it is refused, the "lender" is in default and the debt is no longer valid: The debt is discharged because the lender is in default.

By law, (15 USC 1692g § 809. Validation of debts) you have the right to request a verification and validation of the debt. If the loan was not granted by a real person, as a corporation is not a real person, then they, essentially, cannot verify and validate the debt. It is impossible.

Therefore, you make an offer to pay off your debt obligation, pending verification. Then, when the lending institution does not verify and validate the debt, you send a fault letter, giving them the opportunity to cure their fault. Then, when they do not do that, you send them a default notice and demand the discharge of all debt.

That is how it works.

The Real Secret

The real secret behind how it works is in the discovery process. You are going to discover why it works, how it works, and you are going to be taken by the hand through the process the first time through to completion for an unsecured debt.

We base everything from U.S. Supreme Courts decisions, Title 15 United State Code (USC) section 1692, the Fair Debt Collections Practices Act, section 1601, the Fair Credit Billing Act, the Uniform Commercial Code (UCC), section 203, and numerous Banking and Lending laws. There are many cases that have already been decided on when it comes to the issues of "money"", credit", and "banking". The collection of interest on credit issued by a bank or a credit card company is in direct violation of all usury laws! The laws are very specific concerning the corporate authority of banks and credit institutions. THEY CANNOT LAWFULLY ISSUE

CREDIT! When you tell them, you discovered their fraud, THEY HAVE TO LISTEN AND RESPOND! It is your LEGAL RIGHT to have them certify a lawful debt exists. They can NEVER DO THIS!

LATE BREAKING INFORMATION

IN THE LAST DAYS...VISIONS...

A. B. "Al" Cuppett
US Army/The Joint Staff (OJCS), Retired
RR 1 Box 34-T
Madison, VA 22727
7-31 July 2001 [Update-3]

Subject: Sister Anita's 'Modern' Nazi SS Transport Dream, circa 2001

Introduction: Be advised that Anita, when she wrote the following letter had never seen the video, Straight from the Joint Chiefs, wherein you will see the four-box car building; nor had she ever heard my lecture-sermon about Beech Grove.

On 6 Aug 1994, at 1555 hours, I arrived at AMTRAC's Beech Grove "repair facility" in Indianapolis, on the only day of the month which was designated as "Open House"; then "open" to show the public that Linda Thompson's video "America Under Siege" was just misguided paranoia; i.e., the place isn't a "final solution termination camp". NO! Then why was it completely "sanitized" after Thompson's 1993 video and my 1998 video? Why were the fences changed, the Red-Blue Zone signs, etc, taken down, after spending $5.9 million "renovating" the 90-year old place into such a configuration?

The AMTRAC guard, J.D., who had a NATO-style black uniform 'in-waiting' in his locker, escorted me through the complex. I saw the aviation 25-knot wind socks [trains don't fly], bricked up windows, new gas [heating] furnaces with 6-inch gas pipes, NSA-style high security turnstiles, a two-tier barbed wire fence system with inward leaning tops, which, with the building door locks, made it a TRIPLE security facility; uhhh, for railroad cars -- and more? The 'more' was the last building we observed, at which the guard told me, "This is the one building that's equipped for holding rail cars. You can put four [box] cars in there at a time"! My later-noticed, strictly-by-chance, photo reveals powered air vents in the roof of that "box car" building! You can get the 2 videos "Straight from the Joint Chiefs and Black Ops and Prophecy" by writing: the Prophecy Club at PO Box 750234, Topeka, KS 66675, or call: 785-266-1112. The two videos will amaze you.

In early July 2001, I received the "Anita's Dream" letter. Her words are quoted herein in italics whereas my comments will be in brackets. Please realize many "Holy Spirit-sent" dreams are depicted in parable-like fashion, and are purposefully analogous to the actual subject, as the revelation of the precise truth, as it shall happen in real life, could be detrimental to exposition of the dream, to others"; i.e., it could cause undue alarm! Quote:

Dear Brother Al, 30 June 2001

Hi there again. I pray that all has been well with you. I am writing because of another dream that I had last Sunday at 2 A.M. normally all my dreams will give me a sense of urgency to read the newspaper the next 2 weeks because my dreams usually happen within the next 2 weeks. (Only 2 of them have taken longer than that, but those times the dreams themselves told me how long it would be before something happened.)

The last dream I had let me know that I did not have to read the paper. 'It won't be in the paper', God let me know. To me it was obvious what it was about. At the time, I thought to myself, 'I should write Al about this. He is dealing with the Jews and [word omitted for 'life preservation' concerns]. To wit, I am dealing with dear Jewish folks, but they have been in darkness for 2000 years and few can grasp what is about to happen to them - and us!

Since then my life has been hectic. I have been tired and did not even bother to tell anyone at church my dream until just last night... By the end of me telling the people... about the dream I was shaking so much that it would not stop for about 10 minutes. Then I thought, "I've got to tell Al', because at the time I had the dream I wasn't really afraid at all, but now [at that point] I was almost terrified.

Last Sunday at 2 A.M., my alarm went off to get me up for work. I shut it off and figured I would get up at 2:15 (the time my 2nd clock was set for.) Then came the dream. -- I was walking up to a parking garage with a lady I assumed was my sister (although she didn't look like my sister but) I assumed it was her because the garage reminded me of the P....... building's parking garage in downtown Des Moines..... (My sister used to work for P......, that is why I assumed it was she. [The woman did not "look" exactly like "her sister" because the 'deed' the woman was doing was not what any sister should ever be doing do to a sibling; thus, the identity problem.] We were part of a group of 4 people. My "sister" was the leader [of our group].

As we came up to this garage entrance my sister seemed disgusted and was complaining how no one was allowed to bring anything into this building that was bigger than a loaf of bread. [Remember, in Europe, how few possessions the Jews were allowed to carry, as they were loaded up for "transport" to the camps?] Then she gestured with her hands just how long, tall, and wide that would be. As she said it, I saw a person driving an SUV inside of the building the wrong way through an exit ramp. So I thought, "Well, this story is bunk because Look! There's a person taking an SUV inside", but I said nothing to my sister. [The "SUV" with driver, sighting, tells you that although the particular people making this 'journey' cannot take anything very big inside with them, the SUV driver obviously is not included in this ("Red/Blue List") "Category" of folks making the 'journey'.]

Once near the building I saw a whole bunch (50-100 or more) of other people inside. We 4 were directed to turn to the right down this concrete hallway. On one side of the hallway the concrete had windows carved out in it so you could see outside really well, but to our left it was a solid wall of concrete.

We went down this hallway for a short while then my sister said, "We've got to turn around. We're going the wrong way." Well, okay... To me, so far this was a very innocuous dream. My sister had a bad attitude, a disgusted attitude during this whole thing (but that is just the way she is when things do not go absolutely 100% perfect.) I continued behind her because (before [in real life] she kicked me out of her family because I was becoming 'too religious' (her words, not mine). I would always go with her on errands and stuff. She always directed our every move. I [have always] just kept quiet and kept her kids entertained. (To me this [her attitude] was normal.)

Well, so I am following her. We are now back at the parking garage entrance where yet more people are being directed down the hallway that we just came from. In addition, I see more 'leaders' gesturing to their groups about the shape of the bread loaf thing (just as my sister had done to our group). I thought, 'Man, they're all being told the same story as they enter this building". [The reversal of direction in the groups' travel was placed in the dream so 'Nita would see just what you see here. That is, they're all getting the "same story" and they're all going the same "'final place"! Just like in Europe 1939-1945.] Nevertheless, note here [at this point, at the 'entrance' or 'beginning'] nobody's [yet] afraid. It is just as if they think they are on a little trip... an errand... a brief excursion. No big deal. [That is exactly what the Jews in Germany believed, as they left their homes for the last time.]

Now I notice the hallway we are now walking down is completely made of stainless steel. There are NO window openings [There were (somewhat cheery) 'windows' earlier, but now it gets progressively more restrictive... the further the journey, the less chance of escape! This was the scenario in Europe... Here, now, steel, and NO escape!], no doorways, (We are now headed West instead of East [Note: The 1939-45 Holocaust was in the "East"; the 21st century Holocaust will start in the Western Hemisphere first! See the direction change below]) I keep looking from side to side expecting to be coming upon a stairwell to go higher up in the parking garage (even though we don't have a car parked there. I have no idea why we are there.)

There are no stairwells. We abruptly come face to face with the end of the hallway. It too is made of stainless steel. I am still looking for a stairway. I look up and see a jagged hole in the ceiling about the size of a dollar coin. [This 'feature' probably dream-signifies 'No escape'] Some water is dripping from it. [Significance unknown.] I see some light coming through it from above and think, 'Maybe that's the stairwell. Maybe we can get up through there'. (It was impossible of course, but that is what I thought.) [Again, the "meaning" of this "jagged hole" may be "No escape now"; or maybe a "shower head", thru which Zyklon-B was inserted into the "showers", as I saw at Dachau in 1960.]

As we stood stopped there, I looked behind us and saw many, many people coming to a stop behind us in the hallway as far as I could see. We just stood there, thinking, 'Okay, now what?' My sister, then (still disgusted with the whole trip) said, 'It USUALLY doesn't go this fast."? I noticed that whatever "hallway" we were in was MOVING but it did not feel like it. [The clever deception deepens as the journey progresses.] It had gradually [See what I mean by the deception deepening progressively?] picked up speed, and now we were all standing with one leg bent and one leg straight in order to not fall down from the momentum.

I wondered to myself, 'We're on a train?', and it reminded me of trains that go through the Swiss Alps [Dream significance: Reminiscent of Europe no less.] [And then, somehow, she determined] (We were out in the woods.) Suddenly, we were at a standstill. The stainless steel walls of 'the train' [Gunderson Steel of Portland, OR, makes the [non-rusting] steel rail cars, complete with the shackles and chains the UN and FEMA plan to use in the USA. This is a now-confirmed fact!] were gone, and we were standing on a platform of some kind, to our left. The platform dropped off at a 90-degree angle about 4 feet to a set of railroad tracks that had four cars on it [them]. The tops of these [cars] were open. They reminded me of old coal mining tubs. They flared out on the top. They were made of iron. They [the side walls] were only about 3 feet high (excluding the rail wheels). There was room to seat about 12.. 4 abreast. [Here the Beech Grove AMTRAK "four-boxcar" building now surfaces in her dream.] In addition, there was an opening to climb through like a doorway, an open doorway [without an actual door].

There were many people on the platform. My 'sister' and I had become slightly separated from the other 2 in our group. Then she told me, "We're in car #2. (As she looked at a ticket she had.)[This must signify that the people were each "accounted for", or were specifically identified, and had their car/NAMES also, specified; meaning all those on the 'trip' had been listed or targeted.] However, I thought, "There are so many people; we'll have to scramble to get to our car and save seats for the other two in our group". (Because even though we were first in the line, the 'railcars' were not in order. From our end, they were numbered something like 4, 2, 3 1) I only saw 4 cars. Not enough for all. [What is new? The Nazi's "Juden transporten" rail car movements were always crammed to the max.]

Some guy shouted for everyone to look at their tickets and get in their cars. Then there was some noise and a great commotion as people jumped off the platform to where the cars were. As my sister and I sat in the #2 car (which had seats of steel benches about 4 inches off the ground [floor],looked up at the crowded platform and saw a tall sandy-haired guy who anxiously shouted, 'MY TICKET! I DON'T HAVE A TICKET!' (There was something very important about having a ticket. This guy was almost frantic. [You will see why later.]) My sister said snottily, 'That's too bad". Then the one male member of our group came into our car. (I never saw the 4th member of our [1+3] group. [Is 1 of 3 to be 'spared'; like Zech 13:8-9?]) Anyway, the male stood up looking down at the steel seat looking none too happy about the rough accommodations, [Just like the Nazi SS' "final solution" scenario] on this trip of ours, and he looked at my sister and in an angry tone said, 'I don't like this'. He expected her to do something about it.

She looked up at him and said forcefully,' Am I going to have to call a guard?" The male kept quiet as I thought to myself, "Guard? What guard?' Just then, I could sense that armed guards were standing on the platform... It instantly reminded me of the Nazis. They [the guards] all had on Nazi helmets! Right then my 2:15 alarm clock went off. The [Holy] Spirit in me told me, 'This will not be in the newspapers.' I bought papers since then anyway because the dream was so disturbing to me.

After I have dreams, the Lord reveals to me piece by piece what they mean. (1) The man with no ticket would be shot to death once the railcars moved off (to the East now) and away from the platform. [The SS were always brutal about details/obedience to their commands. The guy had failed to safeguard his ticket; thus, he would be "dispatched". The cars now start moving "East", means the Holocaust will later commence in the "East".] (2) All of these people assumed they were on a little journey. They were led there by people they trusted just like a sister. [Warning to all Jews/Israelis: Do not "trust" or accept US government/UN sponsored free ship transport to Israel. Only the first ship will arrive. Later voyages will not. Why? Those on the first ship will call back to the US and report they got there. That will make it seem like a legitimate process to those hoping to escape. Remember, this is the Satanic/deceptive New World Order we are dealing with!] (3) By the time they realized what was going on or were uncomfortable about the trip, it was too late for them to escape. [Going to any international airport to escape the US, where the UN foreign police shall have absolute jurisdiction, per an intelligence/FBI report. Folks, getting on a "free cruise" to Israel, will bring about the results noted in item (3) just above.]

[Here folks, read and pay attention.] I [later] checked my mail and I saw that your 'Straight from the Joint Chiefs' video had arrived. Within the next two days, I found time here & there to watch it. The part about the 4 rail cars in the 'repair station' simply floored me. I had never heard anything about that [the Beech Grove AMTRAK facility] before. I believe this stuff [the "transport trips" in her dream] is happening now, or is about to happen really, really soon. There is an extreme sense of urgency to warn people.

When I told people at the church, [Sister Winkleman pointed out to me, 'Your sister's been on this trip before'. I asked her, 'What do you mean?' In addition, she said, 'She [your sister] said, 'usually it does not go this fast" (This is the 2nd time that one of this family has pointed out something in my dreams that was very important. [This deceiving 'sister' is dream-significant, or representative, of those Judas Iscariots/Benedict Arnolds who will betray "Believers" and/or Jews, on ideological grounds; or for profit, or personal gain of some sort, just as Anita's fourth point brings out below.]

(4) There are people ASSIGNED to dupe these people into these 'little trips'; and they go along trip after trip after trip [continuing to deceive/betray and trap the unwary whenever possible]. That is why my 'sister' was so disgusted and anxious to just get it [the dirty deed] over with already (sic). [Reminiscent of the 'Cappos' in the concentration camps, who fed their own ethnic people into the gas chambers, etc. They were obviously disgusted with it all, but they did 'the deed', in that ungodly and horrible scenario, to prolong their own lives.]

That is all I really have to tell you. Well, I have to go. God Bless and take care. My prayers are with you and your family. Stay strong.
Sincerely,

Anita

P.S. A year ago in March, "Sister W" appeared to me in a dream pitching hay. She looked at me and said, we have another year to get ready." I wondered 'For what?' Martial law? Moving to Israel? As March of this year came and went, I asked the Lord, 'What are we waiting for? Nothing has happened. A year has passed.' I put my trust in Him to let me know.

The next morning (around 2 AM again) He gave me a dream about a huge man shrouded in black and riding the black horse in a medieval courtroom. The Lord told me in my spirit, 'This is it. This is what you were waiting for. Pure evil is here. Heads up. Pay attention...' Now this dream comes about railroads. This is all so important that I do not know how to convey the urgency. People have to pay attention now more than ever. Do not be duped. If something seems not quite right then people should question it RIGHT AWAY! Be smart. Be awake. Tell them please. Thanks. Unquote... ---- I will tell them 'Nita, but my Jewish friends have been in spiritual darkness for 2000 years, and they run right to the Rabbi with their concerns and he, in error, or commission, continues to misguide them. What can I do?

Signed

EPILOGUE

16 October 2003

As another foreboding 29th of October approaches, President George W. Bush is still obeying instructions in order to keep Arafat in power, thus stressing Israel, plus ensuring more Jews are killed, and effectively cursing himself, his presidency, and his Country. Bill Clinton, having escaped prosecution, as was promised once he left office, is betting on being the Secretary General of the UN. Hillary Clinton, who also escaped justice, now, with the help of the CFR, and the new World Order, is planning to be elected president; if and when the Electoral College is again Perot-style skewed, as it was in 1992 and 1996. The American people never caught - on and will not again.

General John P. Jumper, who refused to remedy the chemtrail problem herein noted in the book has now been promoted to Chief of Staff, USAF. Happy Trails? I don't think so.

The author, Ray Hope, is busy getting the saints to intercede on his behalf, trusting the Lord to help with the distribution of this book; while checking his pathway, fore and aft, being on the alert for the UN's black operations agents who are surely after him for writing America Sold Out.

The Prophecy Club is still warning Christians to stop sinning and to draw neigh unto the Lord. Al Cuppett, who is writing this Epilogue, is vigorously urging Jews to Aliyah to Israel, and warning true Believers in Jesus Christ, who will listen, to eschew the falling away and to prepare their ark for what is ahead.

He is also waiting for the UN termination platoon to come for him, one day, in their [prophesied] three black choppers, at his home in Virginia from which he will escape to Israel. He also continues to inform all who will listen, as to how we, and the World, got into the situation as this book has just described. Moreover, here, concisely, if you have not figured it out, is how we all got there:

The overall problem is S-I-N. Sin! The ONLY cure to the sin problem is the soul-saving, life-changing, gospel of Jesus Christ, the only begotten Son of God. But alas, the gospel has effectively failed, and Satan, via the Jesuits of Rome have, worldwide, leavened the meal, (Luke 13:20-21), changing the "pure" (Psm 12:6-7) word of God on planet Earth, with perverted bibles, thus binding the power of the Holy Ghost, effectively taking him "out of the way". The whole "kingdom" [of God] has now been "leavened". Moreover, preachers, via "bible schools-Ad Nauseam", have been tricked unto using "Greek and Hebrew" to correct the Authorized Version (AKJV), further destroying the power of the Holy Ghost.

This has cleverly caused the "church" to surely despise The Word of God, sure destruction, as promised in Proverbs 13:13. To top this all off, the old salvation and blood hymns have been replaced [as was prophesied to happen by Stanley Frodsham, Smith Wigglesworth's son-in-law, in 1920], with "praise and worship"; instead of prayer and weeping!! We need prayer and weeping, FIRST, before the altar, not praise and worship!

Remarkably, the two most powerful and effective ancient landmarks, which, for example, brought about the Prohibition of liquor 1917, have been removed (see Prov 22:28) from our midst. New per-Version bibles and praise and worship, when practiced by Christians BEFORE being sanctified holy, with the washing of water by the word (Eph 5:26), have destroyed the [Holy Ghost's] intrinsic power in the church of Jesus Christ in the last 40 years.

Thus, we face tribulation, which the Lord never desired us to have to go through. To wit, the Lord wanted it to progress as found in Luke 13:18-19, not the falling away alternative as found in verses 20-21. However, the unfortunate, but satanically planned destruction of the foundations (Psm 11:3), has brought it upon us.

In closing, in order to lessen our imminent and soon coming travail in the US, we must get back to the old standard (Isa 59:19) AV Bible, with [Holy Ghost-baptized] fasting, praying and WALKING on the old paths, where is the good way (Jer 6:16), and singing the old Holy Spirit-inspired hymns; the ones the church has almost lost since 1960. Thankfully, folks, in this book you have been solemnly warned of the future, and how to strengthen the things, which remain -- until the Lord Jesus Christ returns. Chai Yisrael! FOREVER!

Alexander B. Al Cuppett   (Aleph Lamed)
Saved by Jesus Blood on 5 Jan 1969
US Army-The Joint Staff (JCS), Retired
Purple Heart and Bronze Star, Vietnam, 1970-71

Madison, VA -- 3 Nov 2003

Subject: A closing note to Jews everywhere, as well as to "*born again*" Believers who support Israel

In view of the fact that I cannot find my last letter to Elie Wiesel, I will attempt one last time to alert you to the imminent Holocaust, soon to be sponsored by the Fourth Reich. Herein is a paraphrase of some of that letter to Ellie Wiesel; written in 2002.

"*Moshe the Beadle*", a non-native [to Sighet, Hungary] Jew in Wiesel's book, "*Night*" who then lived in Sighet, was, with many others, rounded up by the Nazi SS. To wit, all non-native Jews were herded onto a train, and then taken to a "killing field", where the entire trainload was machine gunned to death. Moshe, by the Lord's grace, escaped and returned to Sighet. However, when he told his macabre story, the local Rabbis pronounced him a "*madman*". You probably can figure the rest of the story, since Wiesel escaped from Auschwitz in 1945 at about 17 years of age.

Unfortunately, the guidance issued by the Sighet Rabbis is the norm, then and now; when you evaluate the leadership and true spiritual knowledge of most Jewish Rabbis. They made the same mistake in 30 A.D., thus dooming countless millions. Fortunately, two New York Rabbis listened to me; one other called the Nassau County Police on me. Nevertheless, my message has gone out into all the Earth, and it is published here, at great personal risk, for your eyes.

Subsequently, today, in November of 2003, I am warning every Jew in the USA to Aliyah to Israel – now! As a symbol of my desperation to warn you Jews, any proceeds of this book, which could come to me, will go to "assist" and persuade Jews to flee to Israel, because the United Nations and the New World Order are planning to kill every Jew they can get their hands on! This book proves it!

Five years ago, in June 1999, in Jerusalem, I was asked by knowledgeable Jews of the legal and professional ranks to help provide a "*way of escape*" for US Jews. That day I vowed to help "*the sons of Abraham by the flesh"*, based on verse 14, chapter four, of the book of *Esther*; the words of which were Holy Ghost-generated, extemporaneously, directly out of the mouth of a yarmulke-wearing Jewish lawyer. That verse exhorted me to obey! One reason is because the little red headed Jewish girl walking with her mom on Roeblingen Street to Gottlieb's Restaurant, in Brooklyn, to buy lunch, has just as much right to walk that street as does my daughter to walk the streets of Virginia.

Friends, I served the USA 31 years to guarantee that little Jewish girl's "New York" freedom from United Nation's tyranny; and having taken the oath to the Constitution numerous times, I intend to honor that oath until death; the LORD God Almighty as my witness and as my Helper!

Furthermore, I have been advised that this "warning to Jews" page will be inserted into the book - somewhere. Therefore I take this last bit of space to warn Jews everywhere, that when the fear quotient is pumped up in the USA, and "they" are planning to use the Islamics to do it, do NOT accept any, free or otherwise, United Nations or US-offered [by the shadow government] sea transportation to Israel! Under no circumstances! You do not want to suffer the fate of Leon Klinghoffer on the ill-fated Achille Lauro. [I warned of this at the Jewish Hatikva Center in Brooklyn in July 2000.]

Yes, a *"way of escape"* has been established, but most Jews will "stay put" as they did in Europe, and they will pay for it with their lives. Do not make the mistake the Jews in Sighet, Hungary made. Aliyah now, and go to an *"absorption center"* in Israel, while you have time! I beg you now!

Shalom, and Am ISRAEL Chai --- FOREVER …   Baruch Ha Shem,   *Al Cuppett*

It is never too late to stockpile until it is too late.

Items to Disappear First
1. Generators /Purifiers
3. Portable Toilets
4. Seasoned Firewood. Wood takes about 6 - 12 months to become dried, for home uses.
5. Lamp Oil, Wicks, and Lamps Buy CLEAR oil. If scarce, stockpile ANY!
6. Coleman Fuel.
7. Guns, Ammunition, Pepper Spray, Knives, Clubs, Bats & Slingshots.
8. Hand-can openers, & hand eggbeaters, whisks.
9. Honey/Syrups/white, brown sugar
10. Rice - Beans - Wheat
11. Vegetable Oil (for cooking) without it food burns/must be boiled etc.,)
12. Charcoal, Lighter Fluid (Will become scarce suddenly)
13. Water Containers (Urgent Item to obtain.) Any size. Small: HARD CLEAR PLASTIC ONLY - note - food grade if for drinking.
16. Propane Cylinders (Urgent: Definite shortages will occur.
17. Survival Guide Book.
18. Mantles: Aladdin, Coleman, etc. (Without this item, longer-term lighting is difficult.)
19. Baby Supplies: Diapers/formula. Ointments/aspirin, etc.
20. Washboards, Mop Bucket w/wringer (for Laundry)
21. Cook stoves (Propane, Coleman & Kerosene)
22. Vitamins

23. Propane Cylinder Handle-Holder (Urgent: Small canister use is dangerous without this item)
24. Feminine Hygiene/Hair care/Skin products.
25. Thermal underwear (Tops & Bottoms)
26. Bow saws, axes and hatchets, Wedges (also, honing oil)
27. Aluminum Foil Reg. & Heavy Duty (Great Cooking and Barter Item)
28. Gasoline Containers (Plastic & Metal)
29. Garbage Bags (Impossible To Have Too Many).
30. Toilet Paper, Kleenex, Paper Towels
31. Milk - Powdered & Condensed (Shake Liquid every 3 to 4 months)
32. Garden Seeds (Non-Hybrid) (A MUST)
33. Clothes pins/line/hangers (A MUST)
34. Coleman's Pump Repair Kit
35. Tuna Fish (in oil)
36. Fire Extinguishers (or. large box of Baking Soda in every room)
37. First aid kits
38. Batteries (all sizes...buy furthest out for Expiration Dates)
39. Garlic, spices, & vinegar, baking supplies
40. Big Dogs (and plenty of dog food)
41. Flour, yeast & salt
42. Matches. {"Strike Anywhere" preferred.) Boxed, wooden matches will go first
43. Writing paper/pads/pencils, solar calculators
44. Insulated ice chests (good for keeping items from freezing in wintertime.)
45. Work boots, belts, Levis & durable shirts
46. Flashlights/LIGHTSTICKS & torches, "No. 76 Dietz" Lanterns
47. Journals, Diaries & Scrapbooks (jot down ideas, feelings, experience; Historic Times)
48. Garbage cans Plastic (great for storage, water, transporting - if with wheels)
49. Men's Hygiene: Shampoo, Toothbrush/paste, Mouthwash/floss, nail clippers, etc
50. Cast iron cookware (sturdy, efficient)
51. Fishing supplies/tools
52. Mosquito coils/repellent sprays/creams
53. Duct Tape
54. Tarps/stakes/twine/nails/rope/spikes
55. Candles
56. Laundry Detergent (liquid)
57. Backpacks, Duffel Bags
58. Garden tools & supplies
59. Scissors, fabrics, & sewing supplies
60. Canned Fruits, Veggies, Soups, stews, etc.
61. Bleach (plain, NOT scented: 4 to 6% sodium hypochlorite)
62. Canning supplies, (Jars/lids/wax)
63. Knives & Sharpening tools: files, stones, steel
64. Bicycles...Tires/tubes/pumps/chains, etc
65. Sleeping Bags & blankets/pillows/mats
66. Carbon Monoxide Alarm (battery powered)
67. Board Games, Cards, Dice
68. D-con Rat poison, MOUSE PRUFE II, Roach Killer
69. Mousetraps, Ant traps, & cockroach magnets
70. Paper plates/cups/utensils (stock up, folks)
71. Baby wipes, oils, waterless & Antibacterial soap (saves a lot of water)
72. Rain gear, rubberized boots, etc.
73. Shaving supplies (razors & creams, talc, after-shave)

74. Hand pumps & siphons (for water and for fuels)
75. Soy sauce, vinegar, bullions/gravy/soup base
76. Reading glasses
77. Chocolate/Cocoa/Tang/Punch (water enhancers)
78. "Survival-in-a-Can"
79. Woolen clothing, scarves/ear-muffs/mittens
80. Boy Scout Handbook, / also Leaders Catalog
81. Roll-on Window Insulation Kit
82. Graham crackers, saltines, pretzels, Trail mix/Jerky
83. Popcorn, Peanut Butter, Nuts
84. Socks, Underwear, T-shirts, etc. (extras)
85. Lumber (all types)
86. Wagons & carts (for transport to and from)
87. Cots & Inflatable mattress's
88. Gloves: Work/warming/gardening, etc.
89. Lantern Hangers
90. Screen Patches, glue, nails, screws, nuts, & bolts
91. Teas
92. Coffee
93. Cigarettes (barter these for big money)
94. Wine/Liquors
95 Chewing gum/candies
96. Atomizers (for cooling/bathing)
97 Hats & cotton neckerchiefs
98. Goats/chickens

FEMA

A Guide to Citizen Preparedness

Federal Emergency Management Agency
Washington, D.C.

If you would like this document emailed to you, simply write
RAYHOPE@AMERICASOLDOUT.COM and put FEMA DOCS in the subject line and they
will be automatically delivered to your email address. It is a lot of good information and very
informative. Some of it might even save your life and some of it may not.

APPENDIX

Elie Wiesel Letter by Al Cuppett

14 May 2002

Honorable Elie Wiesel
College of Arts and Sciences
Department of Religion
Boston College
745 Commonwealth Avenue
Boston, MA 02215

My Dear Doctor Wiesel,

Baruch Ha Shem... Shalom and Chai Israel

Again, My Dear Doctor Wiesel, In the name of El-him, please read this carefully,

Thank you so very much for responding. I have attached a [copy of] letter (Atch 1) I wrote to then-Prime Minister Netanyahu, in 1999, after I returned from meeting with 'Holocaust-concerned' Jewish professionals in Jerusalem. I had also enclosed (Atch 2) the *"Why the strange troops, police, and events across the USA?"* letter", which I have herewith enclosed for your review. Then-Prime Minister Netanyahu had Bobby Brown, Director of Diaspora Affairs, answer my letter. If Netyanhu was not aware of the black uniformed foreign police forces, etc, marshaled in this country, he was cognizant after he read my letter. However, within two months he was "out", as noted below.

Unfortunately, "THE CLINTONS" sent James Carvelle to Israel to vote-stump for Barak; and *Operation Vote* sent planeloads of liberal Jews, for 180 dollars round trip, to vote for Barak. I spoke to Mr. Brown in June of 1999. He told me, *"Mr. Cuppett, we* [the Likud Party] are out of power, *there is nothing we can do!"* That is, to publicize or take action concerning the coming US police state, and its impact on US Jewry.

There was an incident in Edmonton, Canada, that did not make the press. I have enclosed the report of that event, as well as my letter to Rabbi Loomer, a Reformed Rabbi in Edmonton. Please read them carefully!

Doctor Wiesel, I know you are a busy man, however, as I was reading the book, *"The Secret War against the Jews"*, all my military experience and my scriptural knowledge came together. Sir, the New World Order, i.e., the Fourth Reich/United Nations, is planning a worldwide Holocaust which SHALL make Hitler, Heydrich, Himmler, Dr. Mengle, and [CATHOLIC], Franz Stangl's *"Final Solution"* pale in comparison. To wit, they are planning, NOW, to arrest fleeing Jews at the international airports! Moreover, they shall flee soon as the Muslims here are being coached/ordered to make sure of it!

Sir, I have traveled the country and seen the now empty, in-waiting, FEMA detention centers! I have talked to the [uniformed!] officers of the German/Argentinean *"occupation troops"* in their own language! [I speak five languages.] I have photographed the "Regional Police" in their vehicles! The Germans and the Argentines admit they are here for *"urban pacification operations"*! There are hundreds of thousands of foreign troops/cops here -- now! The *"Project*

Harmony Cops" almost caught us in New York in April 1999, as we warned many Jews in that city. We slipped out by the *"skin of our teeth"*, as Job says in Job 19:20, The *Holy Scriptures*.

In closing, I quote Cheryl S…. of Brooklyn, as she left the '[now-FBI (?) raided and Clinton-closed down] Hatikva Center, where Shifra Hoffman and I had just spoken: *"Al, maybe you're a second Raoul Wallenberg!"* I shall gladly be a Raoul Wallenberg to save my Jewish 'cousins', but now I am *"Moshe the Beadle, II"*, but the Rabbis think I'm a *"madman"*! Has anything changed my dear Jewish brother? In sixty years?

Shalom and Am Israel Chai   *Signed Al Cuppett*

Atch multiple

Chemtrail "petition" to General John P. Jumper by Al Cuppett

                    12 March 2001 [8 May 2001 - Update 1]

TO: General John P. Jumper, Commander, Air Combat Command (ACC)

INFO: GEN Shelton, Chairman, JCS; GEN Shinseki, CSA; Gen Ryan, CSA; ADM Clark, CNO; GEN Jones, CMC; ADM Blair, CINCPAC; ADM Fargo, CINCPACFLT; Senators Allen, Shelby, Miller, and Warner; Congressmen Barr, Paul, Bartlett, Cantor, Goode, and Burton; Commonwealth Federal and Military/Police Officers

SUBJ: *"Treaty on Open Skies"* (TOS) Aircraft Executing Operational Bio-Chemical Missions against the United States

Sir, I have just been informed by a freelance reporter out of Munich, Germany, that she recently interviewed two Russian [speaking] officers who admitted they had been *"flying TOS missions in the United States"*. This report was the final confirmation required to dispatch this letter to the above principals.

To prove I know whereof I speak, be advised I served the United States thirty-one years, nineteen of which were "joint service". Moreover, I served two years as an Air Staff Action Officer in XOKCR/SITI; as well as a Communications (C3I) Action Officer/Evaluator, for six years, on the Joint Staff in then-C3SEO, and J-7/EAD. I received the, *"Secretary of Defense Civilian Service Medal"*, and during my service career, the *Purple Heart, Bronze Star*, et al, on a 15 month combat tour; being stationed 14 years overseas, and serving in over 25 countries.

If you are not familiar with *"TOS"* particulars, be advised that Presidents Bush and Clinton put these sorry 'counter-US sovereignty' *TOS* Agreements in place, legally or otherwise, ostensibly to insure our compliance with 'Nuke Reduction Agreements'. Such pretenses were mainly a "public consumption" issue, as is the 45th RS, 55th Wg, and their three *TOS* compliance *"OC-135W"* planes, w/multinational crews, based at Offutt AFB; and associated with the *"On-Site Inspection Agency (OSIA)"*. The clandestine purpose of the *TOS*, rather than to certify US/foreign treaty compliance at US/foreign military bases, was to allow UN/Soviet pilots to over fly, without restrictions/hindrance, the US populace, operating in several modes; which I'll detail below.

First off, I have *prima facie* evidence, from "All Sources", that Soviet/UN pilots, in foreign planes/choppers, are routinely flying ["civil radar-spoofing", transponder-equipped] flagrantly illegal, low-level, IR-magnetometer-radar sweeps, and yes, "black operations" sorties, <u>against private citizens</u>; thus, searching for stored weapons, equipment, and food, etc! This includes sensor-equipped, Soviet Hip (MI-17) choppers over legal Federal Firearms Licensed businesses! I saw one! These despicable UN-ordered missions are bad enough; however, what follows is far worse.

For at least 8 years, *TOS* aircraft/choppers have been conducting pernicious, bio-chemical warfare operations all over the USA! I maintain hundreds of reports, many 'first person', as do other military retirees, including retired flag officers, of numerous attacks on our population; over both cities and rural areas. People are being surreptitiously sickened, and yes, <u>killed</u>, because of these "spraying" operations. The leftist US press is purposely covering the truth, and the US military, the "*only super power*" (what a joke!), can do nothing! Nevertheless, sir, while I have breath, I shall write!

On 29 January 2001, these "carpet-spraying" operations finally came to Central Virginia! Investigation reveals these tanker-configured aircraft are now spraying "*chemtrails*" of "*mycoplasmas/fungi spores*" in most areas of the USA. I am a licensed pilot, and have seen/endured, various aerial sorties myself, for over seven years! These operational sorties also "feature", among other pathogens, Hepatitis, upper respiratory irritants, ad nauseam, etc.!

If you did not know about this, you do now. Moreover, if you do not dispatch an armed F-15, or two, out of Langley/ACC to "splash" a few of these <u>flying murderers</u>, you will never qualify for the "*Admiral Mike Boorda Trophy*". Boorda knew these UN operations were going on, and was planning to do something; but alas, died, not by "*suicide*", but with three bullets in his body! If the action/info addressees above sit by and do nothing they're no more honorable than the traitorous Illuminist "leaders" who allowed these pernicious UN-Soviet terrorists/troops/cops/pilots into this country; in by the hundreds of thousands, no less! <u>Gentlemen, when the "bio agent" is Anthrax [*spores*], it will be too late!</u>

Very respectfully, with warm regards,

P.S. [Jewish] ADM Mike Boorda gave his life for the USA. How many "Flag Officers" will give their country for their lives? You need to make a decision, soon, or we will not escape this "expedition" against us. In addition, I tried to keep this to a "one page" staff paper. I could have written you 50 pages! Please review the attached '*USA Event*" paper also.

The following letter pertains to the one above.